THE PHYSICIAN'S CONCISE
HANDBOOK OF PSYCHIATRY

The Physician's Concise Handbook of Psychiatry

by

JAMES A. BRUSSEL

M.D., F.A.P.A., F.A.C.P.

BRUNNER/MAZEL, INC.

New York, N. Y.

To Louis Mindell

Literary Counselor and FRIEND

CONTENTS

THE PHYSICIAN'S CONCISE
HANDBOOK OF PSYCHIATRY

Foreword

A PRIMARY OBJECTIVE in writing this book has been to present the
outstanding elements of psychiatric knowledge for physicians, from
interns to general practitioners to specialists in all fields of medicine,
not to "teach" them, but to provide them with a concise, compact
reference to use when there are problems of psychogenic elements
in the diagnosis of patients. Again, it is a common experience of
practice to find that patients—seemingly the "same" in all respects
—react in diametrically opposite fashion to the identical therapy
regimens and medications. Similarly, there is the not too uncommon
exception whose emotional condition, say one of depression, is ag-
gravated by the very antidepressant agent most often used to
combat depression.

Straightforward, easily understood language is used, holding
complex so-called scientific terminology to a minimum. Yet simpli-
fied language does not oversimplify concepts, particularly those
which are frequently elusive in nature and content. There are many
excellent psychiatric textbooks available to the medical profession.
Too often these are ponderous, wordy, detailed volumes which are
useful to the specialist in psychiatry or to researchers. When a nonpsychiatric physician needs psychiatric information in a hurry, it
is the short, down-to-earth reference he requires. We hope this book
is the answer to that need.

There is no partiality to any one discipline of psychiatry in these
pages. Where schools of thought clash, both are cited. Where a
particular concept is the exclusive conclusion of one discipline, that
is clearly identified. The Freudian concept of the unconscious is de-

scribed as such, but interpretations and applications of psycho-analytic theories by various schools and the different approaches to these theories are fully discussed; such matters as organic methods of treatment, psychotherapy, etc. are given full consideration.

This book is not intended to make a non-psychiatric physician into the equivalent of a board-certified specialist in mental disorders. It is an exposition, a guide—an explanation of everyday behavior and that of neurotic, psychotic, and personality disorders. It is also hoped that this book will materially assist physicians in handling relatives of patients in instances where the former are as distraught and emotionally disturbed as the latter.

The Physician's Concise Handbook of Psychiatry should also be an aid to medical students, interns, residents, nurses, and others in their professional contacts with psychiatric patients.

JAMES A. BRUSSEL, M.D., F.A.P.A., F.A.C.P.

CHAPTER ONE

Underneath the Mind

A PATIENT MAY tell you his thoughts, symptoms, likes, dislikes, and his troubles as he knows them consciously, and relate them in great detail and without exaggeration or minimization, all of which help you in making a diagnosis and formulating a plan of treatment. No one, however, is exempt from involuntary self-deception—"lying" without the realization that what is honestly said is falsehood. For the physician to uncover the roots of what patients believe and reveal consciously is a very difficult task. The individual feels that he has complete control over his thoughts and actions. It is a shock when he finds out that his thinking and behavior can frequently be traced back to very early experiences of which he is now totally unaware.

Even physicians who have studied psychiatry during medical school find it hard to accept fully the idea that within the mind are submerged forces—psychic forces—that can drive one against one's better judgment or even against one's will to act in an unreasoning or unreasonable manner. Every doctor knows the "actor," he or she who can't speak of something as trite as a headache without making a "production" of it. Then there is the patient who calmly and impassively says, "Dr. Williams says I have cancer of the stomach. I've come to you for, oh, another opinion." Conversely, how often do you have a patient who is almost incoherent, profoundly agitated, and tearfully screams, "I've had an upset stomach for *three* days! My God I must have *cancer*." And, we dare add, what about the physician whose wife suffers gastrointestinal distress frequently.

Does the husband-doctor give her an antacid . . . or does he urge her to have a g.i. series plus all the diagnostic trimmings because he mentally envisages the "worst"? Let us keep this in mind: the human mind is a tricky mechanism, in all of us . . . psychiatrists included.

Submerged forces exert a powerful, albeit hidden, force. They make up an enormous reservoir of memories in the depths of the mind, and are always ready to rise to the surface, i. e., consciousness.

No experience is ever forgotten. Thus, a bitter emotional trauma in infancy may appear to have sunk into limbo, but it can be aroused in later life during a moment of stress. The emotional trauma has been merely *repressed*, kept out of consciousness until a new emotional conflict recalls to memory the earlier experience and brings it again to consciousness. These repressed experiences and their associated emotions are the complexes, of which one of the most familiar is the Oedipus complex which derives its name from Sophocles' *Oedipus Rex* (*Oidipous Tyrannos*) in which Oedipus slays his father, Laius, and marries the latter's widow, Jocasta, whom he does not recognize as his, Oedipus's, mother. When he does discover the truth he blinds himself. By extension, the Oedipus complex describes the boy who is excessively attached to his mother —the Sophoclean theme of incest (unknown to Oedipus, unconscious in the psychiatric patient) serving as the significant factor in psychoanalytic interpretation. Clinical records of many disturbed or neurotic men demonstrate the results of this complex, for these men have been so profoundly affected by their repressed emotions that they are unable to attain suitable (mature) relationships with women. They may never marry or, if they do, may set up unattainable standards for their wives, expecting them to be second mothers —"maternal surrogates." The counterpart of the Oedipus complex in the female is the Electra complex, which is derived from the classical legend of Electra's devotion to her father, Agamemnon, and hatred for her mother, Clytemnestra.

The "normal" child must be understood before we can discuss the "not normal" child. The universe of the newborn is restricted to his immediate surroundings and his mother. At first, she is regarded as part of himself because he lacks the experience and apparatus to "see" her as a separate organism. If the mother is a "good" mother, she provides food, warmth, physical contact, and comfort—the quintessence of security. Because the infant is loved, his psychological needs are satisfied through being enjoyed and fondled. He quickly learns that mother is the symbol of security, happiness, and sustenance. These initial experiences and the accompanying emotion of gratification (pleasure) become indelibly etched in the baby's unconscious and form the nucleus of psychic life which, despite the thick overlay of experiences that accrue as he grows up and ages, is never lost. Deep within him, be he executive, clerk, gym teacher, actor, plumber, or any other kind of worker, the adult man unconsciously carries this mnemonic record that at no time in his life was he so secure, ecstatically happy, and well-fed as when he was an infant in his mother's arms. Practical-minded or philosophically inclined, he will never "forget" this period in his life.

Psychic Development

Two varieties of very early experiences exert a powerful influence in shaping the mind and personality of every person. These experiences are feeding and toilet training in infancy. During the first two years of life these experiences are so dominant that they are associated with two distinct eras of development: the oral stage and the anal stage.

The Oral Stage. Physicians will agree that the outstanding activity of daily life from birth is feeding. The infant swiftly discovers that he is rewarded by smiles and kisses and words (pleasant sounds, to him) when he empties the bottle or completely nurses at the breast. As the diet is supplemented by new items, he learns that his security is more firmly entrenched when he pleases mother by eating the cereal or the egg, or by drinking the orange juice. Her love is gained in direct ratio to his cooperation in catering to his own welfare via the gastrointestinal route. Therefore, from birth there develops from this gastrointestinal association with the mother a symbolic affinity to the entire digestive process which has come to symbolize a measure of security.

If the mother handles the *sucking period* judiciously, the infant will progress normally in his psychosexual development; i. e., there will be no aberrant personality traits in later life traceable to earlier maternal mismanagement. The baby is a despot; almost from the second he draws in his first breath of life he learns that his oral cavity is a superb weapon by which the world, as he knows it, can be subjugated. Since crying and howling usually bring him immediate gratification of his desires and drives, he has a logical reason for holding his mouth in great esteem. If an overanxious mother satisfies every whim of her infant, he goes right along in life, continuing to pamper his mouth—eating well, relying on oral gratification to allay frustration. So, as an adult, he may well become the fingernail biter, the chain smoker, the chewing gum addict, and so on. Because his mouth is his means of "making his way," he is a natural as a raconteur, glib talker, high-pressure salesman, teacher, executive, teacher.

Now consider the opposite situation. Suppose a mother studiously ignores her baby's screams, doggedly determined not to "spoil" her child? His unconscious believes that mother doesn't love him, that howling for her attention is a futile maneuver. As a result he may develop the feeling that he is inferior and, therefore, rejected. These are, of course, unconscious reactions. As he develops, he must rely on himself and, as he depends more and more on his own guidance, he retreats further into his shell. As an adult he is introverted—a misanthrope, perhaps the researcher, writer, artist, the "man in the background." Should he pay back pain with pain and reject society completely, he becomes the recluse, perhaps the schizophrenic.

When the child's teeth begin to erupt at, on the average, seven months, he starts to go through the *biting period* which may last for a year or more. He discovers that teeth are an excellent weapon by which aggression can be expressed; he can and does bite his parents or another child. If his bite is met with a bite (which can be a biting word or gesture), the youngster may interpret the exchange as a fight or a game, and want to continue it. If his bite gains him disapproval, and his mother manages to see that he doesn't resort to this behavior again, he learns that biting is not an acceptable or profitable way to assert himself. He also learns that his mother is pleased if he doesn't resort to such aggressive conduct. This is, of course, a lesson all of us must learn, and, in the main, we do profit by it. However, if a child has to learn this lesson by being subjected to severe punishment and rejection, he may lose self-confidence and become a submissive and timid person. This may turn him into an adult who hasn't the knack of making friends; his interpersonal relations are tenuous at most and the ordinary give-and-take of life is beyond him.

However, the baby whose biting aggressiveness is not curbed, even encouraged, may become the ruthless adult, the sadist, who sweeps all opposition and resistance aside with "biting" sarcasm.

The Anal Stage. A baby is delighted, almost from birth, once he learns that with his excreta he can "create" something. For some time he is "allowed" to follow this pleasurable pursuit, unaware that his mother does not share his joy. When she initiates the toilet training program, he learns for the first time that she disapproves of his creative pastime. There is no pat answer to the question: "Doctor, when should I start training my baby?" The age this program should commence depends upon the individual child, his emotional and physical development, and how regularly or irregularly other items in his daily life are consummated. Most babies gradually gain control of bladder and rectum as they grow older, and a majority of mothers seem to be able to determine when their infants are ready. Generally, this is at the age of twelve months or older. In any case, two psychological forces come into play: (1) the pupil wants to please its teacher, and (2) conversely, the baby becomes possessive toward his bowel productions and wants to keep or control them himself.

No matter when toilet training commences, it is the first check—and an emotionally dramatic one—on what, until now, has been uncontrolled excretory activity. His emotional apparatus encounters the feeling of insecurity for the first time and, later on, this initial threat to his security may trigger a regression with signs and symptoms of a severe emotional disturbance, even wetting and soiling. Toilet training is not all trauma; it is the child's introduction to responsibility and self-reliance—the basis of his realization that there are times when the demands of reality (society) require him to give thought of others and to control himself. How a child responds to a toilet training program does not depend on *what* his mother does, but *how*. It calls for consistency and persistency that are liberally larded with affection and understanding. The grimly determined mother who is intolerant of "slips" by the student and expresses her annoyance by harshness and physical punishment may well be molding a future adult who is bitter, who feels that this is an unappreciative world whose inhabitants are out to "take everything." He becomes the misanthrope, the hoarder, the asocial person. If mother is a perfectionist and places her baby on the toilet at the exact same minute every day, she may be creating a precisionist who will be implacably intolerant of error, a stickler for promptness, and a fussbudget on cleanliness and neatness. Conversely, the mother who changes a soiled diaper when "she gets around to it" may be creating a future adult who will be a slob, careless, irresponsible, lazy, unreliable, and procrastinating. Obviously, neither extreme of training is desirable. A middle-of-the-road course is the answer, the exercise of common sense and compassion. "Moderation" is the word. It implies the proper combination of love and firmness.

Subsequent Stages. Together, the oral and anal stages, just discussed, are called the *autoerotic (self-love) stage*. As the child grows this is expanded and extended—particularly as grandparents, relatives, and family friends admire him—into *narcissistic* (or *narcistic*) *stage*. The name derives from the legend of Narcissus who, when he looked into a pool of water, fell in love with his reflection (himself). Around the age of three or four, when the youngster "goes out into the world" and meets and begins to mingle with others like himself, his libido (psychosexual energy) shifts from himself as the primary object to his playmates. Narcissism is simply projected; this is the *homoerotic stage* (love of the *same* sex, not the male sex). Now, for the first time, the child learns that if society is going to accept him he must subordinate his egocentric drives to those of the crowd.

At puberty, or shortly before, the child enters the *heterosexual* or *genital stage*. The direction of the youngster's libido is unchanged (i. e., it is outward); the objects are different. In the homoerotic stage, libido is centered on mirror-images of the individual; in the heterosexual stage it broadens to include the opposite sex, and this is known as *heteroeroticism*. Heteroeroticism (heterosexuality) is the ultimate adult stage of psychosexual deevlopment, when social adjustment encompasses a world of men and women. Once the adolescent achieves this level, he can be expected to go on to and through adulthood emotionally matured to meet the requirements of reality.

For purposes of completion it is necessary to go back to a very early period in the child's development and consider the resolution of the *Oedipus situation (complex)*. This is a major contribution of psychoanalysis and one that is poorly understood. It stands for the pathologically protracted and intensified attachment of a son to his mother; to this psychoanalysts add unconscious incestuousness—a bone of contention between Freudian analysts and those of other schools. In addition to the boy's possessiveness for his mother, there is a compensatory hostility for the father, he who usurps her attention (love) so that she cannot devote her affection to the boy all the time. She had, however, given all her love to the boy (so far as he could "see" from his restricted world) when he was an infant. He never ceased liking this pleasurable devotion and when he discovers that his father is also a recipient, the love-mother, hate-father emotional reaction commences. How this Oedipus situation is resolved is not known, but several factors apparently make the resolution possible. First, there is the racial (phylogenetic) recognition of father as the top authority, the head of the family. As the child grows, he senses this (an ontogenetic experience). Likewise, he learns that the father has a penis—phylogenetically recognized as the symbol of authority—and the boy becomes the admiring rather than the hostile son. The girl unconsciously interprets her lack of penis as the symbol of inferiority, experiences unconscious fear of organ deprivation (the *castration complex*), and, as a result, this evokes jealousy of the penis-bearing father (*penis envy*, in Freudian analytical parlance), and she is drawn to him. When the boy and girl reach heterosexuality at puberty, these parent attachments are healthfully projected to adult pursuits and object attachments.

THE UNCONSCIOUS

Consciousness is awareness of what is happening inside and outside oneself. This is a glib definition, but psychologically there is more to it. William James said: *"Consciousness . . . does not appear to itself chopped up in bits. Such words as 'chain' or 'train' do not describe it fitly as it present itself in the first instance. It is nothing jointed; it flows. A 'river' or a 'stream' are the metaphors by which it is most naturally described. In talking of it . . . let us call it the stream of thought, of consciousness, or of subjective life."*

Consciousness occurs at three levels: the conscious, the preconscious (or foreconscious), and unconscious. The *conscious* is that plateau of psychic functioning that deals directly with reality and is concerned with awareness and perception. Between the conscious and the unconscious is the *preconscious* from which experiences, concepts, and data can be readily recalled. This recallable and recalled material seldom is associated with emotional conflicts or unconscious impulses. Fundamentally it is ordinary memory association. The *unconscious,* the deepest recess of the mind, is the repository for repressed emotional experiences and the instincts; it is rarely subject to awareness. Some psychiatrists subdivide the unconscious. The most acceptable of these is Carl Jung's. He divided the unconscious into the *collective* or *racial* (phylogenetic) *unconscious,* and the *personal* (ontogenetic) *unconscious.*

There are many psychoanalysts who differ violently with Freudian therapy. However, few argue with Sigmund Freud's fundamental concept of the unconscious, particularly as the explanation of the persistence and power of early experiences in life. Freud divided the psychic apparatus into the id, ego, and superego. The *id* is the inner repository of libido; it is the core of personality, the transmission panel for instinctual desires, impulses, and drives. Not unlike a growing tree that develops a bark as a result of its exposure to the outer world, the id develops a hardened exterior as a result of its exposure to the restrictions, dicta, and taboos of society. This psychic bark is the ego, the mental self, the side personality reveals to the world it lives in. The *ego* mediates between the id and reality, gradually learning which impulses and desires the id is permitted by the superego to release. The *superego* develops from birth—even before birth—and is the mouthpiece of the world of reality in the psyche. It starts with the mother, expands to include the father and members of the household, and finally other authority figures. Thus, the superego enables one to distinguish between "right" and "wrong"

—between "acceptable" and "unacceptable"—according to one's family's principles and mores and those of environment. In essence, then, superego is conscience.

The superego applies its moral yardstick to the "helpless" ego which is at its mercy. In its broadest application, superego represents the demands of a person's morality. Freud said in his *New Introductory Lectures on Psychoanalysis*: "*Our moral sense of guilt is the expression of tension between the ego and the superego. Human sexual behavior is an excellent example of this. The infant and young child are amoral; sexual self-play and curiosity are openly expressed until parental restriction teaches the youngster— over and over—all that is included in the word 'modesty'.*" Repetition steadily leads to automatic obedience, and society's dicta about sexual and other conduct sink into the unconscious and become part of the superego structure.

Therefore, anything learned from parents which eventually becomes an integral part of the superego never ceases to govern the ego later on, even long after parents are dead. What the parent is to child, the superego will be to the ego.

DEFENSE MECHANISMS

What sets one person apart from another, psychologically, is known as individuality. This is the heir of personality whose catalytic and integrating force is the ego. It is the ego that enables one to differentiate between the self and that which is not the self. Each new emotional experience develops in a person those characteristics which make him unique—make him "him"—and he holds his ego in great esteem. Any attack upon the integrity of the ego causes discomfort, if not profound feelings of guilt. To withstand the assault, to "ride with the punch," the mind calls upon its "dynamisms" or "mental mechanisms," devices which constitute most of the functioning of the psyche. This functioning (behavior) includes aggression, defense, and compensation, singly or in combination. Mental mechanisms have, as their motivating force, emotion (*e*, out + *moveo*, move), which is also behind their content of thought. Emotion is also known as "*affect*," which may invest any thought content or object, a feature known as *cathexis*. One mental mechanism, repression, has already been described (p. 2).

When the psyche is under stress or is confronted by trauma it calls upon mental mechanisms to meet the challenge. It must be remembered that this cause and effect scheme of things is a normal process; it may result, however, in abnormal thinking and activity. Thus, a person who is subjected to a tongue-lashing may refuse to utter a single word in rebuttal or self-defense—he "preserves his dignity." A catatonic schizophrenic resorts to mutism as a categorical defense against the communication to others of his ideas. The symbolic reproduction of repressed ideation is another example of using a defense mechanism. The principle defense mechanisms, about to be presented, are the psychic tools by which one adjusts to reality and the many situations, expected and unexpected, encountered in life.

Identification is the original form of emotional tie with an object. At birth and for a time thereafter, an infant is totally identified in his emotional life with his mother and his delimited environment. For the first few months of life the baby devotes his attention to differentiating himself from the environment, in identifying himself as opposed to all that is not himself. The "I" in the normally developing child becomes more and more crystal clear (but in psychosis, such as schizophrenia, the patient regresses to infancy and its vague personal identity with and feeling of close relationship with environment). As an unconscious mental mechanism, identification in normal persons is self-appropriation of another's qualities, whether the latter be animate or inanimate, or the transference of these qualities from one person or object to another. Thus, a reader identifies himself with a novel's protagonist; children "play house" and behave as do their parents. When the unconscious accepts, on a permanent basis, any feature or belief, it becomes part of what psychoanalysis calls the *"ego ideal,"* i.e., the ideal and idealized person we would like to be. Ego ideal is an image incorporated into the ego, constructed in the early years from the attributes of significant persons in the environment, such as relatives, teachers, friends, clergymen, etc.

Introjection is the psychic adoption of environmental qualities by a person. An example is the fastidious business man who feels uneasy if the usual and orderly arrangement of items on his desk is disturbed. Through introjection, an individual seems to draw the outer world into the circle of his interests and thus reacts disproportionately or inappropriately to environmental details. Introjection can turn toward oneself emotions such as hostility or anger which originally were directed toward another person or object.

Projection is the mental mechanism which enables one to attribute one's ideas or impulses to another. It gives what seems to be objective reality to that which is really subjective. The externalization of an idea or an emotion via projection to make it appear as originating in someone else implies that the idea or the emotion is undesirable. Thus blaming someone for a mistake one has made. Once the undesirable trait is externalized it is thereafter regarded as having originated from a source other than the self. Projection is well exemplified in a particular type of paranoid patient who is troubled with unconscious homosexual drives. He projects these impulses upon some man or men in the environment and then resists these impulses as though they originated from external sources. Projection functions in the unconscious and is completely defensive in nature.

Introjection and projection are diametrically opposite. Many affective expressions are characterized by such pairing of mental mechanisms. The affect seems to swing from one side to another like a pendulum. Common pairs are love and hate, masochism and sadism, introjection and projection, etc. One's capacity for opposite types of expression is known as *ambivalency,* an emotional state of the nature of "damned-if-I-do, damned-if-I-don't." It is a prime breeding ground for indecision and insecurity if it becomes the dominant control of the psychic apparatus.

Displacement is the attachment of inappropriate emotions to various objects or ideas. Here we have the ball player who strikes out blaming his failure on his bat, the trainer who blames his dog's inability to learn tricks or the animal's unwillingness to cooperate. In these instances, the affect is shifted from a proper to an improper place, most always in the environment. Displacement is a mental mechanism which enables a normal and a "not-normal" person to defend himself against personal deficiencies and shortcomings.

Substitution uses a response or replacement (frequently something trivial or unrelated) for the original goal or desired object when the goal or object is not obtainable or acceptable to the person. Substitution often calls other mental mechanisms into play, and it functions in such psychic activities as dreams. Its most colloquial synonym is "sour grapes."

Sublimation makes possible the modification of an unconscious primitive (infantile) impulse so that it becomes socially acceptable. This modification, an ego function, makes it possible for the original and unacceptable drive to be realized and accepted in reality. Therefore, in sublimation the ego acts with the id, not against it. Sublimation is normal psychic activity because it helps the id to find external expression of a drive and its associated libido. An excellent example is the outward expression in athletics of inner aggression.

Transference is the unimpeded exchange of emotions. It is a psychoanalytic synonym for love; it is the prime psychic activity which fosters progress in psychotherapy and analysis. During treatment, by means of transference, the patient is able to transfer his emotions to the therapist who, at any one particular moment, may stand for a parent, an enemy, a lover, anyone in the patient's life who is being discussed at the moment.

Conversion is a mental mechanism which makes it possible for the psyche to convert a painful emotional conflict whose overt expression would be socially inacceptable into physical expression such as symptom. This is a compromise: the id finds externalization of its tension, and society's dicta are not violated. Thus, the clerk who helps himself to some change in the cash register may, at a later date, develop numbness or paralysis of his hand. The neurosis, *conversion hysteria* (closely related to what is known as psychosomatic illness) involves unconscious feelings of guilt and the need for punishment. This latter phrase must be clarified. It does not mean that the unconscious yearns to be punished; it is simply a deduction of the unconscious: since I am guilty I will be punished. This is not unlike the little boy who filches only one cookie from a jar that contains dozens. His mother could never possibly miss one cookie, yet the child says to himself, "Boy, I bet I'm going to get it!" Conversion is a masochistic mechanism in which realistic, consciously painful, external gratification alleviates the unconscious, but no less painful, emotional conflict.

Rationalization is the process by which a socially acceptable explanation (not necessarily a true one) is given for behavior. It masks the genuine reason from a person himself, as well as from others in the environment. Most of us believe we perform certain acts for reasons other than those which actually motivate them. It is an inborn tendency to do and think as we wish, and then find an acceptable explanation for how we behave and for what we say. Rationalization may be a deliberate procedure (actually a falsehood) or an unconscious procedure. This is one mental mechanism physicians have to think of as patients recite symptoms or furnish explanations why a treatment regimen which helps others does nothing for them. But, doctors should realize that their own rationalization may influence their clinical judgment and their interpretation of what patients say to them.

What are known as "alibis" are not included as mental mechanisms. Alibis are excuses made on the conscious level; mental mechanisms exert their effect through operations that originate and function beneath the surface of awareness. In another way, the man who creates an alibi isn't deceiving himself, although his aim is to deceive his listener. The man who speaks or thinks in response to an unconsciously functioning mental mechanism *is* deceived; his listeners may or may not be. Above all, if he was not able to deceive himself he would suffer anxiety, tension, perhaps a somatic expression of his nervousness (psychosomatic disorder) . . . even a frank mental disorder. A man is firmly convinced when he tells himself (and others) that "he never wanted the promotion (which he failed to achieve) because the job was just too much for one of his age." This man is no different, in his mental mechanism functioning, than the one who becomes completely absorbed in stamp collection instead of mingling socially—he is unable to establish healthy interpersonal relationships. What we don't realize is that mental mechanisms are constantly working, keeping us at least superficially adjusted—and all the while we are not aware of it.

Similarly, the mental mechanisms presented above are not examples of "abnormal" acting or thinking. Everyone of us resorts to all of these mechanisms in everyday life. In fact, they often are responsible for truly constructive gains for the individual; much of the great work of the world has been achieved by persons who attained compensation for some frustration through the mental mechanism of sublimation.

Masochism and Sadism. Within the psychic apparatus there are two opposite forces; they are contrary to each other, they are also complementary. These forces are masochism and sadism. The former is overtly manifested as kindness, tenderness, solicitude . . . love. Sadism is seen as domineering activity, despotism, tyrannical behavior. Masochism, in its extreme, is suffering pain to ease a love object's pain. Sadism is pleasure derived from inflicting pain, from the nasty verbal dig to actual physical assault. Love and hate typify them, but this is something of an oversimplification. Psychologically, a fine balance between these two emotional forces adds up to emotional maturity, emotional adjustment. Also, the completely masochistic person, he who is the "loving" individual, is not normal. In colloquial parlance he would be "too sweet to live with." An outstanding example of masochism is Joan of Arc; Adolf Hitler was a paragon of sadism. In mental disorders, it is the paranoid who is extremely egocentric, smug, liberal with his insults and criticism; masochism is frequently observed in the depressed and agitated woman who suffers involutional melancholia and continuously berates herself for all the evils in the world.

Individuality. Every psyche has the principal components we have discussed. More, members of any species have many characteristics in common, characteristics which persist throughout each individual's life or which may be manifested only at certain periods; these characteristics add up to what is called "the norm." Deviations from the norm, in whole or in part, are said to be "abnormalities." This concept seems to provide a neat definition, but when it is taken at face value, unsupportable generalities result. "Like carbon copies" sounds logical; but it isn't if each carbon copy is carefully scrutinized. If we study human traits (physical, intellectual, or emotional), we are struck not by the similarity of people but by the seemingly endless number of individual differences. The more we investigate the human mind, the more certain it becomes that no two psyches are the same. It follows, then, that no two personalities are the same.

Character and Personality. In everyday speech these two words are used synonymously. In psychiatry there is quite a difference between them. Personality is the sum total of behavioral traits by which one is recognized as an individual. In psychiatry, although the end meaning is the same, a dynamic mechanism is implied. Besides the external picture that a person presents as his compromise with environment, personality is also regarded as the complex of internal forces that makes it possible for man to satisfy the desires of his instincts and, at the same time, satisfy the dicta of the society in which he moves and lives. Personality is easier to understand when we pause to remember what *persona* stood for in ancient Greek drama. It was a mask worn by an actor to inform the audience what mood or character of the role he was presenting; contemporary programs and many theaters often show reproductions of the masks of comedy and tragedy. Man, if he wishes to survive, must comply with the external world, and so he creates an image of himself. This image, the ego, is his personality as his fellow-men see it.

Character implies a rather special meaning of the composite of a person's traits as they relate to the customs of his society. In psychiatric classification there are "character disorders" which include behavioral and attitudinal features which clash with society's dicta. Actually, this is the only recognized use of "character" in psychiatry.

Environment and Personality. Granting that there are exceptions to the rule, certain personality types are recognized on an environmental basis. Such types may be ethnic, national, provincial, communitarian, or familial. How much biological foundation plays a role in environmental personality types is not known, but all of us recognize the ones in constant use. For example, there is the tropical personality, surrounded by lush vegetation which leaves him free of the need to hustle to find food, warmth, and shelter. So he lives by the standards of *mañana* and *siesta;* he is "hot-blooded" and given to romanticism, excitability, and is not traditionally practical. Guitar-strumming and songs of the tropics reflect the influence of environment in shaping his personality. On the opposite side is the "Scandinavian type," found in a rocky, cold, harsh terrain which makes the hunt for food, warmth, and shelter the paramount interest of life. The Scandinavian is customarily coldly practical, unexcitable, and stolid. He doesn't have much time for idling, and even his music reflects the rigors of his existence.

Within nationalities there are well-defined types. Catalonians, Basques, and Andalusians are Spanish, but they each have different and easily recognized physical characteristics and emotional constitutions. We see these differences in our own country when we compare the Texan, the Missourian, and the New Englander. These intra-group differences can be found all the way down to family groups. There is, for example, the large family whose members are said to be alike as peas is a pod, yet one of them becomes the black sheep of the household. We wonder why all the children aren't the same. After all, their bringing-up, education, and socioeconomic background were the same. This is something that has never been solved, but medicine, rather than admit ignorance, explains this familial aberration by pointing to the black sheep's personality difference as "constitutional" — "he was born that way." Other explanations for this variation (in families or entire communities) are slum conditions, inadequate education facilities, etc. Yet, none of these explains why everyone exposed to the same disadvantages doesn't develop quirks of personality and resort to asocial and felonious behavior.

CHAPTER TWO

Psychopathology

DESPITE THE DISCOVERIES of causes of psychiatric disorders by researchers, it is still an unanswered challenge to define mental "disorder" or "disease." Actually there are no precisely labeled packages of psychiatric afflictions: even the American Psychiatric Association's classification of disorders is muddled and vague in places. In fact, psychiatrists are so dissatisfied with the classification that they are continuouly changing it (a "new" change is being made at the time of this writing) and wrangle among themselves as to the selection of diagnostic terms. Some of these pendulum-like alterations will be mentioned as we come to the more important ones in this book. That is why the long, formal APA classification is not reproduced herein. It is no easier for the certified psychiatrist than it is for his non-psychiatric colleague to place a positive label on a psychic affliction ranging from a mild, fleeting sensation of uneasiness, through a depression, to a full-blown psychosis with all the "trimmings" — hallucinations, delusions, and deviant behavior. It's the variability and lack of specificity that block the road to nosological determination. What psychiatry lacks are the Wassermanns, blood cultures, and Schicks, i. e., positive determinants. As long as there have been psychiatric "staff meetings," psychiatrists have been arguing over diagnoses.

From earliest times until late in the nineteenth century it was thought by laymen and doctors that anyone who behaved peculiarly or talked incoherently was "possessed of evil spirits." All we can say today is that disordered thought and action are overt manifestations of mental illness. Prompt inquiry into diagnosis and the institution of therapy as early as possible are contemporary standards that go far in recognizing psychiatry as an established medical specialty vis-à-vis its esoteric status of not too long ago. The distrust and skepticism have not, however, completely evanesced. We still hear remarks such as *"All psychiatrists think everybody is crazy"* and *"There but for the grace of God go we,"* even though it is no less logical to declare that *"All physicians think everybody is sick."*

"Functional disorder" and "organic illness" have been used so long and so extensively by the profession that the terms have become part of lay parlance. There is one difficulty, however, as the eminent medical historian Robert P. Hudson* points out, and that is meaning. Doctors "tend to act as if their words actually convey identical meanings to other persons" — the physicians included.

The concept of disease is not merely a logical toy. The medical reaction to an organism infected with *staphylococci* is to institute antibiotic treatment. But, as Dr. Hudson says, the problem is not simple. In any specific process, such as pulmonary tuberculosis, the patient is the pragmatist who wonders if he'll survive and be able to pursue his occupation, and whether he has infected members of his family. Tuberculosis is not an abstraction to him; it is something very real — an injustice in an imperfect world. Most Americans regard religion thus: he has faith in its existence, but fails to comprehend why he should be singled out to prove it. The first consideration of disease, therefore, depends on the patient's relationship to it.

Then there is each physician's concept of disease, depending on his psychological constitution which is influenced and molded by his background, morals, religion, education — everything and anything that points his footsteps through life in a particular direction. Syphilis is an infectious disease. So is streptococcal pneumonia. The doctor may be extremely sympathetic to the patient with the latter and abhorrent of the luetic. Any doctor, general practitioner or specialist, has a different emotional reaction to the hypochondriac who is depressed and the advanced senile patient who is also de-

---

* Robert P. Hudson, "The Concept of Disease," *Annals of Internal Medicine,* 65:595-601 (September, 1966).

pressed. One's psyche certainly plays a significant role in diagnostic objectivity, as much as it does in adjusting to all other features in life and in one's environment.

Concept of pathology undergoes changes with time. For example, Hippocrates said epilepsy was "sacred." Centuries later the convulsive disorder was attributed to the machinations of the devil. Within the memory of most of us is the dread many employers had of hiring epileptics. Even today, some states will not license an epileptic to drive a car even if his seizures are completely under control.

No two physicians agree (that is, down to the fine points) as to what really is the difference between functional and organic. This, in turn, leads to the challenge of differentiating "normal" and "abnormal" — which, contrary to the idea held by many, is not the private problem of psychiatry. In an attempt to overcome this difficulty, physicians seized the idea of impediment: thus, before deviation from normality could be diagnosed, some restriction of a patient's physical capacity must be in evidence, or, at least, some limitation of his ability to function in society. Dr. Hudson pointed out that impediment was a step in the right direction, but not the solution. Many grave difficulties arose very quickly.

For example, what do you do with the stoic who has hypertension, electrocardiographic evidence of a serious cardiac process, who insists that he feels "just fine" and has never missed a day's work in his life? Is he diseased? Sure, he will be, but is he *now?* The next patient proves to have a cardiac neurosis. His mother dropped dead at the age of forty-one. Since then, an endless parade of physical, roentgenological, and laboratory examinations—all normal or negative—have not convinced him that he has the cardiac reserve to get up from a sitting position. With impediment as the yardstick, this patient is sick—very sick.

Silly as it may sound, do you decide the stoic is diseased but not ill, while the neurotic is ill but not diseased? If you do, you must have a concept of illness that is opposed to your concept of disease.

In the latter part of the nineteenth century, medicine developed the functional concept of disease. A change in the function, for instance, of the heart was seized upon as a criterion that the heart was diseased. But when, some years afterward, it became apparent that the psyche could also provoke alterations in cardiac function, this concept lost its alleged clarity. Today, "functional" is bandied about in so many senses that, unless it is carefully explained, its usage only serves to create confusion.

Now how does the concept of disease fare in psychiatry? This problem has become more than an issue among medical historians and more than an interesting point to be discussed by academicians. Some psychiatrists are attempting to redefine mental disease in such broad terms as to be absurd. The sociopathic (psychopathic—and we'll speak of *this* switch in terms later) murderer is classified as a mentally ill person. That idea alone is responsible for the endless parade of "expert psychiatric witnesses" in murder trials, but now some psychiatrists are trying to stretch sociopathy to include dropouts, ennui-filled oldsters, unwed mothers, frustrated divorcées, choleric car drivers, and children whose mothers love them too much or too little. The preamble to the constitution of the World Health Organization (WHO) defines health, not as ". . . the absence of disease or infirmity,' but as ". . . a state of complete physical, mental, and social well-being." If this doesn't define health, it certainly does define coma.

And all the while psychiatrists in and out of the American Psychiatric Association are squabbling over the redefinition of mental illness, none of them takes time out to attempt to produce an acceptable definition of the normal mental state. For example, where does a reaction of anxiety cease to be normal and begin to be a neurosis? Psychologists, like drowning sailors clinging to straws, have returned to our old friend impediment; the chief defect of this concept hasn't changed. Impediment is easily applicable in extreme conditions—where it really isn't needed—but when it comes to finer distinctions, the minutiae of diagnosis, it is almost worthless. Thus, impediment is a guide for the surgeon to whom a man with a compound fracture of the humerus is brought; this is an extreme of "disease." So, can impediment help the psychiatrist in dealing with psychopaths (p. 108) and would-be suicides; it would not divulge why a hard-driving city desk editor is not more efficient or why a fortyish, comely widow becomes involved in a messy affair. At best, impediment turned out to be a crude tool for general medicine; it is even cruder for psychiatry.

Laying down acceptable and workable concepts of "diseased" organisms is very difficult. Those who have tried to achieve these, down through the years, merit our admiration as well as the patient understanding of specialists who are concerned with functions of more "accessible" organs and systems. Certainly it is easier to obtain an idea of pancreatic function in the human by studying pancreatic activity in laboratory animals. The same investigatory process is not as revealing when it comes to the human psyche. Wolfgang Kohler tersely defines the fundamental weakness in any scientific investigation into psychic activity: *"Man is not only a subject matter of science; he is also its author."*

As for human behaviorists, they should own up to the truth that their ideas of disease are still in the fetal stage. Ignorance is most dangerous when it is itself ignored. Careful analysis will reveal that there are significant parallels between today's psychiatry and the imaginative system-builders in the eighteenth and nineteenth centuries.

To summarize this discussion and to question how near we are to a solution, we turn again to Dr. Hudson who cites Oswei Temkin who wrote in 1901: "The question: does disease exist or are there only sick persons? is an abstract one and, in that form, does not allow a meaningful answer. Disease is not simply either the one or the other. Rather, it will be thought of as the circumstances require. The circumstances are represented by the patient, the physician, the public health man, the medical scientist, the pharmaceutical industry, society at large, and last but not least, the disease itself. For our thinking about disease is not only influenced by internal and external factors, it is also determined by the disease situation in which we find ourselves. Sydenham . . . lived at the time of the great plague of London, and the plague . . . has little concern with individual variations. In contrast, the practitioner of our time, who has to deal with degenerative disorders and neuroses demanding much individual attention, may have little use for disease entities. He may be inclined to leave them to the laboratory or the public health man for prevention. With the changing disease situation our thoughts about disease change, too. As Hippocrates said, 'The art consists in three things—the disease, the patient, and the physician.'

To the historian's mind, the history of all three are bound up in the history of the art itself."

The best adjusted person can and does become emotionally disturbed or present a personality change in response to unusual and stressful stimuli, and this reaction may be mild or severe. If he didn't, he'd be anything but "normal." The doctor about to face examination for certification in a particular specialty may "freeze" unexpectedly in a state of panic. He is no different than the patient en route to the operating room for nothing more drastic than removal of a nasal polyp, who becomes apprehensive and tremulous because of an unconscious fear of death. In current psychiatric appraisal, these are manifestations of mental, emotional, or nervous disorders; but the manifestations *per se* are not necessarily proof positive of mental pathology. It is the degree of their intensity, their persistence, and the total clinical picture of the person's adjustment to his life problems that tell the story.

Every physician knows the many gradations of pathology that can be found in pulmonic disorders: coryza and bronchitis, influenza, pneumonia, tuberculosis, to name some of many. Examination reveals various degrees of severity between these disorders and within each disorder. Why can't this idea of degree be applied to psychopathology? There is a barrier: notice how differently people respond to so-called physical pathology on the one hand and psychopathology on the other. He who undergoes cholecystectomy, he who follows a salt-free, weight-reducing regimen for hypertension—these patients do not suffer loss of prestige among their fellows. To the contrary, many persons turn out to be the "life of the party" when they render dramatic descriptions of their symptoms, the midnight ambulance race to the hospital, the treatment, etc., etc. What of the individual whose illness is in the "shameful" zone? Let us picture a woman entering a room where a group is gathered for an evening of socializing. If the other guests know she has been to a psychiatrist because she is mildly tense or depressed, watch how raised eyebrows and a sudden lull in conversation mark her entrance into the room. Someone is bound to whisper to someone, "Does it run in her family?" "Do you think she's . . .?"—with the appropriate facial expression of a question. No, as liberal in our thinking and advanced intellectually as we may think we are, there still are traces of primitive thinking that continue to retard the progress of psychiatry.

Yet one of the most stubborn obstacles to progress belongs to the medical profession and the failure to set up criteria to determine what is meant by "normal" and "abnormal." There is no trouble with adjectives such as "peculiar," "ludicrous," "sensational," and "bizarre." The trouble is in the common, everyday fields of human behavior; that's where agreement is lacking. There are literally thousands of psychological tests, but to date there is none that can give an accurate estimation of personality. We say someone is "charming" or a "jerk,"—qualitative gauges; but there are no percentages, ounces, plus-or-minus signs to give us quantitative estimations. A personality cannot be precise as, say, a complete blood count, because there is no such thing as a "normal" personality to serve as a standard criterion; personality can only be measured in qualitative terms not quantitative symbols. In addition, the subject may "unconsciously" lie when he takes a personality test, so that results are a distorted or untrue representation of his personality.

Normalcy must depend, at least to some degree, on racial and national cultures, and on community mores and social dictates. A mini-skirted American girl would be an oddity on the streets of Srinagar; her Indian counterpart in her full and sweeping sari would not go unnoticed on Main Street, U. S. A. If the traditionally placid and verbally economical Scotchman began to speak explosively, using broad gestures as might a South American, his behavior would certainly be considered abnormal. We cannot exclude cultural identification in passing judgment on another's normalcy. Even basic physical measurements challenge the concept of normalcy. As a fact, what *is* "normal" height? It cannot possibly be an arithmetical average, because if this were true, there must be millions of "abnormally" short and tall people. Therefore, any concept of normalcy must take in a wide strip on both sides of the average. Physicians are urged, consequently, to apply this concept to problems of human thinking and behavior. It will enable them to appreciate that psychopathology, like organic pathology, can be but a hair's breadth away from good health, then farther away and more disabling, and, ultimately, totally destructive to the patient's way of life.

Since no classification could possibly encompass a graduated scale that adequately delimits severity in increasing degrees, we list below the major categories as recognized by the American Psychiatric Association; next to each is the chapter in this book in which the category is presented:

1. *Transient situational personality disorders*   Chapter (4) "Nervousness"

2. *Psychophysiological autonomic and visceral disorders*   Chapter (5) "Psychoneurosis"

3. *Psychoneuroses*   Chapter (5) "Psychoneurosis"
4. *Psychoses*   Chapter (6) "Psychosis"
5. *Personality disorders*   Chapter (8) "Sociopathy"
                                   Chapter (9) "Addiction"
6. *Mental retardation*   Chapter (11) "Mental Retardation"

7. *Chronic brain disorders*   Chapter (12) "Epilepsy"
                                   Chapter (13) "Child Psychiatry"
                                   Chapter (14) "The Involution"
                                   Chapter (15) "Senility"

8. *Acute brain disorders.* In this group are neurological conditions such as brain tumor, brain trauma, encephalitis, meningitis, etc. Sometimes a *chronic* brain disorder is complicated by an *acute* brain disorder. For example, a patient with marked cerebral arteriosclerosis may suddenly suffer a cerebrovascular accident, such as a hemiplegia. For the reader's purpose, it is obvious that acute brain disorders, with and without psychic complications, are usually so acute and patently demanding of prompt medical assistance that such patients would not be attended by doctors who flipped pages of this or other medical texts to determine if the patient is "really sick." The obvious emergency requires immediate action.

CHAPTER THREE

Etiology

GENERAL PRACTITIONER or specialist, patients ask you, from time to time, questions such as, "Doctor, can you do anything for my nervousness?" "I wonder if you can give me sleeping pills," "What makes my father so irritable and hard to live with?" "What have I done that God punishes me with a retarded child?" These are spoken by patients who are concerned over their own emotional and psychic difficulties or those of relatives and friends. This curiosity is a healthy indication of the ever-increasing interest of the public in a sorely needed mental health program, the public health challenge of psychiatry seeking the etiology of mental afflictions. This has made at least one valuable contribution: as in cancer, the earlier that unfavorable indications are recognized the better the prognosis is for preventive and therapeutic measures.

"What causes psychopathology?" This is asked by everyone, lay and professional both. The psychiatrist would be the first to welcome a fast, positive, specific reply. The first barrier to the utopian answer is the double-barreled etiology in mental disease: underlying causes and precipitating factors. Physicians recognize these, but often the latter is taken for the former, even by doctors when they self-diagnose. For example, a physician tells himself that he is jittery, irritable, nervous, insomniacal, and without appetite. "No wonder," he soliloquizes. "Night calls, an overflowing waiting room, covering two doctors while they're ill, no time for as little recreation as reading a novel." Is it that simple? Is every physician who's similarly burdened—even burdened more than that—a "nerv-

ous wreck?" Let that self-diagnosing doctor review his past. Was there always "something" that interfered with his recreation, the forming and maintaining of interpersonal relationships? Was he so shy and diffident, lacking the capacity to laugh and exchange sallies, that he retreated from everyday society and withdrew into his work? The excuse that he is "too busy" or "too tired" when he's invited out is socially acceptable; it satisfies the requirements of society and it answers the unconscious's demand to avoid people. No, hard work hasn't made him a nervous wreck; the excuse indicates he "can't take it"—it's the last straw he can grab to remain (at least, superficially), in the "swim of life." Hard work is the *precipitating factor* in a long parade of frustrations, challenges, irritants, and shocks which in another physician might be the very sparks for the development of good social and psychological adjustment. The cause of our self-diagnosing doctor's emotional troubles lies deeper —buried in his personality structure or within the physicochemical complex that furnishes the mechanism for his reaction to the world in which he lives.

Precipitating factors and underlying causes are both *exogenous* and *endogenous*. Examples of exogenous factors are economic stress, social restrictions, cultural clashes, etc. Examples of endogenous factors are metabolic disturbances, circulatory pathology, and infections. Although contemporary research is focusing on endogenous factors, there is no doubt that considerable interplay exists between exogenous and endogenous elements.

THE CHALLENGE OF ETIOLOGY

Let us get one thing straight right now: *There is no known specific cause of any emotional or mental disorder.* Almost every day we read in medical journals of amazing clues, "significant" indications, and statistical hints. Add to these the provocative theories of the various disciplines of psychiatry. Nevertheless, while the italicized statement above may strike physicians as categorical and evoke their surprise, it remains firmly supported by inescapable proof.

Medicine has always aimed to have a specific treatment or modality of therapy for a disorder that is caused by a specific agent.

Such is not the fortune of psychiatry. As stated previously, psychiatrists can't even concur on names of disorders. For example, New York State's Department of Mental Hygiene has never officially adopted in entirety the nomenclature of the APA's classification. Likewise, some psychiatric entities are so poorly understood that they undergo nosological change periodically. "Sociopathic disorder" is one. At the beginning of World War II it was "constitutional psychopathic inferiority" in this country and "constitutional psychopathic condition" in England. Then, during the war years it became "psychopathic personality," and finally "sociopathic disorder." In 1968 the move was on to bring it back to "psychopathic personality."

Consider the very common terms "psychoneurosis" and "psychosis." How shall we define these? First, some authors don't know whether "psychoneurosis" or "neurosis" should be used, although they are conceded to be synonyms. In the latest psychiatric textbook, *Comprehensive Textbook of Psychiatry*, edited by Alfred M. Freedman and Harold I. Kaplan (The Williams & Wilkins Company, Baltimore, 1967), in the lengthy index for "psychoneurosis" and "neurosis" there is no subheading: "definition." In the section on psychiatric disorders of children, Dr. E. James Anthony omits definition and quotes Malamud who considers it a paradox that there is "a surprising lack of unanimity and clarity" as to what is meant by the concept of psychoneurosis in the light of the prevalence of this disorder and the glib use of the word "neurotic" by persons in all walks of life. Fine, but where is the definition? In the same text, Dr. Harold I. Lief, writing on psychoneurotic disorders, quotes the APA's definition of anxiety, but not of psychoneurosis. Dorland's *Medical Dictionary* defines psychoneurosis as "Mental disorder which is of psychogenic origin (*isn't psychosis, too?*) but presents the essential symptoms of functional nervous disease . . ." In my *Layman's Dictionary of Psychiatry* (Barnes & Noble, 1967) psychoneurosis is defined as: "A mental disorder which reflects an unconscious attempt to achieve, through compromise, at least superficial adjustment to an unconscious conflict . . . but unlike a psychosis it does not destroy the integrity of the personality or break the individual's contact with the environment." Perhaps this definition is no better than none at all. Nothing embarrasses a psychiatrist more than to ask him to define psychoneurosis and psychosis. He can tell you, in very great detail, what each is *not* compared to the other, but he cannot give a crystal-clear, terse differentiation. In 1966, medical reports said that the annual convention of the World Psychiatric Association was marked by "nosological anarchy." The International Classification of Diseases is revised perennially by Britain's Dr. E. Stengel who admits that "many psychiatrists will disapprove parts of it." Some psychiatrists, including this writer, have reached the point where we often regard a diagnostic tab as meaningless and no help at all in the diagnosis of or in formulating a regimen of therapy in disorders that vary from patient to patient, since no two minds or life experiences are alike.

Physicians often remark, "Surely there can be no doubt as to etiology when an organic condition is the reason for psychopathology." Such as what? Arteriosclerosis? Syphilis? Brain trauma? Senility? No, not these nor any other. Take the diagnosis, "psychosis due to cerebral arteriosclerosis." It is a misleading misnomer. If cerebral arteriosclerosis provoked a psychosis in every person, then all Americans over the age of sixty or sixty-five would be in institutions. The same applies to senile psychosis. Tertiary syphilis may affect the cardiovascular system or cause amaurosis or deafness and many other nonpsychiatric complications. This is the case with every organic illness that may be, but not necessarily is, complicated by psychosis. In most patients, a detailed, probing anamnesis will reveal that in earlier years he had indications of an emotional or mental disorder or personality quirks that were potential sources for psychopathology; the later organic pathology simply is the final clinical straw that breaks the personality's back.

There are, however, certain syndromes that seem to be exceptions to the above. An example is pellagra. Correction of the dietary deficiency results in reversal of symptoms, including the psychiatric. But it should be noted that this deficiency originates from the "outside" although it affects organs and systems inside the body. Instances of psychopathology seem to arise from within the body.

Research is investigating the question of metabolism as an etiological factor in psychiatric disorders. More of this will be mentioned when we discuss mental retardation. It is fairly well established that metabolic alterations do occur in psychiatric disorders. External excesses or deficiencies which are severe and/or protracted can effect certain metabolic illnesses. Among these are narcotism, alcoholism, and malnutrition; but so can innumerable socioeconomic and personal factors which cause tension (as stressed by Karen Horney, whose concept is presented on p. 95). Psychosis can result from toxins and drugs via metabolic alterations. On the other hand, some metabolic syndromes are characterized by mental retardation if treatment is not promptly instituted, whereas the condition can be corrected by a special diet. As for schizophrenia, there are seemingly endless suggestions as to etiology: heredity vs. constitutionalism, environmental influences, individual susceptibility, endocrinological dysfunction, and even viruses and DNA and RNA are not excluded. Biological etiology was first suggested by the German-English physician, J. L. W. Thurichum in 1884. Today's heritage of that postulate includes the investigations into nerve-endocrine and biochemical deficiencies.

Contemporary research is concentrating on the following. It is fact that some hallucinogens can and do create a schizophrenic-type reaction which can persist in susceptible (whatever that means) individuals; to the contrary there are pharmaceutical agents (see Chapter 7) which counteract some of the symptoms observed in schizophrenia. It is postulated that these drugs exert their effect at the level of the enzymes which control body biochemistry. It is also fact that embryonic brain development and proper pre- and postnatal metabolic functioning depend on a constant enzymic process. Many investigators have shown changes in the biochemistry and metabolism of schizophrenic patients and implicated such hormones as norepinephrine and serotonin, compounds which affect the enzyme systems.

Recently, Dr. Robert Heath and his coworkers at Tulane University demonstrated that another provocative feature in schizophrenia may be the production of protein antibodies by the patient's own body against his own brain tissue which leads to changes in mental function. These proteins play a significant role in the body's defense system, as does histamine (see p. 79). We also know that certain hallucinogens form "deposits" in nerve cells. A natural sequitur to this fact is the question: Does electric shock therapy effect its antidepressant influence by "shaking" these "deposits" out of nerve cells? It's a good question; its answer must await further research.

What are the roles, if any, of heredity and environment in schizophrenia? Some workers claim that a psychosis is due to a heritable inability to react to fundamental and basic environmental situations; others are more cautious and stand by for more definite evidence—if research can provide it. There is a statistical suggestion of likelihood of schizophrenia: only one in one hundred persons in the general population is schizophrenic, but a person with a schizophrenic sibling has a one in seven likelihood of developing the psychosis—that is, of possessing a genetic make-up which would bring about schizophrenia in an unfavorable environment—while a person who has a schizophrenic identical twin has a one in three or four chance.

The efficacy of chemotherapy in psychiatry is inalienably associated with nucleoproteins, specifically deoxyribonucleic acid (DNA) and ribonucleic acid (RNA). These and similar agents are allegedly linked to thinking and memory, particularly as to the hereditability of these functions. Some investigators go so far as to claim that memory depends on brain chemistry. Freud, of course, said that emotional experiences that cannot be recalled have been repressed—an idea far from the materialism of biochemistry. At any rate, current biochemical knowledge seems to suggest that some day, through the action of chemicals, physicians will be able to exert some influence or control over whatever elements are involved in memory and retention.

Some scientists fear that some day research will produce a compound which could be used to control the minds of an entire population. On this subject, Dr. David Krech, Professor of Psychology at the University of California, warned at a recent scientific meeting, *"I do not believe that I am being melodramatic in suggesting that what our research may discover may carry with it even more serious implications than the awful achievements of the atomic physicists. Let us not find ourselves in their position of being caught foolishly surprised, naively perplexed, and touchingly full of publicly displaced guilt at what they had wrought."*

Other investigators have been looking into the action of hallucinogens (see Chapter 10). These compounds are structurally related to such biologically active agents as adrenalin and serotonin which modify the transmittal of nerve impulses. Such research does uncover some explanations of the mode of action of certain drugs such as ataractics; it also may be the ultimate route to etiology.

PHYSIOLOGY, EMOTIONS, AND PSYCHE

The endocrine system, through its hormones, is involved with the emotions and the psyche. This is, in fact, the physiologic foundation on which the tenet of psychosomatic illness is based. The patient who says, "Doctor, there's something wrong with my nerves," is not expressing his symptoms in totally unscientific terminology when you consider the association between the central nervous system and the other systems and organs of the body. From the psychological point of view, the autonomic nervous system makes it possible for the organism to "stay alive"; it allows the body to pursue its ordinary, habitual "involuntary" life, to respond to sensory stimuli, and to "charge" organs for "basic" living (heart, lungs, gastrointestinal, tract, etc.). This is the organism "living automatically" without the need for thinking. On the other hand, the sympathetic nervous system functions just as the word "sympathetic" implies—warmly, emotionally, thoughtfully—by innervating the endocrine system and voluntary muscles and, of psychological importance, it is profoundly involved in emotional control.

Even in research the pendulum of thinking swings a full arc. Many years ago neurologists proposed vagotonia and sympathetonia as causes of mental disease. Today, as we lean more and more to the holistic concept in medicine, these views are assuming such prominence that they merit consideration.

Vagotonia. When the vagus nerve predominates over the sympathetic nervous system or is stimulated, the signs and symptoms that result are known as vagotonia. These include myosis, cool, dry, and sometimes cyanotic skin, bradycardia, hypotension and, with decreased pulmonic aeration, a proneness to respiratory diseases, notably tuberculosis. Vagotonia also causes alternating constipation and diarrhea. Psychologically, the vagotonic is dull, indifferent, without ambition, asocial, and shy. He is the tall, lanky person, whose perpendicular development is disproportionately greater than lateral development. Kretschmer called this the *asthenic habitus* which is essentially the same as Sheldon's *ectomorph* (*hyperonto-morphy*).

Sympathetonia. Stimulation of the sympathetic nervous system results in outpouring of impulses to voluntary muscles and the endocrines. Of the latter the adrenals are of psychological significance. Their hormones (adrenalin, e.g.) cause mydriasis, perspiration, erythema, tachycardia, hypertension, increased respiratory rate, tremors, and loss of sphincter control. These manifestations are seen in persons suddenly exposed to overwhelming emotional situations—shock, fright, anger. The sympathetonic is the rotund or pleasantly plump person, whose girth is disproportionately greater than length. He is Kretschmer's *pyknic habitus;* Sheldon's *endomorph.* The sympathetonic throws himself into life wholeheartedly, "hotly," *sympathetically.* He is seen as the choleric foreman, the wildly yelling spectator at the ball park, the raconteur, the high-pressure salesman, the "eager beaver," the exhibitionist. He is a prime prospect for malignant hypertension, hemiplegia, and coronary occlusion.

The Central Nervous System. By now the physician realizes what is meant by "holisticism": the study of the organism as a whole, not as a conglomerate of components, but as an element of the universe in and to which he attempts to adjust with its climate, geography, cultures, ethnic differences, etc. For purposes of adaptation, man uses his body, mind, emotions, and glands, together with his phylogenetic heritage of instincts and drives, all pieced together to make existence possible. The doctor will find in this book references to pharmaceuticals, emotions, environmental factors, disease, and so forth, which directly affect the organism so that he responds in one direction or another through and with his nervous system.

The same results can be effected by stimulation of the sympathetic nervous system and by depression of the parasympathetic nervous system. The two systems are better understood when we take into consideration that the vegetative nervous system, phylogenetically the older of the two, is fundamentally concerned with instinctive and affective life, while the parasympathetic system is concerned with nutrition and race preservation and is the means by which the organism "moves" in life and is able to cope with environment.

The Combined Aspect. The organism's chemical, physical, psychic, and emotional features are clinically inseparable. This concept, combined with the association of endocrines, muscles, emotions, and the nervous system, enable us to appreciate what is meant by psychosomatic illness (see Chapter 5), which the APA classifies as "psychophysiologic autonomic visceral reactions."

In the Pursuit of Cure

While research, such as we have discussed, strongly suggests that a "cure" lies "just ahead" in psychiatry, we must keep biochemistry and allied sciences in their proper perspective; such research has only begun. But this is not the entire story. Suppose that science *does* discover that the poison *y* in the body causes psychopathology, or that the lack of *x* does the same thing. Such a chemicophysical find could not possibly explain why one individual will present his psychosis as a schizophrenic process and another as a manic-depressive reaction. It couldn't explain why one schizophrenic is hebephrenic and another paranoid and a third catatonic. Science has made it possible for medicine to accurately determine norms for erythrocytes, for pH levels, for protein contents of various body fluids; but it has yet to lay down determinants for "normal," "subnormal," and "abnormal" psyches. We can categorize thousands of clinical entities by changes in blood and spinal fluid and other organismal elements, but in psychiatry diagnostic categories serve statistics far better than they do clinical knowledge.

Current promise of biochemistry and physiological investigation and their enormous contribution to psychiatry's therapeutic armamentarium might induce some physicians to have increasing disdain for the dynamic interpretation of normal and abnormal mental functioning, and to believe that the end of psychological therapy is not far off. Nothing could be further from the truth. Normal functioning of the mind and body has been regarded for centuries in the light of psychological functioning. The dynamic approach—no matter if it is Freud's, Adler's, Horney's, Jung's . . . anyone's—will remain a useful means to explain why and how man thinks while he exists chemically, physiologically, culturally, spiritually. Biochemistry may analyze the body fluids down to the nth degree; physiology may delineate hormonal secretion and metabolism, but how the psyche acts and responds to these functions will always be related and interpreted in the dynamics of psychology. No matter what a person's illness is, no matter what organ is not functioning properly, he is gripped by unconscious dread of death, and the most effective antibiotic won't neutralize this fear, nor will the statistical fact that no one ever dies from his sickness . . . "There's always a first time." You can soothe the id with a compromise; you can't deceive it outright.

Let us go further with our wishful dream of a symptomatic panacea in psychiatry. Let us assume it is uniformly effective; will it be able to remove a patient's reaction to emotional conflicts? Will it solve life's problems for him? A patient comes to you because of persistent headache. You can prescribe an analgesic which is effective as long as the patient takes the medicine. But not until the *cause* of the headache—spinal curvature, faulty vision, etc.—is discovered and eradicated will the headache stop and the patient be able to stop taking the analgesic. This, unfortunately, is the prevailing situation in psychiatry. We can effectively neutralize agitated depression with electric shock therapy and tranquilizers. That is symptomatic relief. However, if the patient undergoes psychotherapy and the underlying cause is discovered, a complete clinical "cure" can be claimed. If, however, the patient goes no further in treatment than symptomatic alleviation, there is an excellent likelihood that he will suffer depressive bouts again . . . and again. This lesson is one of the reasons this book was prepared for our non-psychiatric colleagues. There are other reasons, as we shall see.

CHAPTER FOUR

Nervousness

IN THE LISTING in Chapter 2, the first group of psychiatric disorders is *"transient situational personality disorders,"* colloquially speaking, *"nervousness."* This is the mildest form of emotional disturbance and one that all physicians frequently encounter in their patients. It is a response to life's challenges—trying moments—that all of us undergo from time to time. The student who fails college entrance exams, the young lady whose engagement is suddenly broken, are examples. The ego is hurt and "licking its wound" may be done by moping about the house, staying in one's room and shedding tears, or angrily kicking the waste basket across the floor. But, time healeth most (not all, as we shall see) wounds, and in a few days the student settles down to studying, the young lady is dating again, and the irate individual is back at his usual occupation, realizing he should have kicked himself instead of the basket.

These are examples of everyday tensions and anxieties. Why even consider them? You could say they are "normal" reactions to disappointment and frustration. So they are, but with some persons these reactions begin to drift into the indefinable area of "not normal" because the emotional reactions last longer than they should and are incapacitating (the victim cannot go about his usual daily routine). Most of these patients require nothing more than the common sense counsel of their physicians. If, however, the doctor feels that the anxiety is persisting and the patient cannot get back to his routine of life, formal psychotherapy may be indicated. This is particularly true if the patient is becoming *more* anxious and tense, and he is doing less and less. These may be prodromes of a severe psychiatric illness.

Transient situational personality disorders provide perfect examples of differentiating between normal and abnormal. Take that student who flunked college entrance examinations. How long should you regard his grousing and anxiety in terms of time as normal? A week? Two weeks? A month? Suppose he doesn't "snap out of it" at all? Just what does the APA classification mean by "transient"? How deep is an emotional response that is "profound" or "severe"? Your best guide is the comparison of his pre-situational personality with that which results from the trauma.

Anxiety and tension are the commonest and most frequently occurring emotional reactions. The surgeon experiences these when his scalpel inadvertently severs an artery. So does any mother whose son is in a combat zone. Anxiety gives birth to tension which is an essential of life and almost as vital as hunger and thirst. The person who lacks the capacity for anxiety cannot recognize and respond defensively to the many events and people that pose threats to him throughout life. The two basic self-protective emotional responses are anxiety (the conscious manifestation of unconscious fear) and tension (the mobilizer of one's mental and physical resources).

Dr. George S. Stevenson said that everyone experiences tension in response to appropriate provocations, and that such tension is more intense at some times than at others. An occasional period of anxiety and tension may be unpleasant, but it is normal and is not a cause for concern. Dr. Stevenson pointed out that anxiety and tension may be beneficial. Cyrus Field, in his attempt to lay a transatlantic cable, suffered one failure after another. With each failure, he could have become deeply depressed, embittered, and overwhelmed by a sense of futility—and given up the project in disgust. But, *anxious* to realize his cherished dream and stimulated by *tense* preoccupation with his work, he tried again until he succeeded in transmitting international communications beneath the waves.

Thus, everyday anxiety and tension are the generators that impel most of us to work, to achieve, to get ahead. Their overt expression is doggedness and persistence. Many persons want something at least "just a little better," the externalized drive of internal demand for nothing less than perfection. Anxiety and tension are periodic manifestations of the obstetrician as he begins to apply traction on forceps, of the orthopedist when he turns to an X-ray to determine if a fracture has been properly set, of the gambler who is about to throw dice on winnings he is permitting to ride more than three times.

These are normal reactions; when do they become abnormal? When they become excessive, when they occur frequently, when they disturb the individual, and, above all, when they don't disappear after a reasonable time (after the precipitating stimulus has abated or vanished). It will help physicians in dealing with their patients' everyday anxiety and tension to ask these persons the following questions propounded by Dr. Stevenson to which I have added expository comments.

1. *Do minor problems and small disappointments throw you into a "dither"?* Here is the business man who maps the next day's work on a tight, timetable schedule. He might be late for only one appointment or be late because of a traffic jam. This is temporary failure, albeit failure. He becomes frenzied, completely disorganized, and frenetically dashes from one task to another, actually accomplishing nothing. He simply falls apart at his "emotional seams."

2. *Do you find it difficult to get along with other people and are people having trouble getting along with you?* Meet the complainer. He speaks of his trouble in terms of the second part of the question when it's the first part that actually is his trouble. Everybody is out of step except him. For example, in a group practice the participating physicians have agreed to rotate weekends on call, an arrangement fair for all. Dr. Grimshaw doesn't think so. When his weekend turns up he asks for an exchange; it's never the "right" weekend for him. His constant attempts to switch the schedule, his irritability and sullenness when he is rebuffed, make it impossible for him to adjust democratically to his occupational environment. His attitude spreads to every corner of his work. But it's *his* feelings that are always hurt, and he blames everyone but himself for what actually is his own maladjustment. He is a prime candidate for a paranoid personality.

3. *Do the small pleasures of life fail to satisfy you?*   Mrs. Miller, housewife and mother, relishes an occasional night out, and she's perfectly content with an inexpensive dinner and a movie—anything for a change and a chance to get away from housework. Mrs. Gorham, on the other hand, can't be content with less than the first tier at the Metropolitan Opera, dinner at the Four Seasons, and after-opera dance-lobster thermidor-champagne at the Waldorf— and, of course a chauffeured Cadillac to transport her and her husband from place to place. Anything less fails to satisfy her. Everyone dreams of an estate on the Riviera, around-the-world travel, and similar luxuries. Well-adjusted persons, however, have a sense of values that enables them to save psychic energy other- wise lost in being unable to settle for the pleasures that are avail- able. Less well-adjusted individuals indulge in costly display beyond their means in order to neutralize feelings of insecurity; they can find security only in material possessions, and most of them go through life missing out on the finer things that cost little or nothing.

4. *Are you unable to stop thinking about your anxieties?*   This is the patient who holds up the busy physician's office appointment schedule. He or she can't be put off with a reassuring phrase such as, "Stop worrying, you'll be all right." This patient is perpetually anxious about his anxiety; he is obsessively buried in it and simply can't face life's challenges. "I used to enjoy the theater, but not now." "I don't know what's happened at home; my husband and I are always bickering. He's changed, doctor." She should look in a mirror and say that—changing the pronoun, of course. This is no patient for the non-psychiatric physician to treat. The patient will become irritable, lose confidence in her doctor, and take up more and more of his carefully apportioned time. She should be urged to seek psychotherapy. The longer she puts this off the worse she will become.

5. *Do you fear people or situations that never used to bother you?* "Believe me, doctor, until very recently, I loved my work, selling in- surance. I liked meeting people, overcoming sales resistance . . . but now . . . I could throw up every time I look at the rate book. And as for potential clients, they get on my nerves. Worse, when my

regular clients call for help, I'm actually nasty to them." You've seen and heard of this patient. He's "losing his grip," he's not as efficient as he once was. He's fallen prey to feelings of inferiority. In a majority of instances he's approaching or in the involution (see Chapter 14). Very often you'll find he has been looking around him and sees men of his own age who started when he did. They've advanced; he hasn't gotten anywhere, and the firm is hiring younger men with whom he can't compete as he once did. Things he used to do without batting an eye-lash are now too much for him. Ahead is the dead-end street of senility and unemployment and of being unwanted. It's disheartening, it's cause for anxiety.

6. *Are you suspicious of people, mistrustful of your old friends?* In essence, this is an expansion of Question 2 that deals with the patient who has poor interpersonal relationships. He is the quintessence of suspicion. Two and two must not only add up to four, he has to be shown how they add up and guaranteed the result is correct. No one is exempt from his paranoid personality, even his physician. "You say this prescription is for Superbo, doctor? I've been reading in the papers how the government is looking into this business of pharmaceuticals. Uh-huh. But is it good for me?" Those who solicit funds for legitimate causes such as Heart and Cancer are really "crooks." Friendship? Love? Hogwash. Even if your assistance isn't asked, don't even volunteer to "set him right." You have one obligation to him for his welfare (and to yourself for peace of mind): recommend psychotherapy. Whether or not he'll accept the suggestion (odds are he won't), you've seen your duty and done it.

7. *Do you feel inadequate? Do you suffer the tortures of self-doubt?* Like the patient in Question 3, this patient is inundated with feelings of inadequacy. She can't make up her mind on the simplest problem (should I have veal cutlet or pork chops tonight?), she is without a sense of responsibility, and eternally doubtful that she can finish anything or do anything properly. If she has nothing more demanding to do than write to the piano tuner to make an appointment, she'll write one note after another, tearing up each one. In the end her husband will telephone the tuner.

Of the above examples, what can the nonpsychiatric physician do for those patients who do not need to go to a psychiatrist right away? Dr. Stevenson offers the following simple, practical suggestions.

1. *Talk it out.* Encourage the patient to "let his hair down." Tell him not to bottle his worries up inside himself. Urge him to find a level-headed person he can trust—a member of his immediate family, a friend, his pastor, attorney, and talk the problem over. Here is one instance where the family doctor is often that level-headed person. Talking it out frequently enables the anxious patient to discover a viewpoint his tense state had not permitted him to think of and may alleviate, even eradicate, the difficulty.

2. *Escape for a while.* This is not the fin de siècle treatment of "take-an-ocean-voyage-and-forget-your-troubles" regimen that went out with the bustle. Nor is it telling a patient to "run away" from a situation; he doesn't need you or anyone to advise that. It is, in essence, "putting off to do tomorrow what you *can't* do today." It's getting away from it for a while, and the "while" may be no longer than a concert, a movie, a weekend of fishing. It is the psychological equivalent of the coffee break, of "all work and no play make Jack a dull boy." This type of anxious patient is a masochist. Faced with a problem he can't solve at once (and has more and more trouble with as he becomes more and more tense), he chains himself to his desk and builds up his anxiety with this occupational self-flagellation. When you advise the patient to take a break you should emphasize that although he escapes for a while he must be prepared to return and tackle the problem. Refreshed and with diminished anxiety, he should be emotionally and intellectually fortified when he comes back.

3. *Work off your anger.* It's remarkable how many adults recognize play and sports as excellent means through and by which children unload their hostility. But many grown-ups can't see a parallel program as a benefit for themselves. The patient is told that working off his anger doesn't imply destructive behavior or going into violent rages. Temper tantrums are the psychological

equivalents of childish conduct and undeniable evidence of emotional immaturity. The patient invariably (granted, grudgingly) concedes that anger accomplishes nothing, alienates friends, and sometimes leaves him feeling silly. "Think before you speak," "Put a bit in your anger's mouth," are clichés, but nonetheless psychologically sound. Encourage the patient to think about his problem before permitting his passion to get the better of him; take a walk and mull it over, play eighteen holes, mow the lawn. Sure, it's cracker barrel counsel; but remember you're talking to an adult whose emotions are somewhere down at the kid level.

4. *Give in once in a while.* "Doctor, it's unbearable. From the moment I come home at night until I leave the next morning, it's fight, fight, fight! One damned argument after another!" Doctors hear this constantly; so do attorneys and judges of family courts. The complainant, however, doesn't believe he can't be right all the time. He's adamant, stubborn. He's like the little hellion who screams and stamps his feet, and shouts, "I won't! I won't!" This patient can be helped by you, but not in a few minutes or by some pat phrase of advice. You tell him, "When you are convinced you're right, you should stick to your guns. There's nothing wrong in that. But, it's not *what* you say, but *how*. You know the adage about catching flies with vinegar or honey. It's the soft rebuttal, the serene attitude of self-confidence, the good-sport, gentlemanly front that convince your adversary. And even when you are dead right, try turning the other cheek now and then. You'll be known as the liberal, the broad-minded good sport. Above all, *you'll* feel better for it because anger builds up tension; you'll experience a sense of satisfaction you've never known before." This is not proposed as a pat delivery in every such instance; it is an example and one which you will enlarge.

5. *Do something for others.* Very often an elderly patient will complain of restlessness, irritability, depression, and generally feel sorry for himself. He is so preoccupied with his empty life that he can't lend his shoulder for a friend to weep on. No sooner does someone begin to relate his troubles than the oldster launches into a long recital of his difficulties. "You think *you've* got troubles?

Bro-ther!" This is the egocentricity of second childhood. You un-earth this when the patient tells you of his loneliness or his dissatis-faction with retirement. He should be encouraged to do something for someone else, at least now and then: volunteer work at the local hospital a couple of days a week, for example. Assure him that this will take the bite out of his troubles and he will become emotionally warm by giving of himself.

6. *Take one thing at a time.*   This advice is almost specific for two varieties of anxious and tense patients. First there is the panic-stricken person who, faced with a new undertaking, becomes so tense that he can't even get the project off the ground. He can't decide what should be done first, which component is major, which is minor. Result: nothing is done. Then there is the "eager beaver" who is dedicated to the self-ordained assignment of impressing everyone, including himself, with his efficiency. Yes, sir. Today's schedule calls for several things to be done, and he darts from one to another, giving none its due—even skipping some—and at the end of the day he hasn't achieved a thing. When these patients recite such events to you, there is one question to ask them: "Is it possible that you overestimate the importance of what is facing you?" Discuss that for a while, and you may find that your patient sees the "light" and changes his attitude toward life's challenges ac-cordingly.

7. *Shun the superman urge.*   This patient is not easy to handle because he is the perfectionist; he can't settle for less than 100 per-cent achievement. He becomes fantastically tense if he accomplishes "only" 99 percent. More, he's his own worst critic. If he isn't a failure, his anxiety helps him to become one. He complains that his work is under par, incomplete, unsatisfactory. He loses confidence in himself and becomes depressed. It often helps if the physician has the patient make an honest inventory and appraisal of his per-sonal assets, determine which ones are those he is best at, and then concentrate on them. They're probably the very items that bring him the maximum of satisfaction anyway. The doctor should point out that it is only the patient, by rigid self-discipline, who can eventually get himself to accept the inalienable truth that no one

is perfect and that he, the patient, must be content with achieving something less than perfection, especially when he knows he has done his best.

8. *Go easy with criticism of others.* This patient is usually one in a supervisory position. "What I do, I expect my employees to do." "If I can work overtime during an emergency, why can't they?" But the "employee" may be a spouse or a child or a fellow committeeman. "Well, wouldn't you become hot under the collar, doctor, if *your* wife was so stupid as to buy that piece of junk as a genuine antique?" Don't try the logic of asking him if he can bake a cake as well as his wife or diaper and bathe and do all the chores required in rearing children. His answer? "Oh, well, that's different. Has nothing to do with what I'm talking about." Of course it doesn't. In his gripe, the other party is inadequate; in your rebuttal *he* would be the inferior one. This patient must be induced to understand that there is a broad range of individual differences among people, that not everybody sees, thinks, and acts exactly as he does. If he bridles at this, then try to have him curb his critical attitude, especially his aggressiveness in expressing it. Banging the desk, cursing others, and indiscriminately mouthing sarcasm will leave him a lonely, unwanted man.

9. *Give the other fellow a "break."* Ever have an office emergency who had to be seen before the first person scheduled on your appointment calendar? If the postponed patient is the anxious individual who compensates for unconscious inferiority by always getting there "first," you're in for a strongly worded complaint. He has to pass the car ahead of him on the highway, then the one in front of that, and on and on forever, as he does in everything else in his existence. When he was in elementary school, he had to get all the gold stars; later he had to be valedictorian; now, if he doesn't get the top salesman award each month his anxiety knows no bounds. And if he wins it this month, he promptly worries that he won't repeat next month. So he is the ruthless, get-out-of-my-way competitor. When you point out that giving the other fellow a "break" is one way of establishing interpersonal relationships, be sure to add that patronization and condescension aren't enough.

The spoil-sport who reluctantly gives in is not the good sport. Yes, competition is psychologically healthy; so is cooperation.

10. *Make yourself available.* This type of patient may be developing a severe psychosis, such as schizophrenia. He complains that he is ignored, left out of things. Close questioning may reveal that he is invited to most community affairs, but should an invitation to one, just one, affair not come to him, he feels that no one likes him. This self-pitying attitude drives him further into isolation; he becomes more and more inaccessible and withdrawn. He is said to be "schizoid." Encourage him to make himself available, even to make overtures on his own initiative; but don't forget "moderation." There is a happy medium between total withdrawal and pushing oneself.

11. *Schedule your recreation.* "Don't ask me, doctor. I don't know what it is; I just haven't got time for recreation." Familiar words? Odd that we hear them more and more in an era of shorter hours, longer paid vacations, daylight saving time, and increased recreational facilities. There is another item. Vacation doesn't necessarily mean a period of time devoted to loafing or travel or all the usual things associated with vacation. A man may delight in working from dawn to dark throughout his entire vacation in his garden, perspiring, straining muscles, etc. Psychologically, vacation is an annual event when one does something pleasurable for which one does not ordinarily have the time. But what about the rest of the year? That's what contributes a great deal to anxiety and tension if no time is allotted to recreation. "All work and no play makes jack"; it also makes anxiety and tension.

Bear in mind that when patients attribute their emotional disturbances to mother-in-law interference, financial difficulty, marriage problems, and the like, that these are precipitating factors. A patient can speak of these to you as freely and unembarrassedly as he can to a stranger standing next to him at a bar. These "reasons" for feeling "rotten" are socially acceptable and frequently strike a harmonic chord in the listener's psychological and emotional sounding board. Anxiety and tension can just as easily result from attitudes and habits in a person that date back to early childhood. Conflicts, as we have stated previously, result from inter-acting forces which can be exogenous and/or endogenous; and if these forces go unchecked—even build up—they tend to aggra-vate each other. Further, if the neurotic process (for that is what anxiety and tension are) is of long standing and deeply "etched" in the patient's psyche, the best procedure is probably psycho-therapy. Sometimes something or someone else less specialized can help. In this category are trained counselors (discussed in detail in Chapter 7), the family clergyman, the family attorney.

The examples and the suggested therapeutic approaches—all stemming from Dr. Stevenson—presented in this chapter are not offered as universal and unwaveringly successful answers to the anxiety the nonpsychiatric physician encounters among his patients. They are meant to be helpful guides, that, and nothing more.

CHAPTER FIVE

Psychoneurosis

IN AN EARLIER CHAPTER the failure of psychiatry to define psychoneurosis was discussed. The name itself, *psyche,* mind + *neurosis,* disorder of nerves, is a double-barreled semantic implication that there is something that has "broken down" in the central nervous system. The same thing is suggested by the popular phrase, "nervous breakdown." Of course there are several syndromes of which this is true; these are neurologic disorders in which gross and microscopic pathology is found, as for instance, in a brain tumor. Added to the confusion is the synonym "neurosis" which is used interchangeably with psychoneurosis.

It is worthwhile to refer again to the earlier discussion of the difficulty in differentiating between "normal" and "abnormal"— and this problem reaches its peak in the neuroses. Compared to the everyday anxieties and tensions presented in the previous chapter, psychoneurotic disorders simply stand out as "deeper" tensions and anxieties. A. A. Brill wrote about Freud in his *Lectures on Psychoanalytic Psychiatry* (Alfred A. Knopf 1946) "*(He) showed that the difference between hysteria (a type of neurosis) and schizophrenia (a psychosis) was only one of degree. Soon thereafter he demonstrated the same relationship between the neurotic and the so-called normal person. In his "Psychopathology of Everyday Life" he showed that many ordinary faulty actions—mistakes in talking and writing, forgetting, misplacing things, and other common errors —are all due to unconscious emotional disturbances, and as such show the same distortion as do neurotic and psychotic symptoms. . ."*

46

In other words, according to Freud there is no such thing as a trivial mistake—that is, one without a reason for its happening.

In the matter of "normal" and "abnormal," man's culture has a dominant role in the development of a neurotic process. Investigators have concentrated for some time on the earlier experiences of the organism, the so-called *critical period*. This was the basis for Freud's explanation of the evolution of a neurosis, indicating there is a period in life when primary and secondary development take place, and that circumstances and events of the critical period may result in abnormal behavior. Expressed in contemporary thought: the critical period is the era of extreme sensitivity which influences all aspects of development.

If a laboratory animal is taken from its mother right after birth and isolated not only from her but its "peers," it will never be able to adjust to the demands of life thereafter. Infants in orphanages soon manifest severe psychological and physical symptoms, despite adequate nourishment and care, if they do not also receive needed maternal-type of attention. By expansion, this is borne out by the common finding that without early social opportunities the organism is not equipped to engage in group activities, and they may go on to be shy, withdrawn, and sexually impotent. Without socially acceptable defense mechanisms he may develop unusual psychic and emotional reactions. This is one of Karen Horney's fundamental tenets in her approach to "the neurotic personality of our time." She said that "a neurosis is a disturbance in one's relations to self and others." Conduct is frequently judged as normal or neurotic, depending on where and when it takes place. The mature adult who whoops like an Indian and grimaces wildly at a lodge meeting would be taken to the nearest psychiatric observation ward if he did the very same things on the street. But conduct must also be judged by the individual's age. A youngster at play makes a buzzing sound and swoops his hand around to indicate a dive bomber. Let an adult do that and he'll be diagnosed as schizophrenic.

Features of Neurosis. Despite the lack of a definition, it is possible to identify psychoneurosis by certain characteristics. These are as follows: (1) Neurosis is a psychic disorder, (2) Some neurotic features are not unlike those of neurologic disorders, (3) The

psyche in neurosis is partially disorganized; in psychosis the disorganization is complete, (4) The neurotic patient has some insight insofar that he realizes his behavior and attitudes are not
"normal"; such insight is lacking in psychotic patients, and (5)
Anxiety and tension are features common to all neuroses.

The following table provides the chief differences between a
neurosis and a psychosis:

PSYCHONEUROSIS	DIFFERENTIAL FACTOR	PSYCHOSIS
Ego *vs.* id.	*Dynamics (according to Freud)*	Ego *vs.* reality
Partially changed; usually intact.	*Personality*	Changed in whole; total disorganization.
Patient relates well with reality.	*Reality*	Patient shuns or with-draws from reality.
Conscious sense of guilt.	*Projection*	Unconscious sense of guilt.
Unaltered.	*Language*	May be disturbed (irrelevancy, incoherency, or neologisms).
Indirectly expressed.	*The Unconscious*	Directly (verbally) expressed.
None.	*Regression*	Present (unashamed wetting and soiling, e. g.).

The most important feature in the above table is the objective
feature which the physician most often observes: regression. The
psychotic ignores the world of reality and regresses through the
various periods of psychosexual development until, as in the most
severe forms of schizophrenia, he finally returns to the most pleasurable, most secure, and happiest time of his life: infancy. Nonpsychiatric physicians seldom see this type of patient (unless they are
attendings or consultants at mental institutions). Like a baby, the
patient must be spoon- or tube-fed, unashamedly wets and soils,
rips off his clothes, and huddles in a chair or on the floor in a corner,
incoherently babbling—often using neologisms which may or may
not be responses to auditory hallucinations. There is nothing pleas-

urable in the world of reality; this dislike may be so extreme that the patient may attempt suicide.

The neurotic patient, however, may not like one or more features in the world in which he lives, but he is quite aware of his environmental conflict. This conflict most often concentrates on a well-delimited area of life problems, expressed in a specific anxiety or frustration. He, like the psychotic, would like to return to the time of life (infancy) when he "never had it so good"; but this is "cowardice," and his unyielding superego will not tolerate "howling for mama" and so informs the ego. The ego, therefore, is faced with the problem of relieving the unconscious of its pain in a manner society (as dictated by the superego) will accept. Reality does, indeed, accept—even commiserate with—physical illness, worry, anxiety. It is almost "fashionable" to be "neurotic" and, like a child looking to its parent for guidance, lean on the psychiatrist or analyst ("I must ask my therapist what he thinks about this"). This, it has been said, is the Age of Anxiety. Thus, a neurosis is a compromise; a compromise that satisfies, at least partially, the unconscious and reality. What the unconscious wants to get rid of is *fear;* it cannot be openly expressed as such because "nobody loves a coward." So fear emerges as anxiety and this "draining-off" process can take many forms, particularly through the soma, as we shall see in psychosomatic illness, discussed later.

THE PSYCHONEUROSES

Allowing for the constant changes in diagnostic nomenclature, this book follows the most frequently used terms to designate the types of psychoneuroses. These are anxiety reaction, dissociative reaction, phobic reaction, obsessive-compulsive reaction, and hypochondriacal reaction. First, however, the subject of anxiety must be considered.

Anxiety. It is a misfortune that the term "anxiety" is one of the rare words in medicine that indicates a symptom, a disorder, and an emotional reaction. In addiction, it is applicable to emotional situations that are normal under certain circumstances, pathological under others, and sometimes "either-or." The anxious mother who is profoundly concerned with her son serving in Viet Nam is quite understandable; it is normal. But should she continue to be anxious after cessation of hostilities the emotional manifestation is, at least, not normal. Therefore, one of the doctor's prime objectives is to ascertain the source of the anxiety: anxiety from without—as in response to genuine stress or disappointment—is to be expected; anxiety from within—originating entirely in the patient's psyche— is a sign of psychopathology. The "translation" of unconscious fear into anxiety, (or its variations such as apprehension, doubt, etc.), was mentioned above. Anxiety from within, no matter how it is expressed, is surcharged with tension. Tension may be defined as "emotional strain manifested in the irritability that accompanies anxiety."

We repeat that the vexing challenge physicians often are confronted with is determining what anxiety is normal and what is not normal. It is not unlike the term "tepid"; we know what hot and cold are, but just how much heat and how much cold are in tepid? Most often a doctor has to consider the circumstances under which anxiety has developed: the provocation, the personality make-up of the individual, and the intensity and length of time of the emotional condition.

There is considerable merit to the psychoanalytic theory of anxiety. This discipline claims that instincts have ideational forms of presentation, that is, ideas are attached to every instinctual impulse, and that in repression, the ideational expression of an instinct vanishes from consciousness (if it is there) or remains in the unconscious. Therefore, there are three possible means for instinctual-ideational expression: (1) complete suppression, (2) appearance in the guise of a particular type of affect, or (3) transformation into anxiety.There is considerable debate among psychiatrists over the interchangeable usage of the terms anxiety and fear. Physicians need not be concerned with this since fear finds outward expression in anxiety. According to Freud, there are three conditions which are almost certain of provoking a later manifestation of anxiety: (1) loss of a love object, (2) the castration complex (see p. 7) of childhood following parental scolding or punishment for normal sexual curiosity, and (3) social fixation.

When the physician sees anxiety, it is seldom at less than maximal strength; it is intense, extreme, and severe. Said Eugen Bleuler: *"Anxiety undoubtedly has different sources. In many cases it is plainly connected with respiratory difficulties as seen in diseases of the heart, in the respiratory organs, and in the blood. Furthermore, anxiety is undoubtedly connected in some way with sexuality, a fact which we knew for a long time but which Freud made clearer."*

Anxiety may be "attached" or "free." In the former, it may be linked to definite ideas; if this association does not exist, the anxiety is said to be "free-floating." Physical expressions of anxiety are the same as the signs of sympathetonia (see p. 32): tachycardia, increased respiratory rate, perspiration, alternating pallor and flushing, etc., which point up the neuro-endocrine-emotional triad discussed previously, and the linkage with subthalamic centers of emotional control.

Anxiety Reaction. Of all the neuroses this is the variety most often encountered by physicians. The patient complains of symptoms, singly or in combination, which cover the entire gamut of syndromes and ailments. The most common symptoms are: diarrhea, urinary frequency, cardiac palpitation, tremors, lack of appetite, insomnia, and various pains, and aches. He looks and acts uneasy, and sometimes says that he feels that "something terrible is going to happen to him," i. e., he has one foot in the grave.

Phobic Reaction. "Phobia" (fear) is applied to responses in which the alleged threat of harm is usually remote and, to a majority of persons, not worthy of attention. It is defined as a morbid, abnormal fear, usually without adequate cause. There are many phobias, some very common and well known (claustrophobia, agoraphobia, et al.), but anyone can make up his own phobia combination such as fatophobia in which the survivor of a coronary attack dreads the slightest drop of polyunsaturated fats in his diet—and these phobia names are carried to the extreme and the absurd. To determine if a fear is neurotic the physician considers several factors. Does a real threat exist? Is the fear selective, that is, is it only in one special situation or in response to one special stimulus that the patient manifests fear? Does this fear and its accompanying tension impair his efficiency in his work, does it disrupt his adjustment to others? The answers to these questions invariably provide the diagnostic differentiation.

Dissociative Reaction.   The patient's tension and anxiety may be so extreme that he contrives to separate himself from his own identity for a time. The classical illustration of this is Dr. Jekyll and Mr. Hyde. In clinical experience the patient is seen as a paradox: one day he is irritable, complaining, domineering, hysterical; on another he is solicitous, generous, sympathetic . . . a "perfect doll." Dissociation may attain the extremes of amnesia or a fugue state.

Amnesia.   Loss of memory is a favorite ploy of many types of criminals, and "goldbricks." However, psychological tests, especially the Rorschach Diagnostic Method, can quickly identify malingering. In addition, the past history of these individuals usually reveals a long list of clashes with the law, poor school and work records, and previous arrests. The true neurotic amnesiac does not have these elements in his history. Instead, the doctor unearths periods of "nervousness," frequent episodes of "illness," etc. Commonly there is a severe emotional trauma that triggers the amnesia. It is sudden in onset and, when memory is regained, the patient cannot recall anything that occurred, what was said to or by him, where he was, and whom he saw, during the period of amnesia.

Fugue State.   Fugue is flight. In a fugue state the patient acts like an automaton, as if in a dream. He may disappear from his environment and, like the amnesiac, cannot recall anything pertaining to the period during his fugue. Examples of fugue state are described in the biographies of composer Robert Schumann and artist Vincent Van Gogh.

Delirium.   This is an acute mental disturbance characterized by confusion, excitement, disorientation, and not infrequently by hallucinations and abject fear; it may be organic in origin (as in fevers or toxic states, especially alcohol) or functional in origin. The delirious patient is uncontrollably excited, incoherent, and out of contact with his immediate environment. The physician has no difficulty in determining if organicity or psychic pathology is the cause. Now and then delirium is feigned, but even here the lack of organic pathology on the one hand, and the usual psychopathic history on the other, facilitate differential diagnosis.

Obsessive-Compulsive Reaction. An obsession is a constant preoccupation with a given thought or a complex of related thoughts, which the neurotic patient cannot "shake." A compulsion is an irresistible urge to some specific action, invariably the overt expression of an obsession. Freud postulated that the underlying factor of obsessive-compulsive reactions is ritualism, man's phylogenetic inheritance which is observed today in primitive tribes and civilized nations. Again, we are faced with the normal *vs.* abnormal problem. An example is the mature man's lodge ceremonies, cited previously. Then there are the everyday familiar ritualisms such as "God bless you!" when someone sneezes. Ritualism becomes pathologic when it is persistent to the exclusion of almost every other ordinary facet of life, intense, and sufficient to be regarded as inacceptable. These extremes are seen in the neurotic who walks, indoors and out, with his eyes riveted on the ground, ever on the lookout for strands of hair; or the man who cannot stop memorizing license plate numbers of passing vehicles, or Samuel Johnson who could not bear stepping on a crack in the sidewalk or refrain from running his cane over every picket fence he passed.

It is obsessive-compulsive reactions that often challenge diagnosis when the law is violated. What of the man charged with arson? He may look like an unassuming, insurance-gouging person who, in actuality, is a pyromaniac whose morbid drive is to set fire. In the latter example, it is felt that psychosexual development has never progressed beyond early levels where libido is fixed; pyromaniacs get a sexual "kick" out of their fire-lighting compulsion. Some authorities regard pyromania as a masturbatory equivalent. When he is "satisfied," the "firebug" regrets his unlawful act, but sooner or later, the irresistible impulse rises again and he must set fire. The same differentiation applies to the shoplifter and the kleptomaniac.

Hypochondriacal Reaction.   This subject need not be dwelled on; every physician knows all about it and recognizes such patients as "incurables" who know more about their (neurotic) illness than the doctor, are never cured, never satisfied, and shift from one physician to another. In psychiatry, there is no patient more refractive to therapy than the hypochondriac. Many of us feel that the neurosis is so deeply entrenched in the psyche, so pernicious, and—often— so "unreasonable"—that we regard it as the somatic delusion(s) of a schizophrenic.

There are several varieties of hypochondriasis physicians recognize easily. However, on occasion, actual pathology complicates the picture and the doctor is embarrassed. One such incident in my own experience is an example. When, as a two-year rotating intern, I became house surgeon for the final six months of internship, I "inherited" from my predecessor a woman with pseudocyesis. Regular as clockwork, she came every month to the receiving room to be diagnosed as pregnant. She held herself so that her abdomen protruded, and complained of "labor pains." My predecessor saw— and dismissed—her for four months, and I continued from there. On my third examination, she screamed her low opinion of my diagnostic ability. The chief of the gynecological service happened to pass by and heard her. He came in and I explained the situation. He consented to examine the patient. Then he took me aside. "She's about six weeks pregnant," he said. I presume that for the rest of her life she boasted to friends that she "carried" her baby for sixteen months before it was born.

The Death Wish.   The death wish—more accurately, death instinct —is a Freudian concept that is assuming alarming proportions in industry, insofar as occupational accidents are concerned. Essentially, the death instinct is an impulse, usually unconscious, for personal oblivion. Suicide or attempt at suicide is not necessarily a consequence. Common expressions of the impulse are: accident proneness, alcoholism, total regression in schizophrenia, etc. Studies, such as those of Halliday in Scotland, show convincingly that a great deal of accidents and lost time through illness in industry are traceable to neurotic behavior patterns of employees. The possibility of malingering always exists, but Halliday cited many examples of workers who "suffered" repeated injuries in spite of posted safety warnings, safety devices and precautions. These are the individuals who are "accident prone." Invariably physical examination is negative. These employees seem to be easily fatigued, so that they are not as alert as others. They may seem "careless"; actually they are not. It is felt that these persons unconsciously *wish* to be sick, *wish* to be disabled—i. e. they *wish* to be dead. Industrial psychiatrists find, almost always, that these individuals are overwhelmed by feelings of "unworthiness" and "inadequacy"; that they're not "fit to live." The "unavoidable accident" seems to be the answer to unconscious feelings of futility. Careful probing often uncovers a powerful unconscious feeling of guilt which, as explained earlier, carries with it the emotional drive for punishment and this is realized in the illness and the accident.

Neurotic Depression. Given a sorrow-provoking stimulus, sadness is a normal, appropriate emotional reaction. Thus, the death of a loved one, the defeat of one's country by another, are adequate causes for sorrow. But normal begins to slip into abnormal when the adequate provocation is lacking. "Doctor, I can't tell you why. I feel so . . . so . . . blue, down in the dumps." Or, when there is a "cause," it is trivial compared to the emotional havoc it wreaks. "I've been indescribably sad ever since our bowling team lost out." Finally, the pathologically protracted melancholia is reason for a doctor to suspect that a neurotic process is involved. In other words, in such a case time does not heal all wounds. An example is the woman who loses her child in infancy, and twenty years later is still wearing black, spends hours on end in church praying, and suffers spells of weeping, and is always sad, deeply sad. Melancholia is also a common complication of the involution (see Chapter 14).

Conversion Hysteria. This category of neurosis is left to the end because it is such a frequently encountered psychiatric syndrome in nonpsychiatric practice. As physicians know, "hysteria" is a misnomer originated by Hippocrates who attributed emotional disorders to malfunctioning uteri because he found these disturbances predominately in women. Freud coined the diagnostic term, "conversion hysteria," to describe the socially acceptable overt physical expression of socially unacceptable unconscious emotional conflict. In other words, soma relieves psyche, and the modern concept of hysteria is, of course, psychosomatic illness.

Psychosomatic Illness.   Doctors know that it's one thing to name a set of symptoms "psychosomatic"; it's quite another to be sure of the diagnosis, and, above all, quite a condition to treat. As Weiss and English pointed out years ago in their excellent textbook on the subject, no physician fails to recognize the extremes of the clinical pendulum's arc: at one end is the purely organic, such as cancer; at the other is schizophrenia, purely functional. In between, and at varying degrees from either extreme, are the many syndromes which are regarded as psychosomatic—or, if one prefers, somatopsychic, depending on which element dominates, psyche or soma. Torticollis, colitis, migraine . . . the list is endless. For the physician, the height of aggravation is explaining psychosomatic to the patient—the hard sell.

"All examinations and tests are negative or normal, Mr. Bradshaw. I feel your wry neck is psychosomatic."

"You mean I *imagine* I have pain in my neck? Do you actually—"

"No, no. It's what is known as—"

"It's from my nerves?"

"Well, in a way, yes . . . but—"

"Don't make me laugh, doctor! I ought to know if I *feel* pain!"

Sound familiar?

Fortunately, not all patients respond in this fashion. For the receptive patient, the doctor should take the time to explain psychosomatic illness, even if the patient is to be referred to and treated by a psychiatrist. The explanation can be something as follows:

"You've been troubled with stomach pain and distress. Medicine knows that a healthy body functions painlessly and, since yours does not, and all examinations have failed to turn up any organic cause, I feel that your trouble is due to emotional difficulties. Let me take a few minutes to explain how the rhythm of bowel function is established and how it can be upset by emotions." Then the doctor goes on to describe peristalsis and how, under various conditions, this smooth action can become irregular, reversed, or otherwise perverted. Emotions can do to the stomach what toxins and irritants can, and results in both instances can be equally protracted and intense.

The doctor then outlines the unconscious esteem of the process of eating in infancy, as explained in an earlier chapter in this book, and the association of eating with security and happiness. The explanation goes on to the matter of the relationship between emotions, endocrines, and the nervous system, so that when the mind is unable to cope with a particularly trying problem and anxiety and insecurity increase, the stomach takes over and tries to vomit out the unpleasant situation—a *rejection* of a painful or distasteful emotion which cannot be disguised in any other manner. "So," the physician goes on, "emotional weakness is, temporarily anyway, hidden by a curtain of physical illness—in your case, stomach pain. You know, of course, that pain doesn't necessarily mean that disease is present. Two examples come to mind. One is the headache that may result from eyestrain—too much reading, particularly under a poor light. Another, is a pregnant woman's labor pains." Then, the point is made that this is the case at hand: under stress the psyche creates emotional impulses which can alter physiological function. *The patient must understand this point,* because one of the prime goals of therapy is to eliminate the patient's preoccupation with his somatic distress. This does not imply that the doctor is to pooh-pooh the pain, for *the pain is real.* The patient's confidence can be promptly and irrevocably lost, and treatment doomed to utter failure, by a remark such as "Your pain is purely imaginary." Nor is he satisfied or reassured by the broad smile and optimistic tone of the doctor who says, "Well, sir, good news! Every test and examination is negative! You're healthy as an ox. You haven't a thing to worry about." Really? Well, the patient *does* have and will continue to have something to worry about: his pain. The "good news" that there is no organic pathology isn't going to be the panacea that promptly results in analgesia. The patient looks to the doctor to explain *why* he has the pain, while diagnosis is being discussed. And the hard-boiled practitioner who gives a patient the "brush-off" by a curt pronouncement that "there is nothing wrong with you" will only succeed in losing the patient and sending him on his way to another doctor. This "shopping around for a physician" is a common pastime among neurotics, especially hypochondriacs.

If the doctor, after pursuing a course similar to that outlined above, has gained the patient's confidence, he can help the patient to review the emotional conflicts that triggered the perverted physiological functioning. In this "re-run" of his personal life, the patient will re-experience all the emotional "pain"—all the frustrations and disappointments, the anger, disgust, sorrow, and he may be able to talk, scold, or otherwise emancipate his psyche of the difficulty. Once the unconscious is unshackled and free of its emotional pain, there will be no further *need* for the quasi-relief it once had to be content with: the somatic pain. Once the skeleton is out of the closet, the house is no longer haunted. But, this takes time, and it usually pays the doctor to refer the patient to a psychiatrist.

Treatment of Psychoneuroses. Nonpsychiatric colleagues will not be needlessly burdened with the several methods of therapy employed in the treatment of neurotic syndromes, the routine, and the technique, because the gynecologist (to use just one specialist for purposes of illustration) doesn't want to practice psychiatry or psychoanalysis any more than these latter specialists have any desire to perform a colporrhaphy. It is true that in the previous pages, an approach—not the entire program, by any means—to treatment in psychosomatic conditions was discussed. But one of the aims of our system of certification by the various American boards is to have the qualified shoemaker stick to his last. However, the nonpsychiatric physician does not, cannot, totally isolate himself from psychiatry. On the one hand he should have a comprehensive understanding of psychic dynamics; on the other, he may be caring for a patient's somatic condition while the latter is undergoing formal psychotherapy. Indeed, if you grant that peptic ulcer is a psychosomatic syndrome, and the patient enters into psychotherapy, that does not imply that he must writhe with pain without benefit of an internist's highly specialized knowledge through which he can find relief. This sort of bilateral, simultaneous treatment is a common procedure in our profession.

But the reader will not be short-changed. All modalities of psychiatric treatment are fully discussed and presented in Chapter 7.

CHAPTER SIX

Psychosis

THE TABLE ON PAGE 48 indicates that the neurotic is aware that his behavior and personality are disturbed, although he lacks insight into the unconscious—and true—etiology of his illness which, as explained, is the compromise that keeps his ego intact. It's his answer to his problem. *The psychotic does not or cannot find such an answer and therefore retreats from it and the world in which it arose, and flees into another world, his world, where he finds surcease from his troubles.* The universe he leaves behind is one that was too domineering, too restrictive, too unfeeling, too insecure. All this vanishes when he lands on his new planet where everything is as he creates it; where *he* is the god endowed with what psychiatry calls "magic omnipotence." Here his associates—whom he hears in his hallucinations (and sometimes sees in his visual hallucinations)— are in complete accord with his ideas and behave as he wants them to. Why shouldn't they? They're his creations. When this psychic interplanetary voyage has been completed, the patient is said to have regressed.

Regression. The full-blown psychotic's personality is described as "infantile," and does, as a fact, resemble an infant's personality. If, before the onset of the psychosis, the patient has made a quasi-adjustment on an adult level, then his reversion to psychosexual infancy is known as *regression.* This process determines what psychosis the patient will manifest. For example, if the prepsychotic personality was peppered by cyclothymia (wide mood swings from elation to depression and vice versa) the psychosis will be an affective reaction. If the patient was a suspicious individual who looked for double entendres, misinterpreted the words and actions of others, and had a "chip on his shoulder," his psychosis will fall into the paranoid category.

In the long psychic trek back to autoeroticism, the patient returns to the highest security and the greatest happiness he ever knew. Once more back in his mother's arms, he reigns supreme, as he did as a baby, with magic omnipotence. At the nadir of regression, the adult-turned-infant must be cared for like a baby, which has been described in previous pages. It is perfectly natural when an infant sits in its crib or on the floor and babbles incoherently, cries when it is hungry, and excretes when the impulse strikes him. It is schizophrenia when the same behavior is seen in anyone at or beyond the chronological age of early childhood. Thinking is "autistic"—ideation that wanders in the world of fantasy with or without elements of reality he once knew. These ideas were described by Bleuler as "autochthonous," that is, mental impressions originating within the psyche independently of external stimulation. Jung suggested that many autochthonous ideas are derived from the collective or racial unconscious.

Infantile behavior is equated with psychosis; so is primitive thinking which permits personal gratification primacy over group satisfaction without bothering with social restrictions. The traditional puerile, wild, unhampered practices of aborigines are well known. In *Totem and Taboo* Freud calibrated equally: psychotic regression, primitive mentation, and infantile behavior. It is not unusual for an undisciplined child to be called a "cannibal" or a "little savage."

The primitive, the psychotic, and the infant, each in his completely egocentric fashion, goes about obtaining gratification exactly as his instincts desire: completely, immediately, without half-measures, and—if necessary—ruthlessly.

Maladjustment.   One factor that helps a physician to determine if a patient is psychotic is his inability to adjust to his milieu, to mingle easily with others; this is in sharp contrast to the neurotic. True, the latter may be a source of irritation to his family, his employer, and his friends, but somehow he manages to get through the day, hold his job, and behave himself to the extent that he does not seriously threaten the welfare of himself or others. The psychotic, as we shall see, simply cannot relate; his judgment is impaired, he misinterprets events and people, and he is asocial; at times he may be antisocial, destructive, and a menace to society. So indifferent may be the psychotic that he looks and acts the slob, and finally reaches the point where he requires institutionalization *"for his own welfare and/or others and/or the community,"* to use the statutory phrase.

However, hospitalization of a psychotic patient is not universally mandatory. Many are quiet and well behaved and can remain at home, even hold down a job. Others undergo psychotherapy on an out-patient or private practice basis. It is this group of nonhospitalized psychotics that has been increasing steadily since 1955 when tranquilizers first appeared. This is discussed later.

Etiology. We repeat, there is no known specific cause for a psychosis. However, there is a long list of conditions which a psychosis may accompany, complicate, or follow. Among organic syndromes are: trauma, senility, arteriosclerosis, epilepsy, brain neoplasm, post-partem state, involution, endocrine dysfunctions, etc. In the vast majority of instances, however, a psychosis appears "out of nowhere"—*sui generis*—as a functional syndrome with no tangible, demonstrable, or discernible organic pathology (including post-mortem examinations). The four main varieties of psychosis are: schizophrenia, affective (manic-depressive) psychosis, paranoia, and paranoid condition. *Schizophrenia accounts for more institutionalized patients than any other mental affliction.* Schizophrenia and psychoses due to cerebral arteriosclerosis and senility account for two out of three institutionalized patients.

Schizophrenia

Schizophrenia, literally "split mind," implies a "divided brain," but the term is really a diagnostic description of the patient's mental life which is, at least at first, divided between the world of reality and the world of fantasy. Or, to put it another way: his somatic presence in this world and his psychic presence in that "other" world.

Schizophrenics are "loners"—asocial, sometimes antisocial—who are introverted, seclusive, and withdrawn. Early in life they may have been precocious (hence, the old-time diagnosis, dementia praecox—insanity of youth), excellent scholars, buried in books, and the delight of fond parents who gloried in their young "genius," he who was always so preoccupied with isolated academic studying. He never had time for sports, dances, or people. Schizophrenics may be sullen, sulky, and retreat more and more from interpersonal relations. They are emotionless; they are impassiveness personified.

Not all cases of schizophrenia are clear-cut instances of this psychosis, especially in the earliest stages. At first the patient may be subject to wide swings of mood, not unlike manic-depressive psychosis. These cases are often (conveniently) known as "schizo-affective reactions." Thirty years ago statistical reports of psychiatric institutions listed a considerable number of manic-depressive psychoses. Today it is a clinical rarity because psychiatrists find that early cases of this emotional psychosis are frequently schizo-affective disorders. Again, incipient schizophrenia may resemble a neurosis, or a full-blown schizophrenic may have many neurotic features. These are known as "pseudoneurotic schizophrenia." Finally, if there is no clear-cut variety of schizophrenia but a mixture of two or more varieties, the schizophrenia is said to be "undifferentiated" or "mixed." The four classical varieties of schizophrenia are: *simple, catatonic, paranoid,* and *hebephrenic.*

Simple Schizophrenia.   The hallmarks of this variety are the extremes of apathy and indifference. Nothing, no one, in his environment has any emotional effect on him. One professor of psychiatry used to characterize the simple schizophrenic as the "backwoods resident who sits in front of his cabin, sitting and thinking—but mostly sitting."

Catatonic Schizophrenia.   Catatonia (formerly "katatonia," which means "breakdown of [muscle] tone) is clinically observed in two main varieties. These are tabulated below:

STUPOR	EXCITEMENT
MUTISM	Which is:
BLOCKING, seen in two phases:	Purposeless
1. *Negativism,* which may be:	Impulsive
a. Passive (fetal posture, schnauzkrampf, etc.)	Stereotyped
b. Active (like the Ganser syndrome)	
2. *Suggestibility,* seen as:	
a. Catalepsy	
b. Cerea flexibilitas	
c. Echolalia	
d. Echopraxia	
e. Cataphrasia (perseveration)	

Some of the terms used in the Table above may be unfamiliar. These are defined, in alphabetical order, as follows:

Blocking. Interruption of thought, unconsciously generated and often encountered in emotionally disordered patients, particularly in schizophrenia, and also during a psychotherapeutic interview. It results in retarded, arrested, or evasive responses. Psychoanalysts attribute it to the threatened emergence of a repressed idea into consciousness and the effect of the superego's attempt to keep it repressed.

Catalepsy. Prolonged maintenance of postural attitudes and immobility, due to psychogenic causes; it is synonymous with *flexibilitas cerea* (see below), but the latter is popularly reserved to describe the muscular condition in catatonic schizophrenia. Catalepsy is not to be confused with *cataplexy* which is psychogenic immobility or loss of muscular tone, causing the patient to fall to the ground; it is usually accompanied by stupor. It is a hysterical reaction.

Cerea flexibilitas. More correctly, *flexibilitas cerea,* this is waxlike flexibility of extremities seen in catalepsy (see above) or catatonia. The patient makes no movement of his own volition and will maintain for an extended time any posture in which he is placed (with upraised arm, e. g.).

Echolalia. Constant repetition of another person's words or phrases; it is seen in both organogenic and psychogenic disorders. Also known as *echophrasia.*

Cataphrasia. More familiarly known as *perseveration,* cataphrasia is pathologic persistent repetition of words or gestures, common in schizophrenia and severe cerebral arteriosclerosis. For instance, new questions may be asked of the patient, but he continues to respond to earlier ones.

Ganser's syndrome. A pattern of reaction named for the German psychiatrist, Sigbert J. M. Ganser (1853-1932). It denotes the behavior of an individual who gives false, usually ludicrous, replies to questions. Though frequently encountered in prisoners who are trying to feign mental illness, it may be encountered during an interview with a patient suffering a psychoneurosis, in which instance the content of the subject's replies and his manner may provide valuable keys to his unconscious conflict. Also known as the *nonsense syndrome* and the *syndrome of approximate answers.*

Mutism. A form of negativism in which there is total absence of speech, usually because the patient refuses to talk. It occurs in response to unconscious dictates, usually confusion and conflict, and is commonly observed in catatonic patients, and those suffering from hysteria, stupor, or depression.

Negativism. A trend of behavior and attitude characterized by refusal to cooperate even with reasonable requests and the tendency to do the opposite of what others desire. *Passive negativism* is characterized by the patient frequently seen curled up in the fetal position, immobile, mute, and exhibiting a fixed, impassive facial expression, but occasionally indulging in the grimace of schnauzkrampf (see below). In *active negativism* the patient, in resisting suggestion, is belligerent, impulsive, and may be homicidal or suicidal.

Schnauzkrampf. Pouting, a grimace most commonly seen in catatonic schizophrenia.

Stereotypy. Thinking, speaking, or acting in an unvaried pattern, commonly observed in schizophrenia, especially the catatonic type; many normal persons may show some degree of stereotypy in action and speech. Synonyms are *perseveration* and *rigidity.*

Paranoid schizophrenia. The patient reacts to unsystematized, constantly changing, illogically associated delusions. He is extremely suspicious, sullen, withdrawn, defiant, uncooperative, antagonistic, and asocial. His belligerent attitude strongly suggests repressed homosexual tendencies. When questioned, he is characteristically evasive—even refuses to give his name when asked.

Hebephrenic (lit. "tired mind") schizophrenia. This type of patient is very indifferent, apathetic, regressed, asocial, and totally unconcerned with his environment and reality factors. He may be silly, infantile, shallow in behavior, giggle, wet, soil, and manifest other extremes of psychosexual regression.

MANIC-DEPRESSIVE PSYCHOSIS

This is an affective (of emotions or of mood) psychosis, also known as *cyclothymia* (cycle of moods). The outstanding characteristics of this disorder, as the name suggests, are exaggerated emotional changes which may be sudden or gradual in onset. Speech and movement parallel the mood, all of which are presented in the following table:

MANIC		DEPRESSIVE
"push" (overproduction) of speech; "flight," "wealth," and "leveling" of ideas	SPEECH	underproduction of speech (because of dearth of ideas) up to complete mutism
elation, euphoria, exaltation, hypomania	EMOTION	melancholia (maybe agitated) to the extent of suicide
hyperactivity, restlessness, etc.	MOVEMENT	hypoactivity up to immobility

Manic-depressive psychosis that is simultaneously marked by features of both manic and depressive types is called "mixed" type; one that goes through a manic phase and on to the depressive (or vice versa) is said to be the "circular" type.

Paranoid and Paranoid Condition. Thanks to popular fiction, radio, television, the stage, and motion pictures, these two words have been incorporated into everyday speech, used interchangeably and indiscriminately, so that their actual clinical meanings are obscure. It is unfortunate that paranoia and paranoid are derivatives of the same source, *para,* faulty + *nous,* mind. The two words imply psychopathology in a person who is indescribably and unwarrantedly suspicious of intentions of others. It is perfectly normal to regard with doubt liars, neighborhood gossips, rumorists, etc. because there is no evidence of substantiation and truth. However, to react the same way all the time and to everybody, under seemingly normal circumstances—and where there is no justification for such a reaction—is obviously abnormal.

Paranoia. Of itself, "paranoid" is a descriptive term that applies to more than one psychiatric disorder. Thus, it is found in psychosis due to senility and to cerebral arteriosclerosis, in general paresis, and in schizophrenia. Such patients' delusional ideas are regarded as only incidental to the main stream of thought. Paranoia, however, is something else. It is a chronic psychiatric disorder, gradual in onset—as a fact, unnoticed for a long time—and marked by unchanging, extremely well organized, logically constructed delusions. The paranoiac is irritatingly smug, overbearingly egocentric, a keen debater, usually having a superior intellect, and with a "mind like a trap" is able to defend himself to the point of defying all rebuttal. The one point that sets the paranoiac aside from all other mentally ill patients is that everything he says or claims would be logical and undeniable if—this is a big "if"—his original premise were fact and not delusional. Thus, a patient maintains that he should be released from a mental hospital because President Roosevelt appointed him to the Secret Service and he should be out protecting the president and tracking down counterfeiters. These two facts are backed up by law; they *are* the duties of secret service agents.

However, President Roosevelt did *not* appoint the patient to the Secret Service, nor did any other president. In fact, his anamnesis reveals the patient was never in Washington, D. C. Tell this to the patient and he will smile patronizingly and produce a letter from the White House reading: ". . . The President has asked me to acknowledge your recent letter and to assure you that he will give it his personal attention . . ." This is the usual stereotyped reply federal and state chief executives make to letters from institutionalized mental patients. So, the paranoiac we are discussing, flashes the White House missive and murmurs, "there, doctor, you see you're wrong."

Paranoia is a "rare" syndrome because the patient seldom seeks therapy and is never "picked up" by the police for improper behavior or threatening the welfare of others. The paranoiac bends over backward to be perfect, to be impeccable in speech and conduct. He relates his delusional trend in reality terms. He doesn't resort to violence; he is litigious, going from court to court as the dedicated plaintiff whose endless lawsuit for his "rights" is founded on a delusion.

Paranoid Condition. If delusions of persecution are constantly changing, unorganized, and covering just about every facet of life, the patient's psychosis is a paranoid condition. In addition to the delusions, there may be ideas of reference and influence, and other aberrant ideas. Many psychiatrists, including this writer, believe that paranoid condition is nothing more or less than paranoid schizophrenia.

SYMPTOMATOLOGY

When a physician sees a patient who manifests other-than-normal attitudes and behavior, the doctor is afforded a look into the patient's past. If he is not mute, the patient's hallucinations and delusions, by their emotional tone and content, will be found to originate from some emotional trauma that occurred early in life (fear, guilt, frustration, etc.). The delusions enable the patient to neutralize his unconscious fears. The neurotic patient is hounded by his superego which, as the "guardian" of the dicta of reality, makes the handling of his difficulty complex and symbolic. The psychotic patient who simply leaves the world of reality is not bothered by the external world. Symbolism, however, is a dominant feature of psychosis as well as neurosis. What impresses the physician as bizarre, "weird," "queer" are talk and actions that are illogical, if not meaningless. But, they are very logical to the patient's unconscious: they stand for something or someone and since these are invariably out of his past—his infancy—they are indicative of regression. Don't try to "interpret" or "understand the patient" by an isolated symptom—a voice that he "hears" or a vision that he "sees." All symptoms, every item in the patient's history, must be studied as one conglomerate. This is the holistic pattern that makes up the neurotic or the psychotic.

Symptoms are externalized expressions of unconscious desires, impulses, wishes, frustrations, inferiority, guilt, and conflicts which are, in final analysis, compromises forced on the unconscious by the superego through the ego. The physician should remember, therefore, that a symptom is a symbol. In his nonpsychiatric practice, a symptom is customarily a fairly reliable indication of pathology as expressed by the patient. Thus, "Doctor, I feel very feverish" is easily checked by a thermometer; a complaint of intense heartburn and a boring type of substernal discomfort a couple of hours after eating hints strongly of ulcer which can be discovered by various examinations. Psychiatric symptoms can be conveniently grouped in nine categories, some which are merely descriptive of the patient's response to the challenges and strains of life. The definitions about to be presented are deliberately made as brief as possible because they are in the nature of a review, since the physician has studied psychiatry as part of his medical curriculum.

1. Disorders of Perception. Perception is a psychic action by which sensations are referred to an external object as their source. It is not to be confused with sensation and conception (imagination) and judgment (inference).

Illusion. A false interpretation of a sensory stimulus, usually visual or auditory. The desert mirage of an oasis and the sound of the wind interpreted as the moaning of a human being are examples.

Hallucination. A subjective sensory experience which has no basis in objective reality. Because any of the senses may be involved, an hallucination may be auditory, visual, gustatory, olfactory, or tactile.

2. Disorders of Thinking. Thought is judged by an individual's expression of thinking in language (speech and writing) and movement. A patient's speech may be coherent, relevant, and logical, i.e., he doesn't jump disconnectedly from one topic to another. Again, we judge thinking by the "amount" of ideas expressed; in the psychotic and mentally retarded there may be a "poverty of ideas." Does the patient's thinking yield to suggestion; is it realistic in content, and is it logical in its sequence?

Delusion. A delusion is a disorder of judgment in which the patient's false interpretation of a set of circumstances cannot be shaken even in the face of the most contrary evidence. The truly deluded patient often displays errors of judgment that are bizarre.

A *nihilistic delusion* is a delusion of nonexistence, frequently encountered in schizophrenia and in the melancholic type of involutional psychosis. The patient may deny his own existence or that of his entire family, of all mankind, or of the universe. A *somatic delusion* is one in which the patient believes that certain of his organs (or his entire body) are disintegrating, and that this is due to some vague external influence. It is also any delusion that refers to the body or its components. *Delusions of grandeur* are those in which the patient pictures himself to be possessed of great wealth, power, or superior talents. *Delusions of persecution* have as their central theme maltreatment by one or more persons.

Ideas of Reference. A psychotic patient's beliefs that remarks and/or actions of others refer to him when such is not the case.

Ideas of Influence. A psychotic patient's beliefs that unpleasant and painful forces are incapacitating him, particularly in the genitalia. Common examples of ideas of influence are thought control, telepathy exerted by others on the patient's mind, disability from outerspace radiations, etc.

3. **Disorders of Consciousness.**   Disorders of "awareness" indicate deviations from normal clarity of consciousness. Such disorders range from perplexity and disorientation, through confusion and clouded consciousness, to stupor and unconsciousness. In this category are delirium, fugue, and dream state, which were discussed on p. 52.

4. **Disorders of Apperception.**   Our psychology colleagues have never agreed on a concept for apperception and a clear-cut definition is lacking. However, it implies unhampered, clear perception of environmental stimuli. If you talk to a patient and he pays no attention to you or fails to recount a particular event into which you are inquiring, his apperception is disordered. Apperception includes attention and thought. In a severely psychotic patient there is little if any comprehension of the simplest questions, although he knows language and what words mean.

5. **Disorders of Attention.**   These obvious conditions run the gamut from rapt concentration through distractibility, to complete inattention.

6. **Disorders of Orientation.**   Psychiatric disorders may present disorientation in one or more of the three spheres of time, place, and person. Sometimes, a disoriented patient may "confabulate" to the point of misidentifying persons whom he knows well.

7. **Disorders of Affect.**   When you judge a patient's mood (elated or depressed) the prime point of consideration is "appropriateness." That is, does the affect match the stimulus? Does he laugh at something sad or weep in response to humor? This is psychotic, but it may be quite in keeping with his unconscious mood. For example, the patient who weeps in response to humor may be expressing sorrow in response to an unconscious melancholic impulse. We repeat, *psychiatric symptoms are symbols*. Happiness and sorrow are seen in various degrees: the former can progress from normal (adequate) joy through *euphoria* (a feeling of abnormal well-being), to "elation" and the self-satisfied affect of "exaltation." Sorrow has a similar opposite counterpart. When we discuss treat-

ment we shall see how extremely important it is to question a patient in detail when the complaint is made that he feels depressed. Too often depression and apathy are mistaken for each other. The patient who is apathetic and indifferent and fails to react to either sadness or happiness is described as having an "inadequate affect."

Panic. This is more than fear; it is the end result of prolonged tension that finally is manifested as utter fright, overwhelming feelings of insecurity, and suspiciousness. Such a patient is prone to projection and disorganization of his ego.

Ambivalence, -cy. This is the coexistence of diametrically opposed trends and feelings (love-hate, tenderness-cruelty, masochism-sadism) toward another person, idea, or object.

Depersonalization. Here, a patient is beset by feelings of unreality and of altered personality or identity. He may deny his own existence or that of the world about him. (*nihilism*).

8. Disorders of Activity. These are expressed in movement and speech and cover a wide range from complete immobility and mutism to wild restlessness and constant babbling of sounds or disconnected words. Examples include *mannerism* (a grimace or other action peculiar to an individual such as nictitation, bruxism, etc.), *stereotypy* (see p. 64), *verbigeration* (incoherent compulsive repetition of certain words or phrases), and others which have been previously defined (catalepsy, negativism, etc.).

9. Disorders of Memory. Defects of memory may be observed as a chronological, orderly pattern, commencing with recent events and retrogressing to earliest childhood. This is "retrograde" memory defect. On the other hand, memory may capriciously vary from day to day, the patient able to recall a remote event at one time and forgetting it at another, all this alternating with periods of clear memory. This is known as a "patchy" memory defect, commonly seen in psychiatric disorders of the senium (and normally in the elderly and in dotards).

TREATMENT

As stated under the discussion of neurosis, the physician will not be burdened with the various methods and modalities of treatment of psychosis. With the rarest exception, the nonpsychiatric doctor does not render therapy to psychotic patients, even the most amenable out-patient individual. However, all the contemporary means of psychotherapy are discussed in the following chapter.

CHAPTER SEVEN

Treatment

THERE IS NO DOUBT that in this era of swift communication and all sorts of medical newspapers and similar media in addition to the traditional journals, nonpsychiatric colleagues have a better-than-average knowledge of psychiatric treatment. However, physicians constantly tell me that patients query them about psychotherapy, most often as it pertains to their relatives and close friends. Though lay persons, they, too, are acquainted with features of psychiatric therapy. But they want to know more; it is surprising the details they seek. Therefore, in this chapter coverage of the subject will be quite extensive. To illustrate what this plan envisages is a question such as, "Doctor, my brother is beginning analysis. Just what is that?" The reply: "Oh, the patient comes to the analyst, usually every day, and for 45 minutes, lies on a couch and talks of anything that comes to his mind." The natural answer to that by the inquiring patient, in all probability would be, "Heck! Why pay a doctor for *that?* He can do that at home!" And so he could. What the physician should be able to explain—and it takes very little time—is the modus operandi of psychoanalysis, its aims, and how it works . . . why it cannot be done at home (even Freud tried it and wasn't outstandingly successful).

There is another point, one I shall approach with no little trepidation: many physicians are unknowingly playing psychiatrist, particularly with chemopharmaceuticals, and this is one subject that calls for discussion—in depth—which follows later.

HISTORICAL HIGHLIGHTS OF PSYCHOTHERAPY

With rare exception and excluding certain therapeutic refinements, there isn't anything radically new in psychiatric treatment. Take the term "shock," for example. Devised by Bini and Cerletti in Italy in the thirties, it was brought to the United States in 1940 by Lothar Kalinowski, German-American psychiatrist; it is therefore regarded as a recent modality of treatment. In 1765, John Wesley, the father of Methodism, created an electric shock machine and stated: "The Wonders of Electricity have wrought unspeakable good to thousands. Nor have I known anyone who has received hurt thereby."

"Shock" *is* old, and until very late meant everything that the word implies and more. Patients have been thrashed, purged to exhaustion (and sometimes to death), and had unspeakable physical torture applied to them in the name of treatment. Nevertheless, shock has never been abandoned. In the sixteenth century Paracelsus tried camphor; in 1885 Hurd turned to a monobromate salt of camphor. A half century ago carbon dioxide was used to augment body metabolism to stimulate depressed and apathetic patients. Most physicians know of the dunking treatment which consisted of taking patients outdoors, even in winter, and seesawing them in and out of icy water. In other countries patients were strapped in a rotating chair and whirled until they became extremely ill or fainted. Doctors also have read and seen pictures of straps, chains, ropes, thongs, closets, and other therapeutic tortures. Benjamin Rush, whose likeness is on the seal of the American Psychiatric Association in recognition of his being the "father of American psychiatry" and who is noted for his campaign for humane management of the mentally ill, built a "tranquilizing chair" in which an insane person was strapped with a hood over his head and forced to sit, completely immobile, for hours. At the end of that time he must have been "tranquilized"—if not at death's door. But let us not review this history with the smug satisfaction that we have left all this behind us. There are still some jurisdictions in the United States where the potentially bone-breaking straitjacket is used.

One of the first volumes in psychiatry in the English language was Dr. William Battie's *Treatise on Madness* (London, 1758) and many of the concepts he advanced are still valid. A milestone that marks the turn toward humaneness in psychiatry bears the name of Philippe Pinel (1745-1826) who "unchained the insane" at Bicêtre. Soon after, T. S. Kirkbride in this country advocated "the proper separation of patients according to the degree of the disease." This recommendation was put into practice at New York Hospital's "Bloomingdale" (now the Westchester Division of the Cornell University New York Hospital), the first mental institution in New York state. No one has ever campaigned for psychiatric humanity as vigorously and relentlessly as Dorothea Lynde Dix (1802-1887) who, when she began her battle, could find only thirteen insane asylums in the United States, and when she finally retired, could count 123, of which 23 were constructed by virtue of her pleas to state legislatures.

Today's "stimulant therapy" can be said to have been born with Manfred Sakel's introduction of insulin shock therapy into the United States in the thirties. Almost at the same time, Ladislaus (von) Meduna was using metrazol to induce short convulsions. Both therapeutic modalities had certain hazards. Metrazol, for example, frequently caused vertebral fracture due to the "splinting" of dorsal muscles which become as rigid as steel at the height of a shock-induced convulsion. The currently favored modality for these shock therapies is *electric convulsive therapy* (ECT, or EST, *electric shock therapy*), although insulin shock is still employed in some mental hospitals.

What psychiatry continues to seek is the fast, one-shot cure— the rapidity and effectiveness that is seen, for example, when meperidine is given for pain. In psychiatry there is no tablet, no hypodermic injection, nothing that quickly converts a severely psychotic patient into a rational, well person. Therapy, as it is practiced today, is a program tailored to individual requirements and embracing the principle of holisticism. Therapy may take weeks, months, or years, during which time radical changes in the treatment program may be indicated and multiple modalities may be needed.

In the specialty of psychiatry as, probably, in no other, diagnosis and prognosis must take cognizance of the patients' unpredictability, their personal outlook, and their emotional status. A dozen patients with identical signs and symptoms of schizophrenia, whose case histories are amazingly alike, will have a dozen varying prognoses.

Then there are the intangibles which present snags in the path of therapy and, therefore, color prognosis. These include the ideas and suggestions of well-meaning relatives and friends, the medical "lore" as disseminated by popular magazines, unfavorable domestic and occupational conditions, and the presence of an organic condition.

All these factors clearly indicate a rule of thumb: one method of treatment never holds an indominatable position of superiority over any other. Tranquilizers have been a therapeutic blessing; they are not a cure, and indiscriminate prescribing of them can lead to clinical disaster. This point will be discussed later and is one that was previously mentioned as a subject which I approach with trepidation. Psychosurgery has its place in treatment—"last" place, since it is used only in carefully selected cases as a "last" resort. Electric shock therapy has been used indiscriminately because many physicians have chosen to ignore Kalinowski's uncompromising statement that ECT is primarily for patients with agitated depression.

Psychiatry envies many specialties' ability to achieve "cure." The appendicitis-surgery-recovery way of medical practice is sheer delight. The relative balance between "recovery" and "cure" is highlighted in psychiatry. Consider the oldster who is hospitalized for pneumonitis, and so severely ill that he is on "critical" for a time. He pulls through and returns home where he is "his usual self." The inference is that the patient has not only recovered but is enjoying good health. He is, if his arteriosclerosis is overlooked as well as his osteoarthritis which, in damp weather, is quite painful, and his diabetes. But the patient left the hospital as "recovered." From what? From the pneumonitis which was the reason he was hospitalized. The elderly person's health becomes a relative matter at *any* time. His "usual self" today is something else than what it was ten or twenty years ago.

In psychiatry how can a patient be considered "cured" of a mental disorder whose etiology is unknown? If we classify the complete elimination of signs and symptoms as a "cure," what if the individual is unable to resume his usual occupation or doesn't mingle with friends? Does "cure" become downgraded to "recovery" or "much improved"? The point is that the underlying provocation for the mental illness remains right where it was, in the unconscious, where no drug can gain entrance.

Without belaboring the point, you will have to tell your patient who is asking you about a relative's "chances of recovery" that the patient who is restored to (relative) good health will retain in his personality, albeit at the unconscious level, undesirable impulses and impressions even though his appearance and reaction to environment seem to indicate that he is adjusting well. The degree of "recovery," in final analysis, is the degree to which unconscious conflicts are rooted out by psychotherapy and the extent of this as reflected in the patient's interpersonal relations.

THE TREATMENT REGIMEN

Psychiatric treatment is not the exclusive domain of the psychiatrist. Nor does this specialist make such a claim. True, certain specialized skills and approaches are his, but in the broadest concept of mental hygiene, every doctor renders psychotherapy in some form, in some way, almost every time he sees and/or treats a patient for a nonpsychiatric condition. In many instances, it is the general practitioner who is the first to detect incipient indications of psychopathology, or to whom a patient or his relative appeal for help or advice. The specialized skills of the surgeon, neurologist, and all other specialists are required where pathology affects some organ or bodily system. Then there are the trained members of the treatment team: the psychologist, the social worker, the psychiatric nurse, the psychiatric aide, the chaplain, the teacher, the occupational therapist, the recreational therapist, and the volunteer worker.

Treatment is effected on two plateaus: the psychologic and the nonpsychologic. The former primarily embraces *psychotherapy* and this *is* reserved for the psychiatrist to conduct. Nonpsychologic treatment embraces methods and means that are directed toward the soma: chemotherapy, shock therapy, dietotherapy, and others which are described in the following section.

The Organic Approach

Since not all psychiatric patients require hospitalization or intensive psychotherapy, the organic approach may be the only form of therapy required. The indifference and apathy that are emotional reflections of hypothyroidism disappear when appropriate administration of thyroid extract raises that gland's activity to normalcy. The delirium of pellagra is cleared up with the dermatitis and gastrointestinal distress when the vitamin deficiency is corrected. Similarly, the patient who is depressed when he accidentally loses a hand regains his emotional composure when a prosthetic appliance is fitted and he learns to use it efficiently. The same applies to all handicaps and lowered functioning whether it be deafness, loss of vision, or paralysis. It is conceded these are cause-and-effect therapeutic results and actually far afield from the more deep-seated syndromes of neuroses and psychoses.

Stimulant therapy.   For the past several years one phase of treatment—"stimulant therapy"—has been enjoying increasing popularity with psychiatrists. This is "shock" therapy, but, as mentioned above, ECT is currently the one that almost exclusively dominates the field. Except in agitated depression, ECT does not affect the course of neuroses. As in most treatment areas, the earlier shock is given, the shorter the course and the better the prognosis. In uncontrollable manics, "blitz" shock therapy (ECT given two or three times daily for a couple of days) is very effective in controlling such a patient's overactivity. A "series of shocks" usually implies ECT every other day for six or more times. In a simple case of depression, six ECTs are often enough; there is nothing harmful if a series has to be repeated, nor is the prognosis bleaker because one series is insufficient. When the patient's depression is eradicated, the emotional improvement is not "recovery." ECT has simply rendered him amenable for psychotherapy.

The procedure of giving electric (or convulsive) shock therapy is as follows: Two electrodes are placed on either side of the head; mouth pads are inserted behind the incisors. A controlled current is applied for a fraction of a second which induces a grand mal type of convulsion. The patient has been secured prior to application of current and, in most cases, succinylcholine chloride (also known as diacetylcholine chloride), a short-acting muscle relaxant, is given intravenously prior to shocking the patient: this materially lessens the severity of muscular rigidity during the convulsion. The convulsion is followed by a brief period of coma. When ECT is given on an out-patient basis, the time between the patient's entrance into the clinic or psychiatrist's office and the time he leaves to go home is, on the average, two hours. If ECT produces nothing more profound than a petit mal seizure (see p. 181), current is immediately reapplied to induce a grand mal seizure. ECT is being used less frequently as antidepressant drugs appear on the therapeutic scene.

Hormones. The use of endocrinological agents is well known to physicians without any further delineation here. A typical example of this sort of organic therapy is the use of estrogens during the climacterium. However, this phase of treatment has created interest in the effects of histamine, which accounts for the use of antihistamines in the control of asthma, migraine, and other allergic conditions which have strong emotional overtones, if not etiological origin.

Pharmacotherapy (Chemotherapy). Chemotherapy, as we regard it today, got its start in 1955 with the introduction of the meprobamates. Physicians know that symptomatic relief is available via tranquilizers; antidepressants overcome depression, and energizers overcome indifference. The public, too, knows of these drugs—so much so, that articles in popular magazines include them in the "psychedelicatessen" (see p. 151).

Previously, it was pointed out that drugs are used with a view to achieving symptomatic relief, but precisely how they work is not well established. For purposes of our discussion, it is not necessary to indulge in a lengthy presentation of pharmacology and chemistry. It is sufficient for the nonpsychiatric physician to know the following simple tabulation of psychiatric drugs:

TYPE	SYNONYM-DEFINITION
Psycholeptics:	Calming, soothing
Neuroleptics	Acting on the autonomic nervous system
Sedatives	Calming
Psychoanaleptics:	Psychoactivators
Antidepressants	Thymoleptics
Stimulants	Psychic energizers

All psychiatric drugs must be used and regarded in the light of four guides: (1) differences of effects, (2) contradictions and side effects, (3) habituation, and (4) indiscriminate prescription.

1. **Differences of Effects.** Frequently, instead of the usual effects, a drug will exert the very opposite effect(s) in a patient. Thus, a commonly prescribed antidepressant is known to occasionally aggravate the depression to the point of profound despondency and agitation. It is usual in psychiatry, when a patient who is seen, say, once a week, is given a drug he has not taken before, for the psychiatrist to say, "Call me in three days and let me know how you are."

2. **Contradictions and Side Effects.** When a two-page spread in a medical journal touts a drug as an "effective antidepressant—one that is relatively safe," do you bother to read the microscopic print that describes possible contraindications and side effects? When you receive samples do you read the finely printed folder inside the box—*all* of it? Do you feel you suffer loss of face if you consult the *Physician's Desk Reference* (*PDR*) or the A. M. A.'s *New Drugs* in a patient's presence? Doctor, it will pay you to (1) read all of the advertisements and (2) consult these references, no matter who sees you do it.

A few examples. Meprobamate is very popular among physicians as a tranquilizer. Some of its potential side effects are drowsiness, ataxia, dizziness, urticaria, blood dyscrasias, fever, chills, syncope, bronchial spasm—and there are others. Attempt at suicide is another "side effect." Another commonly used tranquilizer whose chief ingredient is chlorpromazine is not to be prescribed if the patient is under the influence of narcotics or alcohol. Amphetamines deserve separate mention, and therefore are discussed later. Take, as a dramatic example, a frequently prescribed drug (especially by physicians for patients who are not institutionalized). Its base is chlordiazepoxide. It is unsafe for such a patient to drive a car or engage in an occupation where mental alertness is required while taking this drug. The manufacturer frankly advises against giving the drug to patients who are known to be addicts or addictive-prone. There is a hazard to both mother and child when a pregnant woman is given the drug. *Among*—not all of—the unfavorable reactions that this drug can cause are: drowsiness, ataxia, and confusion (especially in elderly patients), skin eruptions, edema, menstrual irregularities, nausea, constipation, extrapyramidal symptoms, decreased sexual potential, agranulocytosis, jaundice and hepatic dysfunction, blurred vision . . . well, these will do as a starter. Sometimes you wonder if a drug is to be given only to a perfectly healthy person, who, of course, doesn't need it!

3. Habituation and Addiction. We are approaching the point previously alluded to as one to be considered with trepidation. To illustrate the case of a physician serving as the unwitting proponent of drug addiction—pushing a sample across the desk to the patient and thus being a "pusher" in more ways than one—we shall concentrate on two classes of drugs: barbiturates and amphetamines.

Barbiturates. A significant difference between barbiturates and tranquilizers is that barbiturates exert a more widespread influence on higher brain centers. In addition, barbiturates are narcotics, period. We hasten to add, parenthetically—and this is discussed in detail in Chapter 9—that of course we recognize that the personality makes the addiction and it is not the drug that makes the addiction. Taken regularly (as is the case with "sleeping pills"), even "safe" dosages often lead to dullness, sluggishness, drowsiness, impaired memory, and slowed speech. Thought processes, judgment, and understanding become disrupted and retarded. The patient may become irritable, querulous, hostile, morose, and overtly paranoid. If the user begins to increase the intake of barbiturates, he will become slovenly, irresponsible, make mistakes in his work, even quit his job. Other results include nystagmus, diplopia, strabismus, dizziness, and ataxia.

It is a sad but nonetheless factual commentary that physicians often are the ones who start some persons on the road to barbiturate addiction. Says Dr. John A. Ewing: ". . . *(the) willingness to write repeated prescriptions or the failure to limit the number of times that a prescription can be refilled may be a major error on the physician's part.*" There isn't one reputable manufacturer of bar-

biturates who does not print on every container: WARNING. MAY
BE HABIT-FORMING.

Why not say ". . . *IS* HABIT-FORMING?* Because, as stated
above, it's the personality that makes the addict. On this, Dr. Ewing
states: ". . . *dependence occurs only in the emotionally maladjusted
person. These people are seeking relief of unbearable feelings of
tension and anxiety. The drug becomes an escape route in preference
to finding more personal forms of adaptation.*"

How often do you hear, "Doctor, I can't sleep. Would you give
me a prescription for sleeping pills?" The commonest somnofacient
prescribed is secobarbital: "cap. i, h. s." Most physicians consider
secobarbital as a "mild" somnofacient. The largest manufacturer of
the drug doesn't hold that opinion. In the *PDR* he states:

> *WARNING: This is a potent drug, and serious conse-
> quences may result if it is used other than under constant
> medical supervision. May be habit-forming.*

In describing secobarbital's actions, the same manufacturer adds:

> ". . . *is a short-acting barbiturate and acts as a central-
> nervous-system depressant. Depending upon dosage, the
> drug will produce responses ranging from mild sedation
> to profound hypnosis. In large doses, it causes anesthesia;
> with overdosage, respiratory depression which may be
> dangerous will result.*

For a time the patient is able to sleep. Eventually he becomes so
inured to the drug that he begins to suffer insomnia again. By now,
of course, he is "hooked" on barbiturates and he asks his physician
for "something stronger." The new prescription combines amytal or
amytal in combination with secobarbital. Once more the patient
slumbers. Sooner or later this strong combination loses its soporific
effect, and sooner or later, after the strongest drugs have been tried
and found to be ineffective, the patient suffers such intolerable insomnia that he spends his night alternately tossing and turning and
walking the floors, and he is now a neurotic wreck. It is the unfortunate truth that some doctors allow patients to reach this
psychic extreme and *then* expect psychiatry to wave a magic wand

of therapy. Like amphetamine addiction (see below), barbiturism in its later stages is a very difficult condition to treat. Likewise, too often the patient finds final and permanent relief in his quest for slumber in the "big sleep" which is achieved by swallowing a fatal dose of sleeping pills.

Barbiturates not infrequently lead to simultaneous amphetamine addiction. As stated in one text: "The exact number of unstable persons who close the day with a barbiturate to put them to sleep and begin the next day with benzedrine to wake them up is not known, but even conservative estimates make it alarmingly high." (W. J. Coville, T. W. Costello, F. L. Rouke. *Abnormal Psychology*, New York, Barnes & Noble, Inc., 1960 p. 142).

Amphetamines. Twenty years ago a small group of us began to voice our clinical concern over amphetamines as a dangerous group of drugs. Over the years others have joined us, until, in 1967, legislators became interested and began to hold hearings with a view to establishing statutes governing the manufacture and sale of amphetamines. Many psychiatrists, including this one, regard amphetamine addiction as more difficult to treat than heroinism.

As therapeutic agents, amphetamines are relative newcomers to medicine. Their use as psychic energizers is discussed later. These chemicals are used as appetite depressants, as stimulants by car drivers who wish to avoid falling asleep at the wheel, by students who want to stay awake all night when cramming for examinations, and as "pep pills" or "goof balls" by adolescents for "kicks." In the latter group, a popular concoction is the "bennie" (so-named from "benzedrine"), which is made by dissolving benzedrine (or other amphetamine tablets) in cheap domestic wine. The enormous "lift" (stimulation) resulting from this potent mixture is beyond description.

Amphetamines, at this point, lead to the fourth consideration, "indiscriminate prescription."

4. Indiscriminate prescription. For some years many physicians have unwittingly lent themselves to furthering amphetamine addiction. This is seen, for example, when a patient complains of feeling "nervous," "depressed," "down in the dumps," etc., and the

doctor reaches into a desk drawer, pulls out a package of amphetamine samples, and hands them to the patient. "Here," he says. "Try these." And the patient, in a vast majority of instances, is "hooked." The same is true of the overweight patient. Whether or not she does lose weight, she "must have" the amphetamine regularly thereafter.

The dangers of amphetamines are no secret. In the *PDR* every manufacturer of amphetamine products prints the hazards of these drugs. For example, here is what one manufacturer has to say:

> *Use with caution in patients hypersensitive to sympathomimetics and in coronary or cardiovascular disease or severe hypertension. Excessive use of the amphetamines by unstable individuals may result in psychological dependence. ADVERSE REACTIONS: The following are unwanted reactions reported or considered possible: overstimulation, restlessness, insomnia, g. i. disturbances, diarrhea, palpitation, tachycardia, elevation of blood pressure, tremor, sweating, impotence, and headache.*

All of which, we add, may be fatal. Nor does the manufacturer include profound emotional disturbance and a full-blown psychosis as possible sequellae. However, otherwise, amphetamines absolutely safe (!).

The commonest hazard of indiscriminate prescription occurs when a patient complains of feeling depressed. He looks as dejected as he claims to be. His physician writes a prescription for an antidepressant agent, the patient takes the drug—and feels no better. There are times when only persistent inquiry and careful investigation of a patient's complaint of depression can determine the validity of the symptom. Very often it turns out to be apathy, indifference, a let-down of drive, and *not* a depression. The drug of choice in such a case would be one that stimulates; the antidepressant would do nothing for him.

Pharmacological Combinations.   It is not unusual for a patient to be given two or more drugs for his psychopathological condition. The principle behind this regimen is the concept that different drugs act differently on the central nervous system. Other advantages include additive therapeutic action, an enlargement of the effective range of the several pharmaceutical agents, and a diminution of dosage of each agent, which implies less chance of adverse effects.

The risk of either psychological or physiological addiction to psychiatric drugs cannot be overstated. Some psychiatrists say that these agents become a "crutch' for the patient; I prefer the term "addiction" because, as we shall see later, this term is confined to those media which, if withdrawn from the user, result in profound disturbing effects. The patient who takes his tranquilizer or energizer day after day and suddenly is compelled to stop taking the drug is swiftly turned into a psychic wreck. Again, prolonged usage results in decreased effectiveness of the drug and dosage must be increased. Invariably, the prudent and medically sound course to follow is the relegation of the drug to the role of transient alleviation of emotional stress *while* the patient is undergoing psychotherapy. The prognosis, under this regimen, is far brighter.

The trouble with drugs is the ever-present menace of a letdown in psychiatric vigilance. Therapy or analysis may become a superficial mode of treatment because the patient's difficulties seem to be materially eased by pharmaceutical agents. And there is the popular belief that unless the therapist prescribes "something," he, the patient, is being short-changed. But, so far as hospitalized patients are concerned, were it not for these drugs, the "open-door" policy, short-term institutionalization, and the steady decrease in hospital censuses would never be attained.

Psychotherapy

We know of no better critique of psychotherapy than the observations of Dr. Robert P. Knight who, in "A Critique of the Present Status of the Psychotherapies," *Bulletin of the N. Y. Academy of Medicine,* 25(2):100-114 (February, 1949), listed the characteristics of psychotherapy as follows:

1. That in which the therapist stresses an attitude or tries to exert influence by suggestion, persuasion, exhortation, intimidation, counseling, interpretation, re-education, retraining, or reorientation toward life.

2. That which is supportive, suppressive, expressive, cathartic, or ventilative.

3. That which is superficial or deep.

4. That which is brief or prolonged.

5. That which is analytic and may be classically Freudian or a modification of or in outright opposition to psychoanalysis.

6. That which treats patients individually or in groups.

7. That which is directive or nondirective.

8. That which incorporates other modes of treatment such as drugs and hypnosis.

Contemporary psychotherapy invariably incorporates two or more of the above eight characteristics, as, for example, therapy may be deep, prolonged, analytic, and individual.

Psychiatrists have argued for many years over the objectives in psychiatric treatment, with vehemently voiced ideas about the insufficiency of mere symptomatic treatment. To efface the outward manifestations of a psychiatric disorder (hallucinations and delusions, for example) without unearthing the unconscious etiology of the illness is nothing more than scratching the clinical surface; and these superficial lesions will close only to open again. Be that as it may, we must make these overt manifestations the immediate target of treatment, administer whatever agents are indicated, so that the patient is amenable and/or accessible to psychotherapy, which may be a long-term affair.

In the thirties, Dr. Leland E. Hinsie remarked, in discussing the objects and means of psychotherapy, "Psychotherapy is adequate when it enables the patient who had previously enjoyed good health to regain his preclinical status through the complete removal of symptoms. This can be achieved with *children* by (1) removing the unwholesome stimuli, or (2) detachment of their interest from earlier harmful habit patterns. In adults, psychotherapy attempts to remove symptoms by (1) building up latent or unused assets and (2) enlargement of interests in the environment."

It is reasonable to regard psychotherapy as effective when it makes it possible for the patient who has never experienced behavior, feeling, and thinking appropriate to his age level to *gain* (as opposed to *re*gaining) a pattern of responses commensurate with the level of maturing he should have attained. This is achieved by removing or altering the inhibiting factors which have blocked the patient's personality development. We have said that these factors may be exogenous or endogenous. It was Karl Menninger who declared that treatment should provide a means whereby the patient can expiate guilt, find opportunity for creative expression, be given a chance to live out his fantasies, to establish advantageous attachments and suitable identifications, and, most important, to find love. A dominant principle of psychotherapy is the need for deep analysis of the psyche, thus making it possible for emotions to be released from earlier psychic and behavioral patterns. Only after this is accomplished can the patient's emotional interest be directed toward sublimated forms of activity.

Psychotherapy, in its usual course, commences analytically and, with time, becomes synthetic. Examples of analytical psychotherapy are the various schools of psychoanalysis and individual psychotherapy; suggestion and re-education are examples of synthetic psychotherapy. The psychiatrist, himself, must be capable of flexibility, that is, he cannot rigidly adhere to one discipline or to an inflexible approach to and management of the patient, since no two patients are alike. Therapy must be custom-tailored to fit each patient. Since psychiatric treatment is a parent-child relationship, the aim of treatment, broadly speaking, is to influence the patient's attitudes—toward his own psychic and somatic processes, his milieu and the people about him, and toward his own psychopathology ("insight"). The height of therapeutic benefit is achieved when the patient begins to discover why he thinks and acts as he does, which means he is understanding the nature and etiology of his emotional disturbance. If he fails to unearth the unconscious features behind his trouble(s), and even if his symptoms are diminished—even eradicated, his outward improvement is only superficial and probably transient. Therapy cannot change one's instincts, but it can alter the course of flow of the instincts' drives and redirect them toward three objects: the new family unit, other persons, and stimulation of creativity.

THE NEW FAMILY UNIT. The parent surrogate-patient association attracts the patient's libido from his family; libido is also transferred to the nurse, psychologist, and others in the psychiatric team (the latter, of course, in the case of hospitalized patients).

OTHER PERSONS. This term implies "other than himself." Again, for the institutionalized patient, one of the aims of the total treatment program is to turn his libido away from himself (subject libido) and have it flow to others in his environment (object libido). It is the first step toward externalization of the ego's interest and the means by which interpersonal relations are created.

STIMULATION OF CREATIVITY. If redirection of the patient's libido does not succeed, occupational and recreational facilities are called into play. Here the patient begins participation in these creative pursuits, working by himself, but others are in the same room as he is. In this way, he gradually gets to know them by sheer repetition of seeing them day after day. In most instances it is the other patients and the therapists who approach the introverted patient, talk to him, "draw him out of his shell," and in this way attract him to extraversion of libido—and he forms interpersonal relations.

PSYCHOANALYSIS

The so-called formal variety of psychoanalysis is presented first, not because it is favored by this writer, but because it was first historically. As we shall see, other schools of analysis are either modifications of Freudian principles of therapy or, even if they seem to bear no resemblance, are outcroppings of formal psychoanalysis. We shall even present views of specialists who differ violently with Freud. But, no matter what one's attitude, it was Sigmund Freud's pioneering and revolutionary philosophy—for that is what it was—that paved the way for all the others.

Freudian psychoanalysis (analysis). Freud never claimed that his psychoanalytic therapy was infallible. In 1932 he declared, "Psychoanalysis is really a method of treatment like others. It has its triumphs and its defeats, its difficulties, its limitations, its indications." He could even joke about psychoanalysis: "I do not think our cures can compete with those of Lourdes. There are so many more people who believe in the miracles of the Blessed Virgin than in the existence of the unconscious."

Nor did Freud ever say psychoanalysis was the be-all and end-all of therapy. He anticipated the day when organic treatment and chemotherapy would stalk out on the treatment stage: "Analysis as a psychotherapeutic procedure does not stand in opposition to other methods used in this specialized branch [psychiatry] of medicine; it does not diminish their value nor exclude them." He also admitted that psychoanalysis does not always succeed in bringing repressed unconscious emotional material to the surface. Psychotics are unsuitable for psychoanalysis because of "the stiffening of mental life"—their mental processes, firmly entrenched in the unconscious, "seem to be incapable of yielding old psychical processes for new ones." Yet he never held out for a hopeless prognosis for psychotic persons: "It is here, indeed, that hope for the future lies: the possibility that our knowledge of the operation of the hormones . . . may give us the means of successfully combating the quantitative factors of the illness . . ." Freud never claimed that psychoanalysis was the panacea for all neuroses; he limited its application to what he called "transference neuroses" (phobias, hysteria, and obsessive-compulsive reactions), because these patients are not excessively narcissistic and, therefore, are able to externalize libido and are truly desirous of being helped. "Narcissistic neuroses" (especially hypochondriasis) are, like psychoses, heavily coated with autoeroticism and introversion. This comparison of hypochondriasis to psychosis has been discussed on page 54.

Freudian psychoanalysis has the patient lie on a couch with the analyst out of his line of vision. The analysand (patient) is encouraged to speak of anything that comes to his mind. His words are recorded by the analyst in writing or on tape; the analyst seldom interrupts the analysand. Production of material buried in the unconscious is known as "catharsis" and this material is carefully sifted by the analyst for "indicators" such as slips in speech and conduct, and these clues may point to the true nature of the emotional conflict. At the first meeting the analysand is provided with an explanation of the therapeutic procedure: to probe the unconscious in an attempt to unearth material which could not be raised to consciousness in an ordinary interview.

To appreciate the unconscious, to be able to explain what is meant by this term, we have the lucid, beautifully composed, interpretation of Henri Bergson (1859-1941):

"For our duration is not merely one instant replacing another; if it were there would be anything but the present —no prolonging of the past into the actual, no evolution, no concrete duration. Duration is the continuous progress of the past, which grows into the future and which swells as it advances. And as the past grows without ceasing, so also there is no limit to its preservation. Memory is not a faculty of putting away recollections in a drawer or of inscribing them in a register. There is no register, no drawer, there is not even, properly speaking, a faculty, for a faculty works intermittently when it will or when it can, whilst piling up of the past upon the past goes on without relaxation.

"In reality, the past is preserved by itself automatically. In its entirety, probably, it follows us at every instant; all that we have felt, thought, and willed from our earliest infancy is there, leaning over the present which is about to join it, pressing against the portals of conciousness that would fain leave it outside. The mental mechanism is arranged just so as to drive back into the unconscious almost the whole of the past, and to admit beyond the threshold only that which can cast light on the present situation or further the action now being prepared —in short, only that which can give *useful* work. At the most, a few superfluous recollections may succeed in smuggling themselves through the half-open door. These memories, messengers from the unconscious, remind us dimly of what we are dragging behind unawares. But even though we may have no distinct *idea* of it, we *feel* vaguely that our past remains present to us. What are we in fact, what is our *character*, if not the condensation of history we have lived from our birth—nay, even before birth—since we bring with us parental disposition?

"Doubtless we think with only a small part of our past, but it is with our entire past, including the original bent of our soul, that we desire, will, and act . . ."

Thus, in 1909, in *L'évolution créatrice,* did Bergson render what remains the most definitive exposition of the concept of the unconscious. His other great contribution to another school of psychoanalysis will be mentioned later.

In what way and how much explanatory detail the analyst provides for the analysand at the first meeting depends on the latter's intelligence. In addition he is frankly informed that the analysis may take considerable time—months, even years— and that he is not to expect counseling and advice. If a patient tells you that a relative, undergoing analysis, was "told" by his analyst to do something, that is either an outright untruth or a misinterpretation of what the relative said. Analytic sessions are customarily daily, five days a week; each session is 45 minutes (the popularized "forty-five minute hour"). Analysis is regarded as finished when there is an understanding by the patient of the final interpretation. How successful therapy is can only be gauged by the subject's use of the "new knowledge."

Three techniques are used in analysis: (1) *Free association,* the spontaneous association of ideas and thoughts, during which inhibitory factors are removed, so that when the analysand speaks of his thoughts as they become spontaneously conscious, they are verbalized with little or no logical or ethical criticism. It is free association that makes possible *transference,* the unconscious shift of libidinal attachment; a stage in the psychoanalytic technique wherein the analysand transfers his antagonism from the disturbing "characters" in his underlying emotional conflict to the analyst. (2) *Word ("controlled") association,* responses by the analysand to a prepared list of words, and (3) *Dream analysis,* the latter often turning out to be the critical point in analysis because it may reveal the extent of progress made in the analytic investigation and, in fact, may control the entire treatment program by "pointing" the road to be followed.

In orthodox analysis, dreams are said to be the consummation of unconscious or conscious desires. What the dreamer remembers when he awakes is the "manifest content," which is derived from the "latent content"—repressed material that is "served up" to the dreamer in a form acceptable to his ego. This transformation is achieved by mental mechanisms such as *displacement* (the substitution of an innocuous idea for a disturbing one), *condensation* (the merging of the characteristics of two or more persons in the dream into those of one person), *secondary elaboration* (transformation of dream material into a more or less homogeneous dream story), and *symbolization* (the application of persons, things, or events as symbols for material which would be injurious or embarrassing to the ego). These mechanisms make it possible for a dreamer to render a more or less plausible story of his dream, on the one hand, and also to explain the frightening episodes and incongruities in the story.

Transference, mentioned above, is regarded as a critical feature of the analysis. In their textbook on *Practical Clinical Psychiatry,* Strecker and Ebaugh declare: *"transference is the unconscious mis-identification of the analyst, so that the patient may behave and feel toward him in a way which satisfied the experiences and impressions which refer to another."* The analyst's "measuring tape" is the Oedipus complex (see p. 7) from whose character and strength can be determined the patient's potentiality for breaking away from a parental fixation and thus liberate libido for healthy, heterosexual attachments. It is a means, then, of predicting whether or not analysis will be successful.

The final part of psychoanalysis is devoted to the overcoming of *resistance,* and the analyst's guidance of transference into safe and pragmatic channels, so that when the ultimate explanation is made to the analysand, sublimation may be anticipated. Sublimation was explained on page 12.

According to Ernest Jones (1879-1958), Freud's biographer and first English student, the principles of formal Freudian psychoanalysis are: (1) mental phenomena are not chance occurrences; (2) emotions can be detached from an idea, object, or action and displaced to another idea, object, or action; (3) mental processes are dynamic and tend constantly to discharge the energy associated with them; (4) repression; (5) mental conflict; (6) wishes of later life are important only as they ally themselves with those of childhood; and (7) psychosexual trends are present in childhood.

There are five practical points concerning psychoanalysis which, although originating with Freud, are applicable to all analytical therapeutic programs: (1) the patient must have a genuine, unconscious drive to be helped, (2) he must be prepared to remain in analysis for a long time, (3) he must have better than average intelligence, (4) he must have the money to pay for the analysis; otherwise worry over economic stress might be expressed as hostility to and suspiciousness of the analyst, and (5) the patient should neither be a child nor a senile person.

Neuroanatomical Support of Freud.   It is not from psychiatrists or psychologists that a unique support for Freud comes, but, surprisingly, from students of evolution, such as Arthur Koestler, Morley Roberts, Judson Herrick, and William M. Wheeler. If we remember our medical school studies of the brain and its evolutionary evolvement, we recall the contrast between the new and the old cortex. On the new (sensory) cortex the body is represented in the shape of a little homunculus in which the mouth and the genito-anal areas are at opposite ends of the projection area. In the old brain, evolution bent the limbic lobe on itself to give olfaction intimate association and participation in both oral and genito-anal functions.

If you think about this, you find support for the much-debated theory of psychoanalytic theory of infantile sexuality (rejected by so many other non-Freudian disciplines). As Koestler says, *"It seems that the schizophysiology is built into our species."*

The Non-Freudians.   Among the leading dissidents who differ partially or wholly from Sigmund Freud are several whose approach to therapy is not analytically oriented.

Carl Jung.   Carl Gustav Jung (1875-1961) was an early follower and contemporary of Freud. His first bone of contention with Freud was over the concept of "libido." He asked Freud for a clearer definition and the Vienna analyst curtly replied he had explained it in full. Jung eventually followed Bergson's *élan vital* as the representation of libido, thereby stripping it of its sexual context. Among Jung's contributions are his conception of the unconscious being divided into the *personal* and the *collective (racial) unconscious,* previously explained on page 8. Jung also said that the "four basic functions of psychic activity are: *thinking* and *feeling,* which are rational and proceed according to laws of logic, and *sensation* and *intuition,* which are perceptual." Sensation perceives what is; intuition what may be. Jung also gave psychiatry the word association test, and the terms "introvert" and "extravert" to describe personality types. He created "analytical psychology' which stresses religious beliefs and symbolism as explanations of psychopathology, especially as it is seen in the middle and later years, in terms of regression to a collective unconscious—that is, he stressed the influence of phylogenicity in mental disease. Jung lost considerable prestige in later years when he attempted to incorporate Nazism into his principles.

Alfred Adler.   Also one of Freud's original disciples, Alfred Adler, Austro-American psychiatrist (1870-1937), gave more emphasis to the ego (self-preservation) instinct than to the sexual instinct. He regarded psychosis as the result of conflict between the drive to dominate and the feeling of inferiority, the latter due to some inborn organic defect. Out of this concept grew Adler's "inferiority complex," which is bandied about, erroneously, in everyday parlance. Adler said that a person who has a definite handicap, such as a speech defect, becomes preoccupied with this defect and consequently devotes an excess of energy in an attempt to overcome it. In the end, this concentration of psychic energy may turn such a person into a gifted speaker (e. g. Demosthenes), but that if this fortunate event does not occur, he may become supersensitive over his handicap and, being "inferior," may develop the idea that people notice it, talk about it and him, and if this paranoid reaction is severe enough, he may become psychotic. Adler postulated that the feeling of inferiority arises from an inferior ego.

Adlerians and Freudians continue to argue over the idea of inferiority. Freud said, ". . . mothers whom Fate has presented with a child who is sickly or otherwise at a disadvantage . . . try to compensate him for the unfair handicap by a superabundance of love." This implies that such a youngster becomes a retiring, shy, dependent person. For purposes of illustration, Freud pointed to Kaiser William II who was born with a shriveled arm and from his childhood was determined to be the world's most illustrious ruler and genius—even usurping God's position. It seems, however, that

Freud ignored the well-known fact that William abhorred his mother all his life (blaming her for his deformity) and seldom talked to her.

Philosophy, psychology, and psychiatry are not the only sciences that attempt to explain inferiority. Anthropology has something to say, too. There is the suggestion that since "Western" society has become less rigidly structured as the centuries pass by, man has become less secure as he feels compelled to keep pace in an ever-changing, ill-defined social milieu. We call this "keeping up with the Joneses." Constant insecurity creates anxiety, and the individual feels he is not running with his fellowmen and, in fact, may develop the idea that he never could—that he is inferior. Unless he can adopt an attitude toward life that he must be satisfied with what he has and is capable of, and let it go at that, or that he is doing his best to compete in the "rat race" of society, he is doomed to some emotional or mental catastrophe.

Other disciplines have sprung up since Freud because his theory of individualism and man's battle to satisfy instinctual demands in a socially acceptable manner does not completely answer man's reaction to cultural stress. In recent years, political upheavals, economic developments, and social struggles have shifted emphasis from man's inner to his outer world. Furthermore, the individual is a product of his environment, he is molded by his particular cultural influences, and judged by his society's criteria. Horney, Sullivan, and Fromm are the outstanding champions of psychotherapy oriented to sociocultural factors.

Karen Horney. This American psychoanalyst (1885-1952) developed the theory of "neo-culturalism." She set about to modify several Freudian concepts and concentrated on man's cultural conflicts as the principal source of personality disorders; she placed great emphasis on her idea of "basic anxiety" which, she said, is a prominent factor in neurosis. She rejected Freud's idea of libido (as did Jung), his emphasis on early psychosexual development, and, instead, turned her back on genetic psychology in favor of culturalism. There is much to be said for Horney's approach. We refer to our times as the "Age of Anxiety," as they are, indeed. News media seldom have humorous or entertaining items; headlines deal with war, economic turmoil, racism, drugs, and atomic destruction. The *rara avis* today is the mentally healthy individual; "everybody's a nervous wreck" is heard from all corners.

Harry Stack Sullivan. Sullivan, an American psychoanalyst and psychiatrist (1892-1949), while recognizing man as fundamentally a biological organism, emphasized the importance of interpersonal relationships in the molding of a well-rounded personality. His postulate of interaction is very significant in the therapist-patient association where the psychiatrist evaluates his relationship with the patient in the light of the latter's previous interpersonal experiences—if there were any.

Erich Fromm. A contemporary American psychoanalyst, Fromm injects sociology into psychiatry. He, like Horney, feels that man must be judged by his adjustment to his social milieu and its demands, rather than simply as a biological organism. It is mortality that prevents man, ever in conflict with nature, from achieving his goals. Fromm attributes less importance to the alleged motivating force of the instincts and subordinates biology to cultural influences. His therapy does not concentrate on the individual, but takes on a holistic aura because it regards the patient (man, for that matter) as simply an element of Western civilization and values.

Other Non-Freudian Schools. There are other and later schools that also modify or completely disagree with Freud. Prominent among these is Franz Alexander's and Thomas French's *Chicago School,* exemplified by the Chicago Institute for Psychoanalysis where the accent is on short-term analysis. Then there is the *London School,* founded by Ernest Jones, Freud's first English pupil, and the *existentialists.* The latter deny identification with any discipline but advocate clarification of dogma and terms in all psychiatry and doubt everything in the various schools of psychiatric thought. Those who wish to inquire into the details of existentialism are referred to Kierkegaard, Nietzsche, Dostoevski, and, of course, Sartre. Existentialism, in brief, is concerned with ontology, the study of being. The point of departure is human consciousness and mental processes. While most older philosophical doctrines claim that an *a priori* essence precedes or transcends individual existence, existentialists feel that existence precedes essence, i. e., the idea that man has an essential self is an illusion.

Individual Psychothrapy. This is the across-the-desk, patient-and-psychiatrist-facing-each-other procedure of treatment. It is precisely how you relate to your patients; in psychiatry it is known as *intensive* individual psychiatry. The two main lead words are "why?" and "so?" Thus, a patient may tell of a particular act. To get at the underlying motivation, the psychiatrist may ask, "Why?" The patient may supply an answer, he may shrug, he may say, "I don't know." In the latter two answers, the psychiatrist does not pursue the particular issue, but he also doesn't abandon it. At a later time when he feels the patient is ready for it, the question is repeated. An emotional block has meanwhile been removed, making response possible. Likewise, a patient may tell of something he did and stop dead in his account. To urge him on, the psychiatrist might say, "So?"

Individual psychotherapy, contrary to popular belief, is not directed by the psychiatrist. Therapy can be likened to a man walking along a dark, uncharted road. But he isn't alone. Directly behind him, and holding a flashlight over his shoulder is the therapist. When the two come to a fork in the road—the patient always leading the way—it is the patient who decides that they will or will not turn off on the side road. If they do, he must be prepared for the disappointment if it ultimately stops at a dead end and they must retrace their steps back to the main road.

Another comparison patients find easy to understand when they are told that an attempt will be made to unearth the underlying, unconscious cause(s) of their conflicts, is the usual manner in which television programs terminate. A series of cards reveal first, say, the actors' names, then the second card gives credit to the author, the third to the editor, etc., etc., to the very last which furnishes the director's name. "But note," the patient is told, "you can't find out who the director is until *all* the other cards in front of the last one have been removed. More, you can't read the second card until the first is taken away. That's how we get down to the bottom . . . one fact, one event, one emotional experience at a time; each item often 'reminding' you of an associated one because there is an emotional significance attached. That's how we will go: step by step until we get back to where your difficulty started."

Group Therapy. This therapeutic procedure arose from a shortage of qualified personnel during World War II to provide care and therapy for psychiatric casualties. Group therapy usually includes a small number of patients, most often those whose neurotic or emotional difficulties have elements in common. With the therapist as the moderator, these patients talk about their problems. There are several advantages to group therapy: there is great psychological comfort in an aura of "misery loves company," and the shy and embarrassed patient quickly loses his bashfulness and "speaks up." Patients subjectively benefit as they objectively and critically interpret and analyze remarks of the other patients who are in the same emotional "boat," and even offer "therapeutic" suggestions. Group therapy underscores Sullivan's interpersonal relationships, discussed above, in that the individual learns to subordinate his selfish impulses to the will of the group. Then, on the economic front, group therapy is cheaper than individual psychotherapy. Group therapy is a treatment set-up used in institutions, in clinics, and in private psychiatric practice.

Therapeutic Adjuncts. Those modalities of psychiatric treatment which physicians know will be listed without any comment; those not commonly encountered in nonpsychiatric practice will be described. In the former group are: occupational therapy, recreational therapy, socialization, guidance, persuasion, suggestion, and academic education (both for children and adults, including vocational training and job placement).

Hypnosis (hypnotism). Hypnosis is a sleep-like state induced by suggestion, in which the patient follows directions or, when questioned, reveals suppressed or repressed information he cannot "remember" when completely conscious. The latter is a psychotherapeutic technique. The Greek word, *hypnos* means sleep, but hypnosis does not induce slumber.

It is not known what hypnosis is or how it works. Franz Mesmer

(1734-1815) popularized hypnosis (mesmerism) as an instrument of therapy; he termed it "animal magnetism." Mesmer was more mystical than medical. There are many misconceptions about hypnosis. First, there is the impression that anyone can be "hypnotized into doing or saying anything," à la George du Maurier's *Trilby* in the clutches of the fiendish hypnotist and musician, Svengali. This idea is completely without scientific basis and contradicts every fundamental tenet of psychology. As Dr. Herbert Spiegel of the Columbia University College of Physicians and Surgeons says: "Nothing can be done with hypnosis that cannot also be done without hypnosis." More, not everyone is amenable to hypnosis; even the great hypnopsychiatrist Bernheim admitted that. It is the subject's unconscious that decides his willingness or unwillingness to respond to the hypnotist. If this were not so, then a Hitler or an Alexander the Great could have an entire nation hypnotized into complete, unquestioning loyalty. Think of the possibilities if a general could have an army hypnotized into blind devotion to duty, totally unmindful of injury or death. Parenthetically, it would be interesting to watch two such hypnotized armies in combat. And, from a practical point of view, if hypnosis could compel a person to talk against his will, police might have used hypnosis long ago (where "legal") to make a suspected criminal "sing." Total control by hypnosis exists only in fiction and fancy.

In an hypnotic trance, the patient surrenders conscious control of his psyche and is "nonrationally" submissive to his dissociative state. Fundamentally, his psyche is "split," similar to amnesia, sleep-walking, dreams, schizophrenia, or even as in the normal states of absorption in a book or a sermon or a play.

As is the case in shock therapy and with psychiatric drugs, hypnosis is not a cure. It can effectively and dramatically—for a time, at least—remove a symptom, but it does not expose the underlying cause. This is like taking an aspirin for a headache: the pain yields to the analgesic, but there can be no permanent cure until the actual cause (faulty vision, spinal curvature, brain neoplasm, etc.) is found. Suggestion, as a modality of therapy, is quite common; it is simply the means of inducing a hypnotic trance. In an emergency, such as hysterical aphonia, hypnosis is useful to have the patient regain the ability to talk so that psychotherapy can be initiated.

Hypnosis is either synthetic or analytic. Analysis can be conducted while the patient is in a trance, questions evoking replies which reveal repressed feelings and ideas that the conscious mind might otherwise censor and block from emergence. Synthetic hypnotherapy consists of positive suggestions made to the subject while he is in a trance.

Psychodrama. Psychodrama, created by Dr. Joseph L. Moreno, contemporary Austro-American psychiatrist, is a procedure by which patients, individually or in groups, "act' out their problems on stage. Moreno and his colleagues claim that the patient, both as participant and spectator, develops insight into his emotional conflict.

Distributive Analysis and Discharge Catharsis. These are direct contact methods of treatment. Distributive analysis is a question and answer routine; discharge catharsis is descriptive of a patient speaking freely, without interruption, on any subject he chooses; he "cleanses" his psyche of an emotional difficulty. Both methods are fundamentally the chief approaches in individual intensive psychotherapy.

Desensitization. Desensitization has the patient confronting the unpleasant traumata of his past. The patient discusses, at frequently repeated interviews, the material concerning his conflicts originally obtained through ventilation, ("airing" the psyche). These interviews are repeated until the patient can talk of them without undue emotional reaction. We say "undue" because normal emotional response is to be expected and it would be highly undesirable for a patient to lose his psychic ability to react naturally to painful situations. It is the *excess* that is pathological and requires relief. Essentially, desensitization is a procedure used in many medical specialties. For example, the man who has undergone amputation and is fitted with a prosthetic device receives instruction on how to use the appliance, and is encouraged to employ it until he becomes accustomed to it.

In psychotherapy, desensitization has a second application. It is the alleviation of fear or other symptom manifestations in specific situations. The patient is required to face the unpleasant stimulus over and over until he no longer exhibits the symptoms in response to it. Desensitization is carried out with a heavy injection of reassurance and encouragement. Desensitization, fundamentally, is an instrument of treatment to combat fear reactions.

Institutionalization

Not infrequently physicians, particularly general practitioners, find themselves involved with a severely ill psychotic patient who requires immediate hospitalization. Formerly, the execution of forms and the paper work that are needed in the accomplishment of institutionalization were statutorily relegated to psychiatrists. Nowadays, most jurisdictions simply require that the doctor be "a graduate of a reputable medical college, duly licensed to practice in the state, and in the practice of his profession for (specific number) years." While mental hygiene laws vary from state to state, the following is essentially the same throughout the country.

Persons to be admitted to a civil or licensed private mental institution or a psychiatric division of a general or proprietary hospital are classified as "willing" or "unwilling." In the former group are those who voluntarily desire institutionalization or those who do not object to in-patient treatment when a relative or a friend, acting in their behalf, seeks such admission (for example, a relative or a friend of an oldster, or a parent of a minor). All others are "unwilling" patients.

Appropriate institutions can be easily found by consulting a psychiatrist, the local health department, the psychiatric service of a general hospital, welfare and social agencies, etc. Means of admission are tabulated as follows:

FOR WILLING PATIENTS	FOR UNWILLING PATIENTS
Nonstatutory admission	Community, county, or municipal agency certificate
Voluntary admission	Court certification (commitment)
	One-physician certificate
	Two-physician certificate

These admission procedures are defined in the order they appear in the above table.

Nonstatutory admission. An informal type of hospital admission in which the patient (in the case of a minor, a parent or guardian) requests hospitalization because of emotional or mental disorder and simply signs an agreement to abide by the rules of the institution. This patient's admission is no different than that of a surgical or medical patient.

Voluntary admission. Admission voluntarily sought by a patient is granted if he agrees, in writing, to remain in the hospital for a stated period of time (usually from 10 to 30 days), at the end of which time he may request in writing to be released. Such request is granted unless the director or superintendent, on the advice of his psychiatrist(s), arranges for a more binding arrangement (e. g., court certification [see below]) so that treatment may continue uninterrupted.

Community, county, or municipal agency certificate. Upon the written application of a county or municipal commissioner of health or social welfare or public welfare, local health officer, director of a community mental health service, or a physician designated by any of them, a psychiatric patient for whom immediate hospitalization and treatment are required, may be admitted to a mental institution where he may be retained for a specified period of time (usually 10 to 60 days). At the end of this time, unless the patient signs a voluntary application or a nonstatutory application, he must either be returned to the referring source or retained under a more binding arrangement (e. g., court certification).

Court certification (commitment). This type of admission procedure is rapidly disappearing as nonstatutory and other means replace it. Court certification includes a *petition* (made by a relative, friend, public health official, etc.), a *medical certificate* (the physician's examination of the patient), and the *certification* (the judge's order).

One-physician certificate. This is a procedure in which nonpsychiatric physicians are often involved. It includes a petition as described above, and the doctor's examination and reasons why he believes hospitalization is needed. There is an item physicians should know about the one-physician certificate. While this procedure is intended for "unwilling" patients, such a patient, when brought to the institution, must express willingness to be hospitalized. If he doesn't, the one-physician certificate is invalid and a more binding arrangement for admission must be obtained. If the patient consents to enter the hospital, he is retained only for a specified period (usually 60 days). At any time he or someone in his behalf may make written application for his release. The hospital director must, within a specified period (usually 15 days), comply with the request, or if he feels that extended institutionalization is indicated, takes steps to have the patient held on a court certification as described above.

Two-physicians certificate. This method of obtaining hospital admission includes a petition, made as described above, plus the usual medical certificate completed by two psychiatrists or one psychiatrist and one physician. In many states this certificate is valid for an indefinite period of time; in others, a specified time limit is required, so that at the end of this period, the patient must be released or a new form of admission be obtained.

Lay Therapy and Counseling

When a patient or someone in his behalf seeks help or you recommend it, it is possible that you (or he) prefer that he consult a lay therapist or a counselor. The public—and some nonpsychiatric doctors—should know where these agents may serve a useful purpose and whether they are harmful. To the best of our conscious ability, the following discussion is presented with what we believe to be complete honesty and unprejudiced estimation. We have no bone to pick with nonmedical practitioners; we bear them no grudge. In the colloquial tongue, "it's a free country."

Counselors. Let us consider counselors first. So far as a psychiatrist is concerned, he is *not* a counselor; he is a diagnostician and a *therapist.* He is not a deity and so he cannot decide for the patient what is right or wrong. Insight, gained through therapy, should enable the patient to make such decisions for himself. When a patient asks me, "Is that wrong?" I invariably reply, "You've just answered yourself." In other words, if he didn't have at least a modicum of an idea that it *was* wrong he wouldn't have asked the question in the first place.

And a counselor isn't a psychiatrist. Treatment is and should be in the hands of a physician—and more of this later. If the patient wants advice he can turn to his attorney or pastor—or a counselor, with whom he can discuss his problem on a superficial level.

Lay Therapists. Physicians are well aware of the war (and the "indefinite truce") that is being waged by the American Psychiatric Association and the American Psychological Association (it's bad enough that each is "the" A. P. A.). Psychologists want the unrestricted right to practice psychotherapy. So do social workers. Much is made of Freud's so-called approval of lay analysts, a view that was bitterly opposed by others, especially by his early pupils, Abraham A. Brill and Ernest Jones. What most people do not realize is Freud's frustration that forced him to advocate lay analysis. He was extremely anxious to spread his doctrine and gain recognition, but at the time physicians wouldn't recognize psychoanalysis as a legitimate modality of medical treatment. Therefore, Freud was willing to accept anyone who would subscribe to his tenets, if only to popularize it. And that threw the therapeutic fat into the polemic fire.

Why should a psychotherapist and/or a psychoanalyst be a physician first and then a certified specialist? We have reached the point where medical science no longer recognizes the isolated domains of psyche and soma; man is an organism. Then, too, psychological medicine is now colored and influenced by biology, biochemistry, anatomy, metabolism, and a dozen other divisions of science. How can psychotherapy be undertaken, therefore, unless the therapist is well-grounded in these aspects which are components of contemporary medical education? Think of the tests, examinations, consultations, and prescriptions that may be involved during treatment!

Psychiatrists, primarily physicians, can and do physically examine patients. Granted, most persons are referrals who have had thorough physical examinations, but if, during psychotherapy, there is a need for re-examination, the *doctor* (i. e., the psychiatrist) is equipped—by training, experience, and apparati—to do this. The lay practitioner retorts that he will not treat a patient without first securing "medical clearance" by a doctor. Fine. What if clinical features arise during therapy which only a physician can recognize? Suppose a patient begins to complain of listlessness, fatigue, and apathy, and his original physical examination was well within normal limits. Is this a somatic expression of an unconscious psychic conflict? Is it an expression of hypothyroidism? Would the lay therapist think of having a PBI estimation made? *Could* he order it? Take another patient whose physical "check-up" is normal. During therapy he begins to complain of headache and occasional nausea. The lay therapist, banking on that original "negative" physical, attributes these symptoms to neurosis. But a prompt neurological examination may reveal hints of cerebral neoplasm which, if it is a meningioma, might be successfully operated, whereas waiting until the patient suffers projectile vomiting might be too late.

Again, the psychiatrist must be a medical detective. We cite two actual cases from our practice to illustrate this all-important point.

Case No. 1. MISS A. J. This 44-year-old single female came to the office complaining of depression, which she attributed to a lack of male companionship. When she came in I could not help but notice that her left foreleg was unusually disfigured by ugly varicosities. During the recital of her past history she claimed she was a virgin. I looked at her and said, "Miss J, when you don't tell me the truth, you aren't deceiving me, you're cheating yourself." She stood up and glared at me angrily. As she was about to leave I said, "I could not help notice the varicose veins in your left leg. Miss J., varicose veins of *one* leg, with very rare exception, are caused by pregnancy or childbirth." She stared at me, and then suddenly burst into tears. There had been, of course, an emotionally traumatic sexual experience. Therapy went well after that.

Case No. 2. MRS. S. A.   The day before I saw Mrs. A. for the first time, I happened to read a medical report by a physician who said that poorly treated or untreated gonorrhea in the male which eventually subsides—the "burned out" case of g. c.—creates a change in the pH of seminal fluid which, thereafter, can cause erosion of the female cervix. Mrs. A was a comely 48-year-old widow, the mother of two teenage daughters. She complained of uneasiness, a feeling that her children were drawing away from her, and a vague sense of guilt. Part of her past history included celibacy during widowhood. Mrs. A. was late for her third session, but she excused herself on the grounds that she had been to her family physician to have a cervical erosion cauterized. "Childbirth caused it, the doctor said," she remarked to me. The second coincidence was that her family physician was a medical school classmate whom I met two weeks later at a reunion. He verified Mrs. A.'s account, but happened to remark that prior annual pelvic examinations had been negative. I asked his opinion of the article I had read. He shrugged, then grinned. "Could be. A year ago I fitted Mrs. A. with a diaphragm."

At the next session Mrs. A. happened to open her purse to take out a pack of cigarettes. I saw a pastel colored leather case. "If you've had no sexual experience since your husband died, why carry a diaphragm?" She stared at me, and then the facts poured out. It wasn't her children who were rejecting her; she had been rejecting them—for a steady love affair. But her fealty to her companion was sometimes punctured by solo fly-by-night sexual affairs, and these stimulated guilt feelings which increased every time she was in her daughters' company. The break in therapy from which progress can be dated was when she asked me, defiantly, "So I'm not a well-behaved woman. Why shouldn't I have fun? I'm free, I don't neglect my home or family. I wouldn't be ashamed to tell anyone what I do."

"Even," I asked softly, "your children?"

After she stopped weeping, we went ahead with therapy which soon terminated happily for Mrs. A. I ask lay therapists: can you play medical detective?

Finally, there is the matter of writing a prescription. As more and more pharmaceutical agents are being added to the psychiatric armamentarium, the lay therapist is handicapped; he cannot prescribe medication. Oh, yes, he could arrange for the patient to see a medical doctor, but why should anyone be economically encumbered by paying two men what one can do? As endocrines, biochemicals, drugs, and other agents continue to be incorporated into psychiatric practice, the debate between psychologists and psychiatrists will die a natural death.

CHAPTER EIGHT

Sociopathy

THIS TERM ENCOMPASSES the *psychopathic personality,* or as it is also known, *sociopathic personality disturbance.* This is really a group of personality disorders which are primarily expressed through inability or unwillingness to conform to prevailing mores. Colloquialisms and slang provide popular but more understandable designations. These range from the hobo and the bum, through the goldbrick, slacker, delinquent, up to the chronic felon. Psychopathic personality is not unknown among neurotics and psychotics, however, and it may complicate organic brain disease or trauma.

Sociopathy is not the psychiatrist's private domain; it involves every physician and is found in his private office, the clinic, and the hospital where he is an attending or a consultant. Sociopathy is found among what superficially appear to be "the nicest people," and includes in its ranks some of "the nastiest people." There are times when you can spot sociopathy instantly; there are times when it spots you and makes you its victim.

The irritating part of sociopathy is that with all the literature and clinical records pertaining to this entity, we know very little about it: its etiology, its place in nosology, and what to do for and about it. Sociopathologic behavior is found in the outerspace of medicine beyond the scope of the clinical laboratory. It bears the impressive classification of *"disorders of psychogenic origin without clearly defined tangible cause or structural change."* English translation: we don't know what it is or where it comes from. Sociopathy has long been a thorn in psychiatry's side because of its wraith-like elusiveness. Why is a misfit? Is a hipster a psychopath? What creates a criminal? What and why is sexual deviation?

Disordered Personality Features. Previously we mentioned the periodic change in nosological designation sociopathy has undergone. At the very moment this is being written, the American Psychiatric Association is once more returning to an old but always popular diagnostic label: "psychopathic personality." There is something connotative for physicians when the word "psychopath" is used; it is the equivalent of a textbook of description. These personality disorders are described as "constitutional" defects, the hedging adjective promptly exposing psychiatry's ignorance; we don't know if the psychopath is born or gets that way. The two varieties of psychopathic personality are: antisocial reaction and dyssocial reaction.

Antisocial Reaction. Antisocial reaction is characterized by rejection of and refusal to comply with obligations and restraints of society. Obviously, such a broad definition would include an otherwise well-behaved person who exceeds the posted speed limit, perhaps stops on the road to "snitch" an apple from a tree or pick flowers in a "no trespassing" area. Were this so, then few would be exempt from classification in this category. What the term implies, however, is the habitually antisocial person who is "always in trouble," who does not benefit from experience, punishment, or personal injury suffered in an antisocial act, and who cannot maintain genuine loyalties to any rule, code, or person. He is an egocentric hedonist, hard-boiled, irresponsible, and extremely emotionally immature. He devotes considerable energy in rationalizing unwarranted conduct to have it appear or be accepted as warranted. Many psychiatrists would place hipsters in the antisocial reaction classification. In this book, the hipsters are given separate consideration.

Dyssocial Reaction. This variety of psychopathic personality is a behavior-attitude pattern of irresponsibility so far as community law is concerned—even family "law"—and is marked by "asocial and amoral trends." The very codes this psychopath despises are the ones with which he most frequently clashes. In the dyssocial reaction group are the delinquent and the felon, but not all criminals are psychopaths. The same anamnestic features (emotionally unstable parents, homes without a father, severe childhood emotional traumata, and violent hatred of authority) that are found in the background of psychopaths are also found in neurotics and psychotics who express their hostility toward authority in criminal acts.

The sociopathic personality features emotional disequilibrium and gross errors in judgment. Such an individual is the height of narcissism; he sneers at the sentimental, derides the Golden Rule, and laughs uproariously at the idea of being his brother's keeper. You can't plead with, lecture, or set an example for him. Only suckers work and save; the world is his oyster—to take what and when he wants, without permission, and regardless of ownership. His motto is "Here today, gone tomorrow." His credo is "me first." A renowned penologist once said, "[A psychopath] would kill his own mother if the murder meant a buck." The sociopath is basically a paranoid, struts through life ruthlessly elbowing everyone and everything aside, and sadistically glories in inflicting pain. But, should he meet resistance stronger than himself, he snivels, trembles, cringes, and begs for mercy. Why some people behave this way *we simply do not know.*

Many sociopaths are materially successful; some command public respect. Read the list of highly esteemed names and the public officials who were involved in the infamous Teapot Dome scandal in the Harding administration. And what was Napoleon, other than a paranoid psychopath? What a glorious monument to humanity and better living is the Rockefeller Foundation! Read the biography of John D. Rockefeller and learn how he amassed his fortune.

Juvenile delinquency is a natural sequella to this, and a problem of this country in which most physicians find themselves involved. The under-twenty-one age group makes up almost 25 per cent of all arrests in the United States. According to the latest Federal Bureau of Investigation report, while crime is increasing somewhat faster than population, juvenile delinquency is rising eight times faster than adult crime. Psychiatrists and psychologists offer various causes for juvenile delinquency: lurid sex and crime publications and movies, television shows that glorify the felon and illicit sex, comic books, disintegration of family life, crumbling morals and ethics, permissiveness, extremes of progressive education, and many more. Why none or all of these are the answer is obvious: only a fraction of youngsters exposed to these unfavorable stimuli react to them with delinquency. This brings up the question again: is psychopathia an inborn constitutional defect? We wonder if, in the long run, geneticists will provide the final answer as research continues to concentrate on chromosomes and genes and DNA and RNA.

Delinquency, in the recent past, has shifted from penology to psychiatry; more of these offenders are being sent to psychiatric rather than correctional institutions. In most states no penal institution functions without full-time psychiatric and psychologic services. While community remedies such as church-sponsored clubs, scouting, Little Leagues, and such are admirable attempts to stem the rise of juvenile delinquency, they do not seem to be achieving anticipated results. Complicating the unfavorable picture is racism, poor living, working, and social conditions, and economic inequality. This prompts the thought: if a specific cause is not known there can be no specific treatment. Such is the unfortunate situation in psychopathic personality reactions.

In view of the constantly changing nomenclature, we are dividing personality disorders into a trio of gross types: emotional instability, homosexuality, and other sexual deviations. Wherever subgroups or sub-types are cited, they are the ones that were being used in the late 1960's.

Emotional Instability

The average person, under appropriate stress, can and does evince emotional instability. But the "emotionally unstable personality" is descriptive of the person who responds to negligible stress with extreme excitability and ineffectiveness, and the net result is undependable judgment. His relationships with others are marked with ever-fluctuating emotional attitudes—he is the "blow-hot-blow-cold" friend—because of his ill-controlled hostility, guilt, and anxiety. The two main divisions of the emotional unstable personality are: passive-aggressive personality and compulsive personality.

Passive-Aggressive Personality. This is best defined by describing the three main varieties, but all of them bear a strong anxiety component, lending each an aura of psychoneurosis. This complication is often a challenge to diagnostic clarity.

The passive-dependent type is the "wishy-washy," "clinging vine" person who is helpless, indecisive, and forever leaning on others. The passive-dependent asks one person after another to "help him decide," listens to the advice, promises to follow the counsel, and then, the moment he repeats this performance with another person, abandons the first person's advice in favor of its successor. This is repeated over and over.

The passive-aggressive type responds to environmental challenges passively but masks this emotional reaction with pseudo-aggressive disguises such as stubbornness, procrastination, pouting, obstructionism, and inefficiency. In this group is the g. i. griper, the chronic objector, the perpetual complainer.

The aggressive type responds to environmental situations with open hostility, temper tantrums, and destructiveness. He is always resentful, and his past history invariably reveals a profound dependency in his relationships.

Compulsive Personality. The individual with this personality trait is constantly preoccupied with "being right." He is fearful that he isn't conforming; he is the one who has the tortured superego—the guilty conscience. These compulsives try to compensate by working like beavers, but they are so rigid that they cannot relax. Behavior has a definite adolescent tinge, and it is difficult to differentiate this personality type from the obsessive-compulsive reaction described on page 52.

Homosexuality

Misconception, misunderstanding, misinterpretation, and myth becloud a sound comprehension of homosexuality, particularly in our culture. The average person, inundated with quasi-scientific information as spread by magazines and newspapers, alternately fascinated and disgusted by "frank" motion pictures and plays, and aghast at the periodicals exclusively devoted to the subject, hasn't the remotest idea what homosexuality is. Ah, but the psychiatrist does. Does he? We shall see.

Many persons visualize the homosexual as the cosmetized, effeminate, hand-on-hip man who looks for male companionship and sex, and his female counterpart—the lesbian, the "dike"—as the tough, aggressive female who seeks out women for sexual gratification. These individuals comprise but a small percentage of homosexuals. Most homosexuals cannot be identified as such, at least, not by their dress or mannerisms or speech. The first homosexual I ever encountered clinically was during my senior year in medical school. He had been one of Walter Camp's all-American mentions! One of America's toughest Senators in this century was a square-jawed, ruthless, sadistic, hard-hitting man who married, shortly before he died, not to "square himself" with the public but to prevent his wife from having to testify against him in a particular inquiry into some of his financial manipulations.

This book separates homosexuality from all other sexual deviations from the norm because homosexuals, unlike all other sexual aberrants, studiously go out of their way to keep their sexual preference out of the limelight; most of them conduct themselves as well as heterosexual citizens—holding down jobs, taking active parts in community projects, etc. More, they are a major factor in cultural and creative productions and pursuits, contributing much to the worlds of apparel, music, art, sculpture, architecture, and allied areas.

As a word, "homosexual" is a semantic misleader. *Homo* in Latin means "man"; but, although zoological derivatives refer to mammalian species, they also refer to the primates (ergo, *homo sapiens*). A more plausible basis for "homosexual" is the Greek *homo*, meaning "of like kind" or "the same." Homosexuality, in its broadest denotation, is applicable to the Ladies Sewing Society of the St. Theresa's Church, the Knights of Columbus, and soldiers in their barracks. These are homosexual—i.e. unisexual groups. In psychiatry, this sexual oneness is homoeroticism, one of the plateaus in psychosexual development.

There is a belief that sexually active homosexuals tend to associate only with other homosexuals, to live apart from the rest of the community, without homes and families. Psychiatrists frequently encounter homosexuals, male and female, who indulge in homosexual practices even though they are married and have children, hold responsible jobs, and are active in neighborhood matters such as P. T. A. and volunteer service in hospitals.

Carl Jung was the man who pointed up the undeniable fact that no one is completely male or completely female. Jung said that man has his female *anlage* and woman her male *anlage*. *Anlage* can be defined as an element in the personality representing the opposite sex, and reposing in the unconscious. This feature permits a man to be an acknowledged designer of female apparel, to appreciate the refinements of grace and posture—to have his nails manicured weekly and to douse himself with ("manly") scent after a shower; it enables a girl to be a mountain-climbing enthusiast, to be an aviatrix (Amelia Earhart), to be a militant crusader(Joan of Arc, Carrie Nation). However, because of society's dicta and a matter of personal pride, most persons try to cover up traits that smack of the opposite sex.

Etiology.   We could dismiss this part of the discussion by flatly saying "we don't know"—the truth. We could avoid responsibility for dealing with etiology by falling back on "constitutionalism"— the homosexual is "born that way." However, there are certain factors which strongly suggest that they at least foster, if they don't cause, homosexuality. Prominent in this area is alcoholism. Many of the drunkard's actions are disguised homosexual gestures —the hearty slap on the buttocks, the brotherly arm around the shoulder. Although contemporary drinking places cater to both sexes, male and female homosexuals have their "gay bars," easily discernible by signs such as "The Black Panther," "The Green-Eyed Cat," and others. By depressing inhibitory brain centers, liquor makes it possible for unconscious homosexual impulses to emerge into consciousness because the censoring superego is "knocked out." It has been aptly said that "the superego is that part of the psyche which is soluble in alcohol."

Sigmund Freud postulated five possible factors as etiological features behind homosexuality: (1) overattachment to the mother —an unresolved Oedipus situation, (2) overvaluation of the phallus, (3) fear of the father, (4) jealousy of an older sibling, and (5) early homosexual seduction. Examples of some of these are: the mother who devotes excessive time and vigor to scrubbing the little boy's penis when she bathes him, and stimulation of the child's curiosity of masturbation when parents constantly lecture on the evils of it. It is difficult to find clinical reports of homosexuality in which any of these five allegedly causative factors account for the deviation. Which brings us back to where we started: the cause of homosexuality remains unknown.

"Change of sex" is actually rare; it assumes a broad scope because news media delight in headlining a single instance. For example, Christine Jorgenson has remained in the public eye for several years. He—or "she"—is not only a transvestite, but had Danish surgeons perform plastic surgery on his (or "her") genitalia to effect an external semblance to a vagina.

Treatment. To speak of therapy for homosexuality is to misuse the term. Most homosexuals are well-adjusted people and perfectly content with their sexual inversion. When a homosexual seeks help it is usually, expressed on a conscious level, for something different from but linked to his homosexuality. The commonest reason is alcoholism. In most instances the psychiatrist discovers that the patient's problem is a conflict over social inacceptability of his deviation, i. e., he would like to be heterosexual and thus satisfy a rigid superego. This hidebound conscience invariably has as its origin very proper and religious parents. The patient's homosexual urges are too strong to be denied; they are no more or less imperative than the sex drive is in the heterosexual and, therefore, he avoids social condemnation by becoming drunk. It is an "ostrich's-head-in-the-sand" compromise that never fulfills its mission. As an example of the homosexual-alcoholic's superego, he will speak of himself as "gay" and of a heterosexual person as "straight."

Psychoanalysis as a means of effecting sexual maturity in the homosexual is successful only when there is a genuine drive in the analysand's unconscious "to be as others are."

Finally, it must be remembered that there is that gray area known as "bisexuality" in which individuals indulge in homo- and heterosexual gratification with impartiality. They are not as numerous as popular belief has them; a well-known example was Oscar Wilde.

Sexual Deviation

Add to our previous discussion of "normal" and "abnormal" the item of sexual deviation. How much "off-center" must sex be to earn a label of "deviation"? How often must an abnormal sexual act be indulged in to be regarded as deviant? Many investigations (the Kinsey report, e. g.) show that happily wedded, well-adjusted couples experiment with various types of sexuality, occasionally resort to deviation, but most of the time, taking their sex "straight." Is this normal or abnormal? Does a rare indulgence of soixante-neuf by a married couple indicate that they are sexually perverted?

There is no question when a person restricts his sexual conduct *exclusively* to a particular deviant activity. Such an individual usually is abnormal in his total behavior pattern. Clinical histories of deviants are rife with backgrounds of alcoholism, addiction, criminality, and other forms of antisociality. Some of the commoner sexual deviations are now presented briefly.

Voyeurism.   Also known as *mixoscopia,* voyeurism is the practice of deriving sexual gratification from surreptitiously watching others cohabit or from viewing a naked or disrobing person. When voyeurism is limited to this latter practice, it is known as *gymnomania.* The voyeur is popularly referred to as "peeping Tom," a derivative of the legend about Lady Godiva. Certain types of voyeurism are socially acceptable such as "girlie" shows and motion pictures featuring nudity; it is encouraged by miniskirts and filmy negligees.

Fetishism. A fetish is any object employed symbolically to stimulate sexual excitation. It may be part of the body (except genitalia) or an article of clothing or some other object belonging to the desired person. According to Magnus Hirschfield, psychoanalyst, the opposite drive, *antifetishism,* is an unconscious mechanism in which a person with strong homosexual tendencies seeks to conceal from himself his erotic attachment to his own sex by exhibiting aversions to certain atypical physical features in the opposite sex. For example, a man may express revulsion at the appearance of hair on a woman's upper lip or at the sight of a flatchested woman. The expression of distaste serves to veil what is really an attraction to the masculine features.

Flagellation. This deviation seeks sexual excitation and gratification through allowing oneself to be whipped (masochistic version) or through engaging in or witnessing the whipping of another person (sadistic version).

Fellatio. Also known as *irrumation,* fellatio is mouthing of the penis. Obviously, the active participant can be a man or a woman.

Cunnilingus. This is mouthing of the female genitalia, and as in fellatio, may be done by a male or a female.

Pederasty. Also known as *retrocopulation,* pederasty is anal intercourse, usually between an older man and a boy or youth. It is often used synonymously with *sodomy,* which is anal intercourse but not necessarily with a boy, although it is between males. However, sodomy also refers to sexual relations by a man with an animal, known also as *buggery,* to which is related *bestiality* which is sexual intercourse with lower animals.

Exhibitionism. This sexual perversion, perhaps the "mildest" of all sexual deviations, is erotic gratification obtained from exposure of parts of the body that have sexual significance. Whether topless female attire fits in this category as normal or abnormal cannot be said. Exhibitionism—so called "indecent exposure"—is most commonly seen in senile men in whom it is a regressive symptom, a childish form of sexuality employed to compensate for sexual impotence.

Although sexual perversion is included in sociopathy, not all sexual deviants are sociopaths, for perversion is not unknown in neuroses and psychoses. Also, there is that indefinable area which the French call *faute de mieux*—men confined to prison for long terms who use each other for sexual outlet, sailors on ships, unisexual schools, etc.

CHAPTER NINE

Addiction

THE INDIVIDUAL who cannot or will not face up to life's challenges, trials, frustrations, and demands can resolve his difficulties in one of several ways. To begin with, the solution need not entail tragic results; the dissatisfied young man who turns to Yoga to find peace of mind may very well succeed and be totally unperturbed that the material goals he originally desired were not obtained. Another compromise between total emotional defeat and conscious displeasure is a psychoneurosis, particularly a psychosomatic reaction, as presented in Chapter 5. Total retreat from the world of reality is found in suicide or psychosis. Symbolic of self-destruction but consciously considered as "reality erasers" or "changers of perspective" are narcotics and intoxicants which are the instruments of addiction. Whatever the reaction pattern followed, they are irrefutably infantile attempts at self-therapy.

In the beginning of this book we discussed how infantile emotional life is focused on the gastrointestinal system, and the manner in which infantile attachments—libidinal fixations—directly or indirectly remain for life as problem-solving mechanisms. Addiction involves oral or parenteral consumption of something which furnishes transient relief by effecting release from an inhibition, exhilaration, or transportation to a world of fantasy. The addict is the grown-up baby whose desires are gratified via the mouth—even with the addict who takes his narcotic hypodermically, it is invariably discovered that his addiction began with an agent consumed orally, such as a marihuana cigarette.

Definition. The words "addiction" and "narcotic" have been used so loosely for such a long time that their actual meanings are forgotten. *Narcosis* is arrested activity, insensibility, stupor, or unconsciousness from which recovery is possible; it is caused by many conditions and agents among which are brain trauma, hyperpyrexia, alcohol, hypnosis, magnesium salts, ether, carbon dioxide and drugs. Narcotics, within the limits of the word's restricted and popular connotation, are drugs, but they are not the exclusive agents of addiction; they are respected pharmaceutical items in the treatment of disease and disability. Thus, morphine as an analgesic; atropine as a relaxant of smooth muscle, a cardiac accelerator, and a mydriatic, are examples of both categories.

On the other hand, hemp (*Cannabis sativa*) is not a useful pharmacotherapeutic agent; it is a prominent article of drug addiction and habituation, along with its derivatives, bhang and hashish.

In order to avoid an argument on semantics, the terms narcotics and narcotism are used in their popular connotation in this book. However, the problem of defining addiction remains. There is no suitable, all-embracing definition. The popular association is drugs. Some may remember to include alcohol; others tobacco. However, there are such divergent forms of addiction as eating (referring, of course, not to the usual three meals a day, but to the chronic "nibbler," gum chewer, etc.), the amphetamine addict who may have started by merely taking appetite depressants, and the question of where to place those persons who "just can't get along unless they take a tranquilizer regularly," a subject presented previously. Definitions as provided by several accepted references merit review.

Dorland's Illustrated Medical Dictionary defines addiction as "the state of being given up to some habit." The inference, then, is that any ritualism or compulsion such as a daily post-prandial walk, in rain or shine, or morning devotions seven days a week in a house of worship, or a tic, are addictions. *Dorland's* goes on with "drug addiction: a state characterized by an overwhelming desire or need (compulsion) to continue use of a drug and to obtain it by any means, with a tendency to increase the dosage, a psychological and usually a physical dependence on its effects, and a detrimental effect on the individual and on society." The "overwhelming desire" of a heroin addict is not equated, we trust, with the "overwhelming need" of the patient dying of cancer whose pain and agony, according to recent reports, are materially alleviated by LSD. Webster offers a broader (and shorter) interpretation: "State of being addicted; indulged inclination; also habituation, esp. to drugs." But Webster doesn't define "habituation" at all; he simply lists it as the noun of the verb, "habituate" ("to make accustomed; accustom, familiarize"). This is illustrated by a quotation from Sinclair Lewis: "*Habituated* to married life." Coville, Costello, and Rouke state in *Abnormal Psychology:* "True addiction means that the body physiology is so altered by the repeated administration of the drug that withdrawal symptoms occur when the administration is not continued . . . *Habituation* is . . . characterized by psychological rather than physiological need." Brussel's and Cantzlaar's *The Layman's Dictionary of Psychiatry* defines addiction as "Compulsive use of alcohol or a narcotic drug. By extension of meaning, one may be said to be 'addicted' to smoking, eating, or any other kind of self-indulgent behavior, when these acts become excessive and persistent. The significant characteristic of any addiction is the severe reaction of the addict to withdrawal of the substance to which he is addicted."

That last sentence, even though I wrote it, worries me because of the frequently encountered psychological disasters when a patient stops taking a tranquilizing drug. If, upon cessation of medication, a tranquilized schizophrenic returns, almost at once, to his pre-medicated disturbed state—attacks others around him, rips his clothes to shreds, soils, etc.—are these violent manifestations of his illness to be regarded as "withdrawal symptoms"? Yet, the same definition does furnish the single means of differentiating the addictive drugs from other repeatedly used drugs: withdrawal symptoms. In the light of this yardstick, marihuana and LSD are nonaddictive because users can voluntarily stop taking them without undergoing any adverse reaction. (See Chapter 10 for a discussion of these two drugs.) The morphine and heroin addict cannot. Using the same yardstick of withdrawal symptoms, smoking and alcoholism must be regarded as addictions.

The Addictive Personality. Alcoholism and narcotism, the only two addictions included in our discussion, are more easily understood when viewed through the telescope of history which enables us to see what persons, singly and in groups, have done and do, because of alcohol and narcotics, in the endless hunt for Elysian bliss.

According to anthropologists, man, ever since he assumed his terrestrial mode of living, has based his existence on habit, whether it is as harmless as nodding to someone in recognition, as beneficial as washing his body, or as poisonous as habitual drinking. In any addiction, man believes he finds a different and better manner of behavior that enables him to place himself in or out of society as he wishes, in contrast with pre-addictive behavior which was ineffective for him—unattractive or meaningless or unprofitable. Psychologically, he finds something in his addictive agent that he cannot find in himself or believes he does not possess. The addiction echoes his unconscious drive to be not merely "as good as the others," but the "best," and this is more than a hint of unconscious feelings of inferiority. The inner mind is motivated by an all-or-none drive; half-measures are inacceptable. In addiction the user believes he finds "all"; if, however, he finds "none," the only solution is psychosis or suicide. Any person whose unconscious is tortured by feelings of inferiority reacts, at least, with anxiety, and it is this unpleasurable emotion that is neutralized by the addictive agent; the individual is soothed, and once this relief is found available in an agent this latter medium enslaves the user. One of the mental mechanisms that frees the unconscious of guilt for carrying inferiority is projection. This accounts for such excuses as, "I became involved with the wrong crowd, and began using dope," or "When my husband died I started to drink."

No place on this planet is without addiction, whether it is the tundra of Uganda or an air-conditioned apartment looking out on Diamond Head in Honolulu. Drug addiction is unchecked by race, color, faith, socioeconomic stratum, or occupation. Whether the individual is a professor of political science or a tribesman, one is as potentially addictive as the other. The agent may be universal in use or endemic to a particular region.

To give some idea of the wide variety of addictive drugs throughout the world, a few are cited. In Australia there are the alkaloids derived from the pituri plant; African Bushmen and Hottentots use dagga which is obtained from hemp. On the eastern Mediterranean one finds khat tea. In the southwest Pacific, Malaysian and Polynesian addicts prefer the betel nut and the pepper kava.

Narcotic agents, whether stimulating or soothing, are smoked, eaten, chewed, sniffed, or taken intravenously. The most commonly used addictives have been known to and consumed by man for ages: tobacco, hashish, opium, and coca leaves. Furthermore, drug addiction is not confined to those who have but a meager education or who have no interest in scientific and intellectual pursuits. Sigmund Freud, according to Ernest Jones, his biographer, took cocaine and consumed 20 cigars a day. Hashish was the addictive medium of Bayard Taylor, Baudelaire, and Gautier. Among victims of poppy seed were Coleridge and DeQuincy. Poe preferred gin, while Ulysses S. Grant chose whisky. An anecdote concerning Grant and his drinking merits space because it points up a salient feature of alcoholism to be presented later. President Lincoln proposed sending a barrel of General Grant's liquor to all other (less successful) commanders. Yet the general's poor judgment and unsuccessful life after he left the White House are pathetic terminations to what might have been an otherwise brilliant life. This is the common story of most chronic alcoholics.

A brace of ironic twists started heroin on its infamous journey. In 1898, when heroin was isolated in Germany, it was hailed in scientific literature as a "safe preparation free from addiction-forming properties." What is currently known as the "main-line" (intravenous administration of a narcotic) commenced in the 1840's when the hypodermic syringe was invented. Not long after that, Dr. Alexander Wood of Edinburgh gave the first hypodermic injection of a narcotic—morphine—to his wife, who is said to be the first mainliner to die of an overdose.

The "Typical" (?) *Addict.* It is impossible to delineate the typical addict from so-called authoritative reports; these conflict, one with the other. The U. S. Public Health Service in Lexington, Kentucky, describes him as in his late twenties, hailing from the northern part of the country, and addicted to heroin; thirty years ago the USPHS described the typical addict as a forty-year-old southerner addicted to morphine. New York psychiatrist,

Dr. Alfred M. Freedman, says the typical addict is young or middle-aged, having a comfortable background, addicted to several drugs, but, as heroin becomes more costly, turning more and more to hallucinogens. According to Dr. Milton Helpern, Chief Medical Examiner in New York City, and Dr. Yong-Myun Rho, of New York University School of Medicine, addicts are "younger-age groups who comprise the bulk of the so-called 'street addicts' and who use heroin, in contrast to the older 'medicinal' addicts who become addicted to such narcotic drugs as morphine and meperidine hydrochloride." Drs. Helpern and Rho also report an interesting aspect of addiction, in the following table covering the New York City area:

ADDICT	DEATHS (Narcotism/10,000 Deaths-All Causes)
White	
male	11.3
female	3.1
Negro	
male	115.3
female	47.6

ALCOHOLISM

Alcoholism is the fourth most important public health problem in this country, subordinate only to heart disease, cancer, and mental illness. Alcoholism accounts for one out of every seven admissions to civil mental institutions, and in nine states it is the most frequently occurring diagnosis among new admissions. While statistics on alcoholism in the general population cannot possibly be accurate, one report claims that at least six million Americans are alcoholic, and that one out of every thirteen males over the age of 20 is alcoholic. Reports of hospitals, clinics, and allied centers show that alcoholism is soaring at the rate of a quarter of a million persons annually. What seems to be amazing is that only a small percentage (roughly three) of alcoholics are on Skid Row; all others are in business, in private dwellings, industry, and practically every walk of (respectable) life. It is the latter feature that principally involves all physicians in the problem, as we shall see.

From earliest times man has been getting drunk and, at the

same time, battling the problem of intoxication. The first in the long line of intoxicants were probably certain herbs, the use of which became habitual. Soon thereafter the technique of fermentation was discovered, and alcoholism was launched on its endless orbit. There isn't a place in this world where some element is not used as a source of stimulating and intoxicating beverages: cactus, corn, grain, potatoes, rice, sugar are some. There are two cultural exceptions to alcoholism: Mohammedans and Jews, whose religious doctrines are particularly adamant about drunkenness. Alcohol has wrecked nations, devastated armies, jeopardized masterful undertakings, and ruined families by the millions, religions and governments notwithstanding. Nevertheless, it is not possible to categorically state that any single national or ethnic group is more prone to alcoholism than another. France has the doubtful honor of supporting more drinking places per capita than any nation in the world. Habitual use of alcohol is common among the Irish. The director of psychiatric research in Russia, Professor A. V. Snezchnevsky, told me when I visited the USSR recently that the "big problem" is alcoholism, a surprising datum since one would expect the state to be in a position to control mass behavior. The Russian psychiatrist's attitude toward the problem of alcoholism is interesting. Dr. Beljaev Vladilen Pavlovitch, chief doctor of the Fourth Hospital for Mental Diseases in Leningrad, told me (and I quote): "We do not regard [alcoholism] as a psychiatric illness until 'overt' symptoms develop . . . The question is whether alcoholism is an emotional disease. We are investigating this at present at the Bechterew Institute in Leningrad. I feel that people blame alcoholic addiction on misfortune, but I am of the opinion that it is their attempt to win approval of their own personality. If alcoholism is an illness, it begins as a habit, that is, it is a personality disorder."

The Ambiguities of Alcohol. In its natural state or in a concoction, alcohol presents one ambiguity after another. It cannot be detected on the breath; the odor that is smelled is always that of the flavoring agent. Among foods, alcohol is the easiest to digest; digestion is total. In moderation it has its place in medical therapeutics: as an analgesic for rheumatoid arthritis, as an appetite stimulant, as an aid to digestion, as a first-aid agent to revive those suffering from cold exposure (the Alpine St. Bernard dog and his flask of brandy, e. g.), and others. Alcohol, on the one hand, is a leading factor in highway disasters (only 0.04 per cent alcohol in the bloodstream may lower visual acuity as much as wearing smoked glasses); on the other hand, several beer-guzzling volunteers at the Yale Center of Alcoholic Studies *outperformed* their abstinent competitors in a series of special machine-efficiency tests. "Drinker" and "alcoholic" are not synonymous. There are many persons who are steady drinkers who could not become alcoholics no matter how they tried. One New York physician decided to test this statement. He filled his car with two cases of liquor and drove to an isolated cabin in New England where he drank and sang day after day and night after night. However, as Milton Golin, authority on alcohol addiction reported in the July 19, 1958 *Journal of the American Medical Association*, "he was not happy. At the end of one solid month of inebriation, when this doctor returned to his office to measure his craving and physical dependency on alcohol as a drug, only one thing was certain—*he did not want to look at liquor for the rest of his life*." We have paraphrased this reaction elsewhere: the personality makes the addiction, the agent does not.

Finally, alcohol doesn't stimulate the central nervous system; it affects it as a depressant. The first stages of intoxication may resemble those due to stimulation but these are reflections of depression of central inhibition, a direct cerebral action. The later results of intoxication are said to be due to a spread of the depressant effects to other segments of the nervous system. One drink may be enough to make a loquacious orator out of a shy, diffident mouse of a man; his "shyness" has been "depressed" and his inner drive to be the center of attraction is thus emancipated and can express itself.

Where and how alcohol concentrates its influence depends on the concentration in the bloodstream. It is fairly well established that alcohol first exerts its effect on the cerebral cortex, which is the cause for loss of control of judgment and self-control. As imbibition raises the alcoholic content of the body, the effect spreads to other parts of the brain, and posture, equilibrium, speech, sensory perception, and other functions are profoundly disturbed. The last stop on this physical descent is unconsciousness.

Ninety per cent of ingested alcohol is oxidized, as with other foods, and converted into energy. Only ten per cent of the alcohol, as such, is excreted through lungs and kidneys. The rate of oxidation is controlled by the need for energy: the greater the physical exertion, the faster the oxidation. However, the rate of oxidation is independent of the energy required and is relatively the same in everyone. Therefore, black coffee does not nullify drunkenness; it just keeps the drunk awake. Similarly, physical exertion does not speed up alcoholic oxidation.

Personality. To date there is nothing in medical literature that specifically categorizes an "alcoholic personality." Alcoholics, however, do have certain characteristics in common. They are emotionally immature, inordinately narcissistic, and filled with guilt and insecurity. Of course a person may have these traits without becoming an alcoholic. He might become depressed and kill himself; he could find compromise relief in a neurosis; he could project his unconscious conflict out into consciousness and blame others for his difficulty. Furthermore, alcoholism and neurosis, or alcoholism and psychosis are very possible combinations, as we shall see. Sigmund Freud postulated that the compulsive drinker is a paranoid with fixation of libido at the homoerotic level. Whether these drinkers are single or married, they nevertheless gravitate to unisexual bars and resort to intimacy in gesture and in word. It is a fact that many practicing homosexuals are compulsive drinkers; the alcoholic homosexual was discussed on page 115. It is of academic interest to note that Freud would not join any organization that embraced antialcoholism in its aims, whereas Carl Jung was vehemently antialcoholic.

The Psychology of Alcoholism. If we compare Dr. Pavlovitch's views on alcoholism with those of American psychiatrists, we find that Russia and the United States differ on psychological opinion as much as they do on political ideologies. Many American psychiatrists believe that alcoholism is a form of neurosis, thus bypassing the fact that it is first an addiction which has both emotional and physiological elements. When a person discovers that alcohol gratifies some desire or drive, he simply repeats the experience more and more frequently and becomes emotionally enslaved (dependent). It is the coward's escape hatch (inferiority); it is the emotionally enfeebled's crutch (inferiority); it is the Caspar Milquetoast's "six-shooter" (inferiority). Inferiority is, as previously stated, anathema to the unconscious; it is, thus, a springboard for neurosis, too. It is felt, therefore, that back of alcoholism is a neurotic constitution. But while one neurotic may become addicted to alcohol very quickly, another (the "excessive social drinker") may take years to become a complete alcoholic, as we shall discuss. Like every other form of addiction, be it drugs or eating or smoking, the basis of the drinker's search for surcease is unconscious inferiority.

Defining Alcoholism. There is no agreement on what alcoholism is among those concerned with the problem of alcoholism. Psychiatrists, police officials, sociologists, and scientists in general have their respective concepts of this addiction. Certainly alcohol doesn't create addiction just because it's available. Milton Golin, in the same article cited above, declared that "alcoholism is basically a brain disease—insofar as the brain is (1) a physiological organ subject to mental and emotional stresses and (2) a sociological organ subject to interpersonal demands and byplay." Mark Keller, managing editor of the *Quarterly Journal of Alcohol Studies,* regards alcoholism as "a chronic behavioral disorder manifested by repeated drinking of alcoholic beverages in excess of the dietary social usages of the community and to the extent that it interferes with the individual's health or his social or economic functioning." The World Health Organization (WHO) defines alcoholism as: "One becomes an alcoholic when he begins to be concerned about how activities interfere with his drinking instead of how drinking interferes with his activities." An ancient oriental proverb describes the downward progression of alcoholism as:

> *"First the man takes the drink,*
> *Then the drink takes a drink,*
> *Then the drink takes a man."*

Of itself, alcoholism is not a disease. It is one symptom of a complex and all-inclusive pathological situation which involves the drinker's psyche, soma, morals, spiritual existence, environment, and his interpersonal relationships. Clinically, alcohol is seen as the provocative agent in many physical disorders: cirrhosis of the liver, nephritis, peptic ulcer, and many others. Whether an alcoholic will or will not develop one or more such organic complications is not certain. What *is* certain is that his psyche is *always* implicated, as evidenced by the ultimate ruin experienced by his emotional structure. Although there are several types of alcoholism, as we shall see, with organic features, the disease is falling more and more into the psychiatrist's lap for treatment.

This brings to the forefront the problem of fitting alcoholism into the classification of mental pathology. "Psychosis with alcoholism" was once a popular diagnostic term, but it actually was avoiding the issue. One wonders how many patients given this diagnosis were really manic-depressives or schizophrenics. The latest revision of the APA's classification puts alcoholism under "personality disorders," a clinical bow to the current feeling that habitual usage of intoxicants is basically a personality deficiency—the drive to take off into the outerspace of addiction. Earlier we observed that it is *the man who takes the drink,* then *the drink that takes a drink.* Up to this point alcoholism is a personality disorder. When *the drink takes the man* the dead-end of the road of drinking is in sight and destruction of the alcoholic's personality, comportment, and somatic systems and organs begins. This latter stage is diagnostically divided into several types: pathological intoxication, chronic intoxication, alcoholic paranoid states, delirium tremens, acute hallucinosis, Korsakoff's reaction, and one other we dare to insert: the "quiet drunk."

Pathological Intoxication. Colloquially known as the "crazy drunk" and *mania à potu,* pathological intoxication is a reaction to alcohol in which the subject, after drinking even small quantities of an intoxicating beverage, gives vent to excessive emotional display (usually blind rage) along with violent, even homicidal, behavior upon the slightest provocation. Following recovery from intoxication, he does not recall any of his acts but is tearfully remorseful when informed of them. Invariably this type of alcoholic has abnormal personality characteristics even when sober, and, like the epileptic, he often shows "antithetic traits." Frequently, his personality is typically schizoid. During the height of pathological intoxication the subject may react to auditory hallucinations. The attack lasts only a matter of minutes, but sometimes it may persist for several hours.

Chronic Intoxication.   Also known as "alcoholic deterioration," this variety of alcoholism is the last stop on the descent to utter psychic bankruptcy. The patient has an abhorrence of interpersonal relations and of nourishment. At first he misses meals in order to devote himself to drinking; ultimately he refuses all solid foods and nonalcoholic beverages. Malnutrition and general decrepitude are the hallmarks of the end. The motivation of the chronic alcoholic appears to be that of deliberate self-destruction. It is the terminal clinical picture—colloquially known as the "lush"—that fosters the popular idea that the guilty factor is liquor, whereas it is and always has been only the accomplice of the personality. Many researchers stoutly maintain that the only difference between suicide and the terminal point of chronic alcoholism is time.

Alcoholic Paranoid State.   This is the alcoholic who is suspicious, sullen, and irritable; these manifestations strongly suggest the projective mechanism of unconscious homosexual impulses. The alcoholic paranoid is well-known: he is the chronic grumbler and griper, life has given him a "dirty deal"; no one will give him "a break." He may even react to delusions of persecution. The more paranoid he becomes the more he frequents bars and "clubs"— drinking lowers the barrier to the expression of the homosexual drive. Frequently, alcoholism enables him to prove to the world that he is, nonetheless, every inch a "man." He backs this up with fist fights, drunken brawls, and will attack policemen as well as civilians. Clinically, there is a question: is this individual a schizophrenic who is a chronic drinker?

Delirium Tremens ("d. t.'s"). Psychiatrically known as *oinomania,* delirium tremens is an acute manifestation of chronic deterioration. It usually follows a prolonged drinking bout during which the patient has abstained from eating. The "d. t.'s" are marked by agitation associated with lurid visual hallucinations such as "pink elephants" or weird forms that "pursue" the patient. The victim reacts to these experiences with abject fear. There is one common diagnostic sign in delirium tremens: during the time the patient reacts with fear to his visual hallucinations, he presents a "grim humor" in response to his helpless plight, i. e., he laughs ironically in the face of his impending "end." Moreover, he is highly suggestible and visual hallucinations can be suggested to him. Sometimes the patient behaves "occupationally," that is, he tries to perform his usual work in his delirium: the postman "walks his rounds" (by circling the room) and delivers mail by depositing imaginary letters in imaginary boxes. The acute and immediate danger of this condition is the physical element. The patient is markedly prostrate, the weak and rapid pulse indicates the enfeebled cardium, and the extent of his prostration can be gauged by the cold clammy skin and profuse perspiration. Violent tremors persist for a matter of days. When the patient is admitted to the receiving room of a hospital, emergency treatment is focused on the preservation of life, for death due to heart failure is very possible. Often the medical measures must be heroic to prevent a fatal termination. The heart is watched closely, fluids and alkalies are forced intravenously, and spinal drainage may be necessary. If the patient survives this acute critical stage, he sinks into a deep sleep and awakens comparatively clear mentally but extremely weak physically.

Acute or Alcoholic Hallucinosis. Sometimes, following a bout of intense drinking, the individual may react to auditory hallucinations for a brief period lasting from a few hours to one or two days. During this time he is extremely frightened, but, with the disappearance of the hallucinations, this emotional reaction vanishes.

Korsakoff's Psychosis or Reaction. While this variety of alcoholism may be marked in its early stages by frightening auditory hallucinations, the outstanding features are mnemonic defects and disorientation, particularly for time and person. When tested, he seems unable to retain and then recall—even a few minutes later—the simplest statement told him (and he is warned he will be asked to repeat it in a few minutes). He doesn't answer, "I don't know" or "I don't remember." On the contrary he *does* have an answer, albeit entirely wrong, which he renders with an engaging smile. He will even accept suggestions (wrong ones, of course) from the examiner as the correct replies. Invariably the Korsakoff victim's personality is that of a jolly, happy-go-lucky child.

The Quiet Drunk.   Physicians may not find this variety of alcoholism in textbooks; they may, however, in their offices. The quiet drunk is restricted to a rather well-delimited circle of drinkers with definite occupational, socioeconomic, and environmental characteristics. The age bracket is approximately between the thirties and fifties, the members are high level professional men and women whose occupational efforts are concerned chiefly with services rather than the production of goods, and the divorced and widowed. This latter group will be discussed in Chapter 14.

In the first group are the gray-flannel account executives of advertising firms, attorneys, and designers (from architecture to fashions). They are intelligent, intellectual, and interested in many cultural pursuits and entertainment. They are tense from and intensely involved in their respective occupations. They live it, eat it, breathe it, all day long and bring it home with them, and often, unknowingly, carry it with them to social gatherings, the theater, the opera, the movies. Their world is one of creative and original ideas, a highly competitive race in which inferiority in its slightest manifestation is intolerable. The drive, therefore, is for superiority— status, prestige—and he frenetically goes whole-hog for all that stands for superiority: suburbia, country club, custom-tailoring, smart people, and smart talk. Above all, he must be "one of the boys," and so, after a few years in his occupation, say, advertising, (often, having not advanced as rapidly as he—and, long ago, his parents—would have liked) he joins his confrères for a "quick one" at a bar before catching the 5:15 for suburbia. *Mirabile visu!* in that one drink he finds the magic solvent that releases him from worry and frustrations. It overpowers his superego. He can now compete with his peers: tell the anecdote that throws the crowd into stitches, talk convincingly of ideas for advertising lay-outs, make a strong impression. Unconsciously, he finds that if a drink . . . or two, for quite a while—gains him status downtown, why not elsewhere, the club, for instance? The story is old hat. Doctors recognize this man. But alcohol, like most narcotics, demands escalation of dose. Now the descent begins. He finds he cannot get started each morning unless he has a pick-me-up. You'll find him on any weekday morning in the dimly lighted bar of the terminal where his commuter train pulls in, or in a small one nearby. There will be one or two other well-dressed, obviously well-bred men, having a drink. They don't speak to each other; they don't know each other and don't want to know each other. They realize that drinking early in the morning is an indication of weakness—inferiority.

In time, the alcoholic—for that is what he is—can't even wait to reach the city. He arises and, before he attempts to do anything, he must have that hooker. Eventually it'll be two hookers, then three . . . and again, when he reaches the city. Then during the day, and finally, constantly, like the chronic alcoholic described above. Now he is brought to his physician, to whom he should have been brought or come on his own long before. This, then, is the story of the "quiet drunk."

Treatment of Alcoholism. The aim of every means of therapy in alcoholism is complete cessation of addiction to alcohol; there can be no temporizing with this objective. However, until very recently, the various programs of treatment were supposed to succeed in their respective ways; they were not regarded as palliative approaches. Today there is uniformity of opinion that it is one thing to pull an alcoholic out of a bout with liquor; it is quite another to keep him away from drinking. As in other forms of addiction, the underlying reason for falling victim to the habit must be dug out, and psychotherapy is the answer and will be until something better comes along. However, the psychotherapist makes no claim that he is the only one who can succeed in treating the alcoholic. He makes use of as many ancillary modalities as he can. Top priority is given to Alcoholics Anonymous (A. A.), created several years ago by an Ohio surgeon who was, himself, a compulsive drinker, and his friend, a New York stock broker, also an alcoholic. A. A.'s approach incorporates the therapeutic tools of group therapy, suggestion, reeducation, and support. Despite A. A.'s excellent record, its high ideals, and its excellent reputation, a recent report by the director of all A. A. groups in a large city stated that less than 10 per cent of the country's more than six million alcoholics make a start toward recovery. In a typical case, he said, it is five to nine years after the onset of chronic alcoholism before the drinker's wife asks the family doctor or minister for advice. This brings to mind the active participation in current treatment by members of the clergy. Ministers, priests, and rabbis work in close contact with the medical profession. Whereas these prelates may have once quoted scripture and "lectured" the drinker, regarding him as a hopeless sinner beyond salvation, the clergy now regard him as a sick man with the potential for recovery. Dr. Donald W. Hewitt, chief medical adviser for the Los Angeles Charity Alcoholic Rehabilitation Center states: "The physician can refer the alcoholic to someone who will reassure his patient that God is a loving and forgiving Father who is willing to blot out and forgive the sins if the alcoholic is only contrite and repentant (that is, if he has 'insight') . . . An alcoholic is already suffering truly excruciating physical and mental anguish. Portraying God as a stern, unrelenting Deity who demands His 'pound of flesh' for each sin committed will often load down the alcoholic with what he feels is an unsupportable burden that only further drinking can ease for him."

The physician may find that the patient requires institutionalization, if only to get the chronic drinker on his feet and started on the road to treatment. Obviously, the patient must have a well-rounded diet, exercise, and sufficient rest. Tranquilizing agents may be needed for the anxious and "jittery" victim. Drugs such as disulfiram (Antabuse, trade mark) will, without doubt, make it impossible for the patient to even look at liquor, but unless someone stands over him the first thing each morning and compels him to swallow the pill, he will revert to drinking at once. Antabuse is to the drinker what insulin is to the diabetic: a check and not a cure. Physicians are warned to regard new and "amazing" cures of chronic alcoholism *cum granum salis*. For example, Japan's Krume University recently reported that the desire for alcohol as well as tolerance to it, are markedly lessened by a daily dose of 10 to 60 mgms. of cyanide.

Trends in Treatment.   Experience garnered from treatment of alcoholism indicates the future direction of therapy, as follows:

1. Prevention is always preferable to treatment. This is prompting educational leaders to incorporate a reasonable and effective teaching program for high school students, which presents the uses and abuses of alcohol.

2. Family and community friction turn up so often in the histories of alcoholics that it is obvious that therapy must incorporate these elements. One of the pioneers in this type of therapeutic program was Johns Hopkins Hospital where alcoholics and their spouses undergo concurrent treatment. Reports from this hospital are optimistic and gratifying.

3. Group therapy is another promising project. One of the first such programs was pioneered by Central Islip State Hospital, Long Island, New York. The groups include out-patients, and patients who were formerly institutionalized and are on convalescent status.

4. So much remains unknown about alcoholism that research must be encouraged and continued, and in many fields—the community, the family, and the areas of physiology, sociology, and specific therapy. Among current centers conducting this type of research are the National Institute of Mental Health, the National Council on Alcoholism, and the Yale University Center on Alcohol Studies.

NARCOTISM

Narcotism is a specific form of addiction indicating chronic use of narcotic drugs, or chronic addiction or habituation to narcotic agents such as cocaine, heroin, morphine, and opium. A *narcotic* is a drug exerting analgesic and soporific affects. *Habituation* is acquisition of a desire for the effects of narcotic drugs, without physical dependency, following their repeated use for medical purposes. This latter standard definition is unsatisfactory because it is untrue; it is a semantic reflection of a belief among professional and lay persons that narcotism invariably is the result whenever a physician prescribes a derivative of opium or a synthetic equivalent.

This idea is contrary to basic psychological fact. You have written prescriptions, many times, I am sure, for paregoric for patients who are going abroad—to have "something" in case *"tour-*

isme" strikes them. There must be thousands upon thousands of these paregoric-equipped tourists. How many cases of opium addiction have you found as a result of this practice? Do you know of one? In the same manner, at this moment there must be thousands of hospital patients who are receiving hypodermic administrations of morphine or meperidine as part of the usual pre-operative routine, and as many who, post-operatively are receiving the same medication for analgesic purposes—on a q 4 h, p. r. n. schedule. This procedure, too, has not resulted in wholesale conversion to drug addiction. True, there are instances where patients who were introduced to opium and morphine medically, continued it as an addictive practice, but their histories invariably reveal that they had been using these or similar drugs prior to medical administration. The whole concept of "induced" addiction is reduceable to a basic psychiatric precept that it is the personality deviation that renders an individual vulnerable to drugs, not the reverse.

There is another common belief that should be corrected. For the past several years heroinism has been considered the "worst" addiction in this country because of its implication in crime. The prohibitive price of a "fix" forces the average addict to steal so that he has the money to buy heroin. In terms of dollars and cents, heroinism probably *is* the worst addiction. It is our contention, however, that overeating is, by far, the most disastrous addiction because of its production of overweight, a prominent factor in cardiovascular pathology, the leading cause of death. Quite conscious of the possibility that he may be eating his way to the grave, the compulsive overeater complacently goes on his nibbling way, often "dieting" carefully at mealtime. Consider tobacco addiction. Well publicized health statistics, the printed warning on every cigarette package: CIGARETTE SMOKING MAY BE HAZARDOUS TO YOUR HEALTH, the fact that cancer causes one in every four deaths—these are no deterrents to smokers. In fact, the consumption of tobacco in the United States continues to rise year after year. Physicians do not question that smoking is an addiction. Witness the patient who is told he must stop smoking if he wishes to live. The anguish this patient suffers is sheer agony for him; and some of these persons do avoid suffering by continuing to smoke—they opt for death. This is the grip addiction has on an individual.

Addicts are always aware of their addiction, whether it is overeating, smoking, drinking, or taking drugs; they are also aware of the ill-effects. But, like the patient just mentioned, they choose the chance of death rather than surrender the addiction.

Drug addiction statistics are utterly worthless; they have to be based on *known* cases. Obviously, the financially well-fixed user of drugs never becomes a statistic. In 1968, the Federal Bureau of Narcotics estimated the total number of known addicts to be 64,025; others believe this figure is far too conservative. A recent Senate Judiciary Committee investigation of drug addiction put the total at 150,000.

There have been a couple of sociological twists to drug addiction in the past thirty to forty years. In 1955 the U. S. Public Health Service Hospital for drug addicts in Lexington, Kentucky was convinced that addiction was well on its way to becoming an ethnological problem. The hospital reported that the percentage of its Negro patients rose from 8.9 in 1936 to 52 in 1955. This is a startling statistic, considering the fact that Negroes constitute but 11 per cent of the entire population. Therefore, the USPHS concluded, drug addiction could be considered an ethnological problem. Statistics released in 1967, however, indicate that drug addiction among Negroes is commencing to decrease. The statistical reversal is variously inferred to mean that the Negro's status is changing, that there is greater racial pride, that he has an improved understanding of the effects of addiction, and that addiction is equated with loss of status. We cannot support or deny these conclusions. The other sociological peculiarity is that narcotism is predominantly a practice of youth.

If it is permissible to expand the implication of "addiction" (as discussed elsewhere in this book), then psychiatric pharmaceuticals may be the leader of the addictive parade. Statistics are of no help because, for example, the report that in 1966 about 70 million prescriptions for psychopharmaceuticals were written means little when you consider the unreported and unrecorded (in pharmacological prescription records, that is) orders for tranquilizers ordered by house physicians in hospitals and by doctors in clinics, and the handing out of samples by physicians to patients. Likewise, those

70 million prescriptions may not be for as many individuals; it is more likely that a sizeable number were refills.

According to reports from Japan, slightly more than 40 per cent of hospitalized addicts use amphetamines, while 27 per cent are meprobamate "addicts." Again, the question of ataractics serving as addictive agents crops up. The Japanese find that withdrawal symptoms among amphetamine users include antisocial behavior, convulsions, and delirium.

Opioid Addiction (Opioidism).   The term "opioid" is preferable, so far as discussion of addiction is concerned, because it includes and is meant to refer to derivatives of opium. Addiction to opium itself is "opium addiction" or "opiumism."

We can only surmise how extensive opioid addiction is in the United States; statistics, such as they are, provided by the Federal Bureau of Narcotics are the data usually cited. We repeat, these are based on *known* cases, those who have been arrested for possessing or engaging in the opium traffic, and those who are committed to or voluntarily enter treatment centers. The list of addicts' names is maintained by the Bureau on a time basis (a name is retained only for five years after its initial recording). The list has never contained more than 50,000 names in the past five years even though 7,000 to 9,000 names are added annually. Males outnumber females by 3:1. Slightly more than half are Negroes (reminding us of the previously cited USPH report); Puerto Ricans and Mexicans are a small percentage of the whites. A little more than half are 20-30 years of age, one-third 30 to 40, and only four per cent are under 20. A bit less than half the names are registered as from New York State. Heroin is the chief offender, followed by morphine, meperidine, and the other opioids. Another USPH report describes the "typical" addict of the 30's as a white male 38-year-old convict serving a sentence of two years for selling narcotic drugs, and who began his addiction in his late twenties. In 1955 the typical addict was a male Negro in his twenties, a voluntary patient who became addicted to heroin when he was barely out of his teens.

Addictive Drugs

Because they are alkaloids, opium, morphine, heroin, and cocaine have almost identical actions. They constitute a large group of organic, basic substances found in plants. They are usually bitter in flavor and physiologically active. None of them is endemic to this country and all of them are brought in by smugglers working for underworld organizations. Heroin originates in Turkey; the others are harvested and desiccated in China and after a circuitous passage, find their way into the United States directly by smuggling or by way of a series of way stations such as South America and Mexico, also under the guidance of smugglers.

Cocaine. Cocaine is a crystalline alkaloid (methyl benzoyl ecgonine) obtained from the leaves of *Erythroxylon coca* and other species of *Erythroxylon*. Its anesthetic qualities were discovered almost a century ago by the ophthalmologist, Carl Koller. He, however, would not have discovered cocaine's anesthetic properties had it not been for his lifelong friend, Sigmund Freud. There is an interesting postlude to this event.

During his internship, Freud frenetically looked for something he could seize on that would bring him international renown (even the future father of psychoanalysis suffered feelings of inferiority). Freud tells of this incident in his autobiography: "I may here go back a little and explain how it was the fault of my fiancée that I was not already famous at that early age (1884). A side interest, though it was a deep one, had led me in 1884 to obtain from Merck some of what was then the little-known alkaloid cocaine and to study its physiological action. While I was in the middle of this work, an opportunity arose for making a journey to visit my fiancée, from whom I had been parted for two years. I hastily wound up my investigation of cocaine and contented myself in my book on the subject prophesying that further use for it would soon be found. I suggested, however, to my friend, Königstein, the ophthalmologist, that he should investigate the question of how far the anesthetizing properties of cocaine were applicable in diseases of the eye. When I returned from my holiday I found that not he, but another of my friends, Carl Koller (now in New York), to whom I had also spoken about cocaine, had made the decisive experiments upon animals' eyes and had demonstrated them at the Ophthalmological Congress at Heidelberg. Koller is therefore rightly regarded as the discoverer of local anesthesia by cocaine, which has become so important in minor surgery, but I bore my fiancée no grudge for her interruption of my work."

There is more to what medical historians call "Freud's cocaine episode." He had used hypodermic injections of cocaine to relieve a patient's facial neuralgia, and had failed; perhaps he lacked the surgical knowledge (or so Ernest Jones suggests). In the same year, 1885, a young American graduate student, W. H. Halstead, succeeded where Freud had failed. Halstead is remembered as one of Hopkins "Four Horsemen"—and he also became a cocaine addict, thanks to Freud's enthusiastic praise for the drug.

But the Freud-cocaine saga does not end there; the second part is blamed for the disfavor—even the stigma—that is attached to the mere mention of the word "hypodermic." Freud experienced another disaster with cocaine; he had ordered large doses of the drug for a patient who died from overdosage. Anxious to clear his favorite anesthesia (and himself?) of becoming known as "dangerous," he appealed to general prejudice, as his biographer, Jones, put it, "by implicating the hypodermic injections as the real peril." That was the birth of abhorrence for the hypodermic needle. Physicians know very well the frown and sometimes horror of a patient when a "shot" is to be given. "Oh, must you, doctor? Can't I take it by mouth?" In other words, the effect of the drug is the same; the only unpalatable part of medication is the hypodermic.

Cocainism is seen clinically as acute and chronic cocainism.

Acute Cocainism. Following initial giddiness and slight headache, the cocaine recipient becomes euphoric. His perception and interpretation of stimuli are altered; he says his "consciousness is broadened"; his "mind is expanded." It isn't expanded; it's distorted. For instance, a dazzling sun may be interpreted as a brilliant, indescribably colorful bouquet of poppies. These ecstatic and exotic sensory misinterpretations are elements of the overall emotional reaction of euphoria; they are also typical manifestations of the effects of any sympathomimetic agent, and cocaine is one. In his grandiose state the cocaine user claims he can "do great things"— and often he can. He reaches new peaks in his work, speaks and writes impressively and fluently, or performs artistically with supreme verve, originality, and grace. This acute stage of cocainism is known as the "cocaine jag," during which sympathetic nervous system stimulation is seen at its maximum. After the initial period of euphoria passes, generalized weakness of mental functioning, fatigue, tremulousness, and incoordination ensue. In the end, the individual is a morose, irritable, suspicious person who may react to hallucinations. Death is always a possibility, depending on dosage and individual resistance.

Chronic Cocainism. Persistent addiction to cocaine terminates in social bankruptcy; the chronic user of the drug is seen as completely depraved and immoral. He neglects his job, his family, his community relations, and becomes totally divorced from his former role in society. It is not known why male addicts become sexually impotent and females frequently resort to perversions. Chronic cocainism is marked by overtalkativeness, extreme deterioration, and an inability to use acquired knowledge, i. e., intellectual faculties are at a standstill. This may be due to the addict's faulty memory. Emotional reactions vary from mild overactivity and excitement to surliness, suspiciousness, and a snarling manner—the paranoid. Physical stigmata include the "cocaine bug," a feeling that an insect is crawling under the skin and producing intense itchiness which compels the addict to claw constantly at his skin; the "sniffles" sound as though he is perpetually detecting unpleasant scents; and the manifestations of sympathetic nervous system excitation are noted as mydriasis, dry mucous membranes, polydipsia, generalized malaise, and cardiac palpitation.

Opioids. Opium is the air-dried juice from unripe capsules of *Papaver somniferum* or *Papaver album*. Morphine, discovered by Sertürner in 1806, is a colorless or white crystalline alkaloid derived from opium. Heroin is a diacetyl form of morphine. Heroin is most often used and sold as the hydrochloride. Like cocainism, opiumism (morphinism) is clinically seen as acute and chronic opiumism.

Acute Opiumism (Morphinism). Physicians are well acquainted with the classical picture of acute opiumism as provided by Thomas De Quincey's *Confessions of an English Opium Eater* (1822). At first there is euphoria, then the user is overwhelmed by a disinclination to move, rich fantasies, and ending in a deep sleep marked by vivid dreams. When he awakens, the addict complains of lethargy and heaviness. Rarely is he excited or depressed.

This *was* the typical picture of acute opiumism, particularly as seen in joss houses more than a century ago. For the past few decades a different variety of opium addict has cropped up. He is rare, admittedly, and his group comprises a hard core of addicts, especially among intellectuals, who seem to be able to control (often with difficulty, however) their addiction to the extent of resorting to opium only at irregular intervals when anxiety is particularly intense. In other words, opium is used by this group as a tranquilizer rather than as an obscurer of reality. No textbook can do this type of addict justice. Physicians are urged to read the dramatic and gripping description that André Malraux provides in his *Man's Fate*.

Chronic Opiumism (Morphinism).   The end of the road of addiction to opium is the same for all, even Malraux's Gisours: intellectual and emotional deterioration. He is weak, emaciated, pale, debilitated, a wraith of his former self straying in and out of the umbra of addiction. Sensitivity is lowered, pupils are miotic, he is sallow complected, and he has uncontrollable tremors. His body bears the telltale relics of hypodermic injections (smoking opium is rare in this country). He is prematurely old and he is impotent; he complains of bizarre skin sensations. There may be delirious episodes. Many chronic addicts develop full-blown paranoid reactions (also described by Malraux).

Heroinism.   Acute and chronic heroinism are, for all intents and purposes, clinical images of acute and chronic opiumism. Until very recently, heroin—"the hard stuff," or "snow," or "H"—was Public Drug Enemy Number One. This may have been due to heroin's cheaper cost compared to opium or morphine or because of the well-executed sales campaign in this country by the underworld. Later, we shall see why it is losing out to marihuana and LSD.

The Heroin Saga.   Because of federal statute outlawing the manufacture and sale of heroin in the United States, the heroin trade is a complex, cloak-and-dagger underworld commercial venture that encircles the world. It begins on Turkish farms where, as the law permits, poppies are raised from which opium, the first step in the manufacture of heroin, is obtained. According to 1967 figures, opium sells for about eight dollars a pound in Istanbul. It is then smuggled into Lebanon and Syria where it is converted into morphine base; 11 pounds of opium yield one pound of base. From the Near East, the opium base is brought into France where, in laboratories that the *gendarmerie* ignore, the base is converted into heroin, now worth $140 a pound. By devious means and routes, heroin is imported into the United States where the going wholesale price is $700 a pound. In dingy bedrooms, cellars, and back poolrooms, dealers or pushers cut the imported heroin as much as ten times, and retail "fixes" in glassine for $5 to $10—sometimes more —a single dose. Most addicts require several fixes a day to remain comfortable; in a short time dosages have to be escalated as tolerance to the drug increases and its effect decreases.

Heroin's effects—"going on the nod"—are euphoria progressing to sleepiness through its actions on the higher brain centers which govern judgment, self-control, and attention. The indescribable craving, the maddening desire for heroin when an addict needs a fix, and hasn't it or the money for it defy the average physician's power of description. The sadistic mercilessness of the pusher, the eventual relief of the addict when the needle is expertly inserted into the vein are beyond belief. Again, we leave it to popular literature—*The Man with the Golden Arm* by Nelson Algren—to paint the adequate picture of heroinism. Yes, this book is dramatic; no, it is free of exaggeration and distortion. But Algren reveals one fact about heroinism that is not generally known: the habit can be "kicked," permanently. It simply is another proof of the psychological truism that it is the emotionally distressed and twisted personality that invites addiction; not the agent that creates addiction.

Cure implicates a twofold program: withdrawal and rehabilitation. The problems involved are summarized by the New York State Narcotic Addiction Control Commission as: "To understand the many difficulties to be overcome by the addict before he can be cured, one need only consider what has happened to him and his life. He is *emotionally* dependent upon a drug and craves its effects. His body needs the drug, too, and if he stops taking it, he will experience withdrawal sickness or discomfort due to physical dependence. Worse than that, his body has also built up a peculiar *tolerance* that causes him to require larger and larger amounts at each dosage. He adjusts himself to the fact that each time he holds in his possession the implements of drug taking, or the narcotic itself, he is committing a crime. In his never-ending search for money to buy drugs, he commits other crimes, lies to and cheats his family and friends, and eventually permits others to 'try' drugs he has bought."

There is more on the subject of treatment which is left to the end of this section because the topic of amphetamine drugs and of alcohol and narcotics must be considered first.

Amphetamines.   Twenty-five years ago a small number of psychiatrists, including this writer, began to notice the hazards of amphetamines and the tenacious character of the addiction they quickly induce. We were, in the main, ignored, but over the years our ranks have swelled and most psychiatrists currently agree that amphetamine addiction is the most refractory addiction to treat—even heroinism is easier to handle therapeutically. In 1967 legislators became interested, and hearings were and are being conducted to gather expert testimony to help legislators prepare suitable statutes governing the manufacture and sale of these drugs.

Amphetamine is synthetic racemic desoxy-norephedrine or alpha-methylphenothylamine. As a therapeutic agent it is relatively new. It was discussed as a psychic energizer in Chapter 7. Amphetamines are also used to depress appetites in obese persons who lack the emotional maturity to limit their caloric intake, as stimulants by car drivers who wish to avoid falling asleep at the wheel, and as "pep pills" or "goof balls" or "speed" by adolescents for "kicks." Among youngsters there is a popular concoction, the "bennie" (the name is derived from benzedrine), which is a mixture of amphetamine pills and cheap domestic wine. As a stimulant, this beverage defies description.

For some years it has been physicians who sometimes have unwittingly lent themselves to abetting amphetamine addiction. A patient may complain of feeling "nervous," "depressed," "down in the dumps," and similar reactions. The doctor may reach in a desk drawer, pull out a package of amphetamine samples, and hand them to the patient. "Here," he says. "Try these." And the patient may thereupon be "hooked." The same applies to the obese patient. Whether or not they lose weight, they may have a constant craving for amphetamine every day thereafter.

The hazards of amphetamines are well known. In the *Physicians' Desk Reference (PDR)*, every manufacturer of amphetamine products spells out the dangers of these pharmaceuticals. For example, one manufacturer states:

> *Use with caution in patients hypersensitive to sympathomimetics and in coronary or cardiovascular disease or severe hypertension. Excessive use of the amphetamines by unstable individuals may result in psychological dependence. ADVERSE REACTIONS: The following are unwanted reactions reported or considered possible: overstimulation, restlessness, insomnia, g. i. disturbances, diarrhea, palpitation, tachycardia, elevation of blood pressure, tremor, sweating, impotence, and headache.*

The manufacturer fails to include the possibility of a full-blown psychosis . . . and death. But, as you can see, amphetamines are otherwise absolutely safe (!).

Treatment runs the usual gamut of substitution and withdrawal-replacement techniques, combined with intensive psychotherapy. As stated previously, treatment of amphetamine addiction is one of the severest challenges facing a psychiatrist; it is one of the most tenacious addictions known.

Alcoholism and Narcotism. It has been shown, in the preceding pages, how addiction is an attempt to avoid responsibilities which the patient cannot face. In the retreat from life situations, the alcohol or drug addict actually regresses to a point in his infancy where all his needs were satisfied orally. The inadequate personality which renders a person unable to accept reality is a basic weakness, and because of faulty personality development he feels the need of a stimulating or elevating drug or an intoxicant to blot out his problems—to enable him to "forget," to superimpose a false perception on consciousness, thereby distorting or constricting it, never expanding it. While both alcoholics and narcotic users show similar personality structures, there are sharp differences between the two types of addiction, including economic implications, and the attitudes toward treatment.

Attitude Toward Treatment. A drug addict seeks therapy far more readily than does the alcoholic, but the latter is more likely to be cured of his addiction. Too often, the narcotic victim's search for treatment is based on a deliberate plan to reconstitute himself so that he can start the cycle of addiction all over again—his motivation for therapy is based solely on his finances, or lack of them: as the craving for drugs creates escalation of dosage, the greater the monetary burden becomes for the addict. The alcoholic, on the other hand, develops so low a tolerance to liquor that he can almost be said to be "allergic" to it. With time, he loses his discriminating taste for the better liquors and accepts the cheapest brands, then turns to substitutes (hair tonics and cough medicines, e. g.), and finally becomes the Sterno (canned heat) habitué. In this aspect, the alcoholic is in a sorrier state than is the drug addict, for he can continue to cloy his addiction cheaply, whereas the narcotic user needs a larger and larger dose.

Economic Factors. There is a socioeconomic difference between narcotism and alcoholism that makes the former a much graver problem. The difference has a mathematical flavor. We can say that the need for and consumption of alcohol proceeds arithmetically: the supply is plentiful and the cost is not prohibitive, and, for a great number of persons, the craving can be deferred for a time, at least. To the contrary, the narcotic addict's craving is far more compelling and the drug is an exceedingly rare, illegal, and costly item. The person who is "hooked" frenetically darts from pillar to post in search of his narcotic, and the further he sinks into addiction, the more compelling is his need and the greater become his requirements. Sheer desperation and poverty often propel him to criminality as the last means by which he can get the sorely needed money with which to purchase his narcotic.

Combined Alcoholism and Narcotism. Simultaneous addiction to drugs and alcohol is quite possible. Previous mention has been made of the "bennie" and of the "quiet drunk"—the top-flight executive who is alcoholic and takes tranquilizers to soothe his "frayed" nerves. Many popular tranquilizing agents carry the manufacturer's warning, however, that patients are to be cautioned against using alcohol while taking a specific ataractic.

Treatment of Drug Addiction. A foolproof, positive, specific regimen of therapy is not yet available. The problem of addiction has spread in public interest until it now includes jurists, penologists, police officials, judges, and others—besides the medical profession. Among doctors there is great disagreement on therapy programs. Perhaps much of this discord is due to the lack of permanent cure under any treatment program. There have been a few amazing and gratifying instances of permanent recovery (Barney Ross, the ex-Marine hero and boxer, e. g.), but such cases are rare and attract attention chiefly because the person involved is often a public figure.

Above and beyond what was said about the differences between the alcoholic and the drug addict in their attitudes toward therapy, not every addict seeks therapy. Some prominent personages, especially in the world of entertainment, who capture the imagination of large blocs of the population, have the wherewithal to keep themselves in quasi-adjustment by means of drugs. Consequently, they become models to the young admirers who yearn to "live with a thrill."

The boon to therapy has been the sociolegislative recognition that narcotism is a medical problem and not a legal one. Federal legislation, commencing in 1966, laid down the ground rules that stress treatment rather than prison—help rather than punishment —for adults charged with federal crimes arising out of the habitual use of addictive agents. Most states have followed or plan to follow this principle.

Because of the wide variability among addicts, treatment programs must be based on a scale of graduated goals running from maintenance on drugs to total abstinence. These goals imply a broad variety of therapies, each of which must be closely assayed as it is used, for no method of treatment has yet been found that is universally successful.

Likewise, treatment must be geared to what Dr. C. Winick calls "maturing out," i. e., the tendency of youthful addicts to give up their drugs in their thirties or forties, with or without therapy. The reason for maturing out is unknown, but it is no reason to stand by during the addict's twenty or twenty-five most precious years and do nothing other than wait to see if he does ultimately abandon narcotism.

At present, two therapeutic approaches are used: residential settings in which addicts remain while undergoing psychotherapy, and the use of nonaddictive drugs to combat addiction. The problem of custodial therapy centers around voluntary and mandatory hospitalization, particularly for criminal addicts who commit felonies to obtain money for drugs. The voluntary system is not often successful; patients do not remain more than a matter of days. One recent report revealed that 80 per cent of voluntary patients left within 18 days after admission. State legislatures began to enact statutes for compulsory institutionalization. This program is too new to express any opinion, but it will not be surprising if it does not meet with outstanding success, for psychotherapy is the one medical treatment that cannot be "forced" on anyone. Half the victory in treatment is achieved when the patient voluntarily applies for help.

Three methods of treatment are currently in use: (1) immediate and total withdrawal, (2) gradual and partial withdrawal, and (3) the "British plan."

Immediate and Total Withdrawal. Among chronic users of narcotics, this method is referred to as "cold turkey." Anyone who has witnessed this horrible sequence of psychological and physiological events (which may terminate fatally) has been profoundly shaken by the patient's maniacal conduct and physical agony. He is overactive, complains of bone-shaking chills and "hot flashes," has an outpouring of nasal secretion, and screams that he is suffocating. He is plagued by violent abdominal cramps and "dragging" pains in the legs; he sweats profusely and trembles violently. Men sufferers have seminal emissions and females experience orgasms. The patient alternately begs for "just one more shot," weeps, sinks to his knees and implores the world, and suddenly curses, howls, and beats his fist on metal bars and cement walls. Eventually he collapses. (For a dramatic presentation of "cold turkey," readers are again referred to *The Man with the Golden Arm*). All this may last for two or three days after withdrawal is initiated. Then vigorous medical measures are taken to restore the exhausted and depleted patient to good health.

Gradual and Partial Withdrawal. This is slow and incomplete reduction of narcotic drugs, i. e., simultaneous administration of non-habit-forming sedatives in increasing doses and reduction of the patient's customary narcotic in decreasing amounts. A variation of this procedure resorts to faster withdrawal while the patient is subjected to vigorous replacement of vitamins and minerals, and a high caloric diet. Fluids are forced for several days. At first the patient may be resistive, require restraint and feeding by the intravenous route.

The "British Plan." One positive result of this therapeutic program has been passionate controversy among physicians. In England narcotics are provided to addicts, gratis, but only if the patients agree to undergo and continue in psychotherapy until the doctor decides treatment may be discontinued. The philosophy behind this scheme is the belief that the nefarious trade in narcotics would collapse and, since this would mean loss of business for the underworld, the root of the evil would be ripped from its soil. This hasn't been the happy result; in fact, young men, claiming to be addicts, report religiously for therapy, receive their drugs, and then go out and sell them to the genuine addicts. At this time, it is reported that Britain will soon radically change this method of combatting narcotic addiction.

Regardless of the treatment regimen, there is general concurrence that psychotherapy must be a major segment of the program if there is to be any lasting improvement. The addict, alcoholic or narcotic, has run away from the reality of his problems, using his addictive agent as the escape route. He must be brought back, through therapy, to a recognition of the existence of these problems, and must be helped to make an adjustment to his environment before permanent recovery can be expected, or even hoped for.

Methadone. Methadone is an analgesic chemical resembling morphine in action and addictive potential, which was first used to treat heroinism by Marie Nyswander and Vincent P. Dole at the Rockefeller Institute. Its role is that of a replacement. Unlike morphine or opium, methadone does not have to be taken in ever-mounting doses to exert its effect. It is also claimed that continuous use for two and more years produced no deleterious effects and that patients controlled by methadone showed no desire for heroin. However, some authorities claim that these patients are not "cured"; they have merely had one drug habit replace another, though the new habit is much the preferable one.

There are two other anti-addiction drugs, still in the research stage, which must be mentioned. These are Nalline (trade name for nalorphine) and Lorfan (trade name for levallorphan). According to the A. M. A.'s 1967 *New Drugs,* these agents "specifically antagonize most of the pharmacologic effects of morphine and morphine-like analgesics. The actions of nalorphine and levallorphan are similar but the latter drug is more potent . . . (These) narcotic antagonists precipitate an abstinence syndrome in addicted . . . individuals, and reverse drug-induced states of euphoria and miosis. Thus, nalorphine, in particular, is used to detect the use of, and dependence on, morphine and related drugs with an addiction liability." Whether these two agents will eventually be included in the narcotic treatment program must wait for the final answer by research.

CHAPTER TEN

Hallucinogens

TO BE EXACT, "psychedelic" and "hallucinogen" are not synonymous. Even "psychedelic" is an incorrect spelling; it is "psychodelic," but since the former has found acceptance through popular usage, this book uses it. A *hallucinogen* is any agent that evokes hallucinations through any of the five senses. The term instantly brings LSD to mind, but this is not the only agent. For example, a hypnogogic hallucination is a visual experience occurring when one fights sleepiness. Thus, a motorist, late at night, driving on a dimly lighted road on which no other vehicle is in sight, is trying to remain awake. Suddenly he thinks he sees a child dash out from the side and start to run across the road. The driver jams on brakes, sees no child, but he is now awake. This is a common reaction when one is fighting overwhelming fatigue.

Psychedelic (Gr. psycho- relating to the mind + *delos* evident, manifest) implies freedom from anxiety, exceptionally creative mental patterns, and pleasurable, vivid perceptual alterations. LSD, marihuana, and related substances are not the only psychedelics. There are many more, in what is colloquially known as the "psychedelicatessen," that are innocuous and used by the average person. Thus, the overworked businessman who is a classical music enthusiast obtains his "freedom from anxiety, exceptionally creative mental patterns, and pleasurable, vivid perceptual alterations" as he listens to a concert featuring his favorite symphony.

Hallucinogens have been used for eons by primitive peoples. The modern intellectual search for mysticism and a more acceptable world did not turn to these drugs until fairly recently. The impetus was supplied by Aldous Huxley (1894-1963) when he described his visual experiences induced by the use of mescaline, in *The Doors of Perception* (1954). For example, at the height of this cactus derivative's effect, he saw a vase holding three flowers as ". . . Adam had seen on the morning of his creation: the miracle, moment by moment, of naked existence."

Marihuana

I have yet to find a medical report or a modern textbook in which there is a complete presentation of the subject of marihuana. Likewise, questioning dozens of colleagues has failed to find one who has taken one puff. I know of one other psychiatrist beside myself who has taped an interview with a patient while the latter was under the influence of marihuana. Much of what is believed by the public about this drug is sheer myth; some of the marihuana legend is perpetuated by doctors, even in some of the latest psychiatric publications.

For instance, Dr. Alfred M. Freedman and Ethel A. Wilson, writing on "Addiction and Alcoholism" in the recent textbook *Comprehensive Textbook of Psychiatry,* (Baltimore, 1967: The Williams & Wilkins Co.), state: "Although many young people who become narcotic addicts actually begin the use of heroin by the age of 16, a large proportion have used marihuana before becoming heroin addicts." The implication is that marihuana is the gateway to heroinism. These authors cite a study in which 77 per cent of marihuana users began their practice before 17 years of age. There can be no doubt about this, but what has this to do with the claim that these same people give up marihuana for heroin? In the same textbook, Drs. Arnold J. Mandell and Louis Jolyon West flatly declare: ". . . . the great majority of addicts to substances like heroin . . . started out by using marihuana."

These writers and all other authorities, including educationalists, sociologists, and police officials, concur that marihuana is rampant among young people in and out of school. If this is so (and there is no valid reason for believing otherwise), then heroinism would, by now, be Public Problem Number One. Statistics, such as those cited above from the USPH Hospital in Lexington, Kentucky, show that known cases of heroin addiction have not exceeded 50,000 in the past several years despite annual additions of 7,000 to 9,000 names to the register. It is the general feeling that heroin addiction has decreased in the past two years while marihuana and LSD usage has been soaring. Despite these incompatibilities in mathematics, psychiatrists and others continue to broadcast about marihuana being the introductory medium to heroin.

The main trouble, I feel, behind these inconsistencies is lack of firsthand experience on the part of some writers. Some medical authors, in an attempt to convince their audiences that they "dig" the subject, toss in words which are supposed to add a youthful zing to their productions—and end up with colloquialisms that are old hat and no longer used. For example, you read of "Mary Jane" for marihuana; "reefers" for marihuana cigarettes. Some are more up to date with "smoking pot," which was replaced by "turning on," and this current phrase may be out of date when this is published, as may be "grass," the newest hipster appellation for marihuana.

The International Police Organization (Interpol) reports that there has been a marked increase in the quantity of marihuana being smuggled into the United States. This is puzzling, since *Cannabis sativa* (whose flowering tops and, sometimes, leaves are the source of marihuana) will grow anywhere on earth, indoors and out, requires no tender horticultural supervision, and is insensitive to climatic changes. The current price for an ounce of marihuana (actually about ¼ ounce in a one ounce container) is "a nickel" (five dollars) which yields six to ten cigarettes. These are made by the user on a little machine which has been sold for many years by tobacco shops for the purpose of rolling homemade cigarettes from ordinary tobacco. The smoker, when he inhales the fumes, holds his breath as long as he can to absorb as much of the marihuana as possible. When he comes to the end of the cigarette, he holds it with his fingernails or a pin—even tweezers, to get all there is in the cigarette. The full effect is felt within fifteen to twenty minutes. The aroma of smoked marihuana is easily identified: it is pungent and reminiscent of incense.

Marihuana produces mental exaltation, intoxication, and certain bizarre sensations—double consciousness, disturbance of time and space appreciation, and a false sense of performance efficiency.

Reports of marihuana users who, with little previous training or skill, played musical instruments or danced divinely while under the influence of the drug, are entirely unfounded. Microcosmic and macrocosmic experiences have been commonly described, but I have never had a patient recount such experiences. Since many of my patients are New York East Villagers—to be described later—I consider these individuals deeply "indoctrinated" veterans who know the effects of marihuana very well. Twenty years ago, because a patient (in the army) "challenged" me to, I smoked a marihuana cigarette. I felt giddy and slightly nauseated, that and nothing else.

While the expression "stoned" implies "intoxicated," the marihuana user is able to converse, walk from a tape-recorded therapy session without any difficulty, and remember all that has been said by him and by the psychiatrist. During the 45-minute session he does become relaxed, seems to be more amiable, and, in many instances, is quite "tolerant" of the therapist. Marihuana is not an addictive agent and has no known adverse effects physically except that in a considerable number of chronic users there may be photophobia which makes it necessary for the sufferer to wear dark glasses most of the time.

LSD

Lysergic acid diethylamide (LSD 25)—LSD or simply "acid" —was first isolated in the United States by Jacobs and Craig in 1934. In 1938 Stoll and Hofmann, Swiss chemists, were working on the drug when Hofmann "was seized by a peculiar sense of vertigo and restlessness." He left the laboratory and rode his bicycle for what seemed to him to be thousands of miles to his home, where the unusual reaction persisted. A few days later he went back to the laboratory, measured out what he empirically believed to be a minimal dose (a quarter milligram), and swallowed it. Once more he experienced the same reaction. His dose was much larger than today's average dose, a tenth of a milligram. The term, "psychedelic" (mind-freeing) was coined by Dr. Humphrey Osmond, director of research at New Jersey's neuropsychiatric center at Princeton.

Because of the federal ban on the manufacture of LSD, it can only be secured illegally, although anyone with a knowledge of high school chemistry can make LSD. The usual method of taking LSD is by ingesting a cube of sugar impregnated with the drug which costs about a "nickel" ($5.00) a cube.

Effects of LSD. Taking acid or "tripping" is usually done in groups. There is a psychological reason for this. The indescribable spacelessness apparently is frightening and the sense of utter isolation—"floating alone in the cosmos"—can be eliminated only by physical contact. As one investigator put it, "LSD trippers must hold hands." A trip, from beginning to end, can last as long as twelve hours; the actual period of the drug's influence varies from four to seven or more hours. The setting can be provided by Nature or by the group. This, LSD users declare, creates an atmosphere conducive to meditation or a sense of wonder and discovery. The setting is achieved in many ways: just before dawn on a lonely stretch of beach so that the peak of LSD's effects coincide with the beautiful rising of the sun; a room without illumination other than a candle or a single electric light that casts its rays on an art object or a vase of flowers or something colorful. Other props include multiple moving pictures, several different musical records playing simultaneously, flashing lights, or a powerful, esoteric perfume. Thus does the trip begin—a "voyage within the self."

What started as alleged experiments by psychologists Timothy Leary and Richard Alpert became the International Foundation for International Freedom (IFIF) and, by 1966, Leary's cult: League for Spiritual Discovery (LSD). The union of drugs and religion is not novel; man has been combining the two for ages. For example there is bufotenin, an hallucinogenic herb whose action is sympathomimetic, used as a stimulant in certain primitive ceremonies.

LSD users are mostly young persons, particularly university students, some young college instructors, and the hipster set of whom more later. These people describe ecstatic experiences (spacelessness, timelessness), a heightened sensory perceptivity, which accounts for the visual hallucinations and the original descriptive term: a psychosis in miniature. As with all other similar agents, LSD does not expand consciousness—"expand the mind." LSD does blot out consciousness at first, and then this is followed by distortion because perception is distorted. Many artistically inclined LSD users are amazed to discover that their performance ability is not enhanced by the drug; if anything, it is impaired. One concert piano student exclaimed when she heard a recording of herself playing while on acid, "My God! Is that *me* playing so horribly?" Some time ago a television program showed an artist painting while sober and while under LSD. An established art critic dubbed both productions "terrible," adding that the LSD work was "worse."

The effects of LSD are admirably described by Dr. Daniel X. Freedman* as follows: "It is the intense experience without clouded consciousness—the heightened 'spectator ego' witnessing the excitement, which is characteristic for these drugs in usual dosages. Thus there is a split of the self—a portion of which is a relatively passive monitor rather than an active, focusing, and initiating force, and a portion of which 'receives' vivid experiences. Some people seem to repeat this long after the drug state, standing apart from life and its 'games' or relying on the group to direct events, they turn away from the prosaic world—or else are turned away by society. The striking self-centeredness—the experience of the self seeing the self —can be elaborated in a variety of ways, from detachment to symptomatic narcissism. The dominant experience of seeing can be expressed as convictions of revelation—i.e., psychological, mystical, aesthetic, or religious 'insights.'

"During the drug state, awareness becomes intensely vivid while self-control over input is diminished, fragile, and variably impaired. Thus there is always the lurking threat of loss of inner control—loss of control of integral stability. This is variably experienced and symbolized. At its height, it has been called 'dying the ego' and is often reported in bad trips or in phases of mystical experience with the drug. For some, such experience is dread transcended; for others, it is unwelcome or denied anxiety and dyscontrol. Many anxious concerns and problems after the drug state center around issues of control, autonomy, self-directedness, and decision making.

"In the drug state, customary boundaries become fluid and the familiar becomes novel and portentous. Any event or category of events which comes to one's attention—sensory, sexual, or cognitive

---

* Daniel X. Freedman, M. D. "On the Use and Abuse of LSD." Arch. of Gen. Psychiat. Vol. 18:3, March 1968, p. 333,

—takes on a trajectory of its own. Qualities become intense and gain a life of their own; redness is more interesting than the object which is red, meaningfulness more important than that what is specifically meant. Connotations balloon into cosmic allusiveness. This can be experienced religiously, aesthetically, sensually, or in a variety of clear or confused frames of reference.

"After the drug state, we may find pseudoprofundity, or omniscience as well as more tolerance for the novel, the unusual, or for ambiguity. We also can find an associated inability to decide, to discriminate, to make commitments . . . Such a tendency to avoid distinctions could lead to alienation and retreatism, even if these were not preexisting traits as they are very often. For many, the drug experience may represent a beginning—an attempt to feel intensely—which without luck or experience, cannot easily come to a useful conclusion (just as neurotic acts may be viewed as unguided attempts at self-cure).

"Certainly when hidden meanings perceptually contaminate the response to the explicit conventions of everyday life, 'focus' and goal-directed efficiency are impaired. Judgment is not enhanced during the drug state and isolation or apartness bring their own problems: accordingly persons who continually overvalue the modes of experience of the drug state could develop and reinforce poor practical habits. Pseudoprofundity, philosophical naivete, impractical detachment, and inadequate foresight and judgment or impulsiveness in dedicated users were already evident to an observer [Dr. N. Gordon] of the Harvard scene of 1963. The consequence of long-term and frequent use of the drug—involving possibly 5% to 15% of those experimenting with LSD—would probably have to be evaluated in this context."

A few years ago LSD was scientifically investigated as a possible medium of psychotherapy. It was soon determined that very often the drug made it possible for a patient to bring unconscious repressed material into consciousness, the realization of which provoked deep depression, sometimes a severe psychosis, even suicide. There are many previous emotionally traumatic experiences which should remain repressed—"sleeping dogs should be permitted to continue to sleep." Deaths have also occurred from overdosage. However, as users learn to take trips using smaller amounts of LSD, admissions of these habituants to hospitals are falling. This has led some observers to observe that "statistics indicate that LSD is losing its popularity." No they don't; statistics can also indicate that acid trippers are keeping dosages to bearable quantities. However, the possibility of fatality from overdosage prompted the A. P. A. to issue a warning: *"The indiscriminate consumption of this hazardous drug can, and not infrequently does, lead to destructive physiological and personality changes. The Association most particularly deplores its use by some persons as a mind-expanding or consciousness-expanding experiment. There is now no substantive basis for this claim. The destructive consequences to some who use it in this expectation have not yet been adequately established in the professional and lay press."*

Two recent clinical investigations have turned up one recommendation and one condemnation for LSD. Research, to date, indicates that LSD can alter chromosomes and, therefore, cause genetic damage. On the other hand, two surgeons found that when subminimal LSD dosages are administered to patients who suffer agonizing pain for weeks, even months, as they await the end of their inoperable cancer, they are not only relieved of all pain by LSD but become amiable and even optimistic with the drug.

Two recently isolated drugs have the same effects as LSD but they persist only for one or two hours. These are N,N-dipropyltryptamine (DPT) and FDET—the latter has no other name as yet. DPT's drug-induced hallucinations are very short compared to those caused by LSD. FDET has no psychic effect. Both drugs cause elevation of blood pressure, heart rate, and respiration. It is possible that FDET, since it has no psychic effect, may be proved to have therapeutic possibilities.

Other Hallucinogens

Morning Glory seed addiction is characterized by hallucinations and stimulation; it is not addictive, despite its designation. The boiled seeds of some varieties of morning glory are used as "mind-expanders." This hallucinogen, however, can cause psychosis. *Sniffing* of stimulants and hallucinogens is not new. For centuries snuff, in addition to its relief of nasal congestion, has been used to give the sniffer a "lift." Two common snuffs are a mixture of bismuth and morphine and a mixture of cocaine and menthol. The practice is so old that anatomists named the space at the base of the thumb on the dorsum of the hand the "snuff box," in recognition of sniffers placing the powder there from whence it is inhaled. *Glue sniffing* is a hallucinogenic practice that can become an addiction. Exhilaration is obtained from the inhalation of glues that contain toluene. This type of glue is used in the assembling of model airplanes, and started as a source of thrills for young children and teenagers who place the glue in a plastic bag and then inhale the fumes of the toluene. Teenagers learned to intensify the effects by drinking cheap wine after the inhalation. Effects include excitability, nausea, vomiting, sleepiness, stupor, unconsciousness, and, at the height of stimulation, a domineering mood or uninhibited behavior. According to the literature, about 40 per cent of glue sniffers experience no effect other than exhilaration. Other sniffing media include ether, ethyl chloride, lacquers, paints, lighter fluid, and gasoline vapor. The latter is alleged to produce vivid visual hallucinations.

Conclusion

The subject of hallucinogens cannot be concluded without reference to the anatomical and physiological reasons why hallucinogens cannot "expand" the mind, or, if you wish, consciousness.

In 1961, John Saunders, former Chancellor of the San Francisco Medical Center, spoke on the promise of tranquilizers and other pharmaceuticals used in psychiatry. In part, he said: "... *Here at our disposal, to be used wisely or unwisely, is an increasing array of agents that manipulate human beings ... It is now possible to act directly on the individual to modify his behavior instead of ... indirectly through modification of the environment. This, then, constitutes a part of what Aldous Huxley has called 'The Final Revolution.' ..."*

As a fact, Huxley was frightened that the joint result of mass media and psychopharmacological agents would be *"within a generation or so for entire societies a sort of painless concentration camp of the mind, in which people will have lost their liberties in the enjoyment of a dictatorship without tears."* This was the reason Huxley championed mescaline and other psychedelics as the route to cosmic consciousness, artistic originality, and mystic enlightenment.

Huxley's ideas are wrong by every scientific yardstick of anatomy and physiology, and, we add, downright silly, because no drug, psychedelic or not psychedelic, can deposit in the psyche mystic insights or profound wisdom or artistic creativity. Years ago, Dr. Clarence Cheney, as director of the New York Psychiatric Institute, used to tell post-graduate students that "You can't get out of a brain what God hasn't put there." And you can't reverse the process: no drug can put into a brain what Nature has not, although drugs can remove obstructions to the normal use and functioning of mental faculties. We cannot be made "superior" to what our mental capacity is, even though drugs can, to a degree, return a disturbed mind to a normal use and appreciation of its capacity. Drugs can dull the shock of disappointment and frustration and permit one to face life's challenges with some equanimity. This is actually a reversal of "The Final Revolution": with drugs we are able to bring psychic disturbance back to psychic balance. Psychedelics do the opposite: they change normal mental perception and consequent action into mental disturbance. We repeat, psychedelics do not broaden consciousness, they distort it by effecting a schism between psyche and reality. Schizophrenia does the same thing over a period of years; so does suicide in a matter of seconds.

CHAPTER ELEVEN

Mental Retardation

Definition. Several years ago "mental retardation" began to replace "mental deficiency" or "defectiveness" which, in turn, had, at an earlier date, replaced "feeblemindedness." Two factors were responsible for this semantic shift. First, both professional and lay groups, especially parents of retarded children, decided that the implication of "deficiency" was faulty heredity, an unsupportable stigma. Second, the older nosological term implied a hopeless prognosis because it suggested an inborn, unchangeable defect that permanently limited the individual's development. When it became apparent that much could be accomplished to improve the outlook for some of these handicapped people, many conditions that were listed under "mental deficiency" or "defectiveness" were placed under the new and hopeful category of "mental retardation." At present it is the accepted diagnostic label and the precise, comprehensive term for syndromes we are about to discuss.

Nevertheless, mental retardation is not a satisfactory classification because it does not refer exclusively to intellectual inadequacy and its resultant social maladaptability; it includes *any* "slowed mind." A slowed mind is typical of the withdrawn and introspective schizophrenic, a confused alcoholic, a dazed drug addict, or a self-centered neurotic, just as it is observed in the acute, moderate, and severely retarded patient. A slowed mind is manifested by the business man who after a few drinks might be too "woozy" to review his accountant's calculations; his *intellectual,* not his *intelligential* faculties have been dulled. In the case of children, the new and broader

161

clinical concept of retardation has fostered increased attention on the *autistic child* which we will consider later in this chapter.

The American Association on Mental Deficiency (which hasn't changed *its* name!) defines mental retardation as *"including all degrees of mental defect due to arrested or imperfect mental development as a result of which the person so afflicted is incapable of competing on equal terms with his normal fellows or of managing himself or his affairs with ordinary prudence."* When a cardiac valve lacks the ability to close and/or open with normal accuracy, the condition is referred to as "insufficiency." That is the state of mentality in those who are said to be "retarded" today: intelligence is insufficient. The most serviceable and connotative diagnosis would be "intelligential insufficiency," and, to take cognizance of the time element, it should be qualified as "congenital" or "acquired."

Prevalence. Various estimates indicate that approximately 3 per cent of the American population is mentally retarded. However, if "borderline intelligence" (I. Q. 70-79) is included, this statistic becomes 4 per cent. Since so many borderlines and mild retardates never become statistics—they achieve minimal adjustment, holding down menial jobs, living at home, etc.—too much reliance on these numbers is inadvisable. However, as an indication of the extent of the problem, consider New York City as an example. In that metropolis more than 3,000 mentally retarded infants are born annually. This means that New York State has to build, equip, and staff one institution for mentally retarded children *every year*—and just for New York City. More, of course, would be needed for the rest of the state. This is not being done, in any state. In fact, most—we repeat, "most"—civil institutions for the mentally retarded have been closed to new admissions for several years!

In the entire United States about 130,000 babies born each year are mentally retarded. Of this total, 5,000 will be severely retarded, 13,500 moderately, and 111,500 mildly. There are about 160,000 mentally retarded patients in civil institutions (figures for those in private establishments and day schools are not available); how many thousands more cannot gain admission cannot be estimated.

Etiology. Because this discussion is limited to congenital intelligential insufficiency, acquired conditions—which physicians know only too well, such as is seen in brain trauma and neoplasm, and encephalitis—are not included.

The adjective "congenital" allows a certain latitude because retardation at birth may be caused by prenatal factors or conditions arising during pregnancy, at birth, or immediately thereafter. The main features behind these instances of mental retardation are, with rare exception, mechanical, bacterial, or traumatic influences, or hereditial and metabolic defects. This wide concept permits nine types for classification, not counting the tenth ("unknown causes").

1. Faulty Embryotrophy. Not until rather recent times have researchers begun to focus attention on passing developmental accidents and toxic infections that occur in pregnancy. Of especial interest are the exanthemata. Accumulating clinical evidence indicates that a sizable number of mentally retarded children can have their retardation traced to mothers who, early in pregnancy, suffered an exanthematous disease. This is quite feasible, since it is a clinical fact that the exanthemata in children can involve the brain's white matter and result in complications such as "measles" (or any exanthematous equivalent) encephalitis.

Hydrocephalus is a common prenatal disorder that is seen in some mentally retarded infants and young children. Defective development of the blood-cerebro-spinal fluid septum results in the accumulation of fluid within the brain, the pressure of which separates the skull bones. Eventually, usually at an early age, this pressure crushes the brain and death is the termination. Hydrocephalic mental retardation is an example of "mechanical" factors: the blocked fluid and its constantly increasing pressure lead to atrophy of brain tissue to the point of little if any functioning by that organ. A popular myth exists among the laity that hydrocephalus is always a congenital abnormality. Physicians know that it may occur, often acutely and progressing rapidly, in a normal adult. For instance, a small, benign intracranial tumor that blocks cerebral circulation can result in deterioration and dementia, various neurological signs, and mental retardation.

Other developmental malformations include microcephaly, oxycephaly (familiarly known as "pin" or "sugar cone" head), and porencephaly. Conditions such as anencephalia and cyclopia are not, of course, compatible with life.

2. Encephalomalacia.   So-called softening of the brain encompasses many injuries that result in deformities and mental retardation at birth. These may constitute clinical entities such as infantile congenital hemiplegia. What role genes play in these conditions is not known, although geneticists are investigating this possibility. Again, to what extent an inexplicable change or shift of the fetus account for these defects is a matter of conjecture.

3. Congenital Mental Retardation.   The most frequently encountered type of mental retardation in this category is *Down's disease* or *syndrome,* named for Dr. J. Langdon Down of London who, in 1866, devised the term *mongolian idiot* (later *mongolism*) for retarded infants whose faces bore Mongolian features. Etiological hypotheses include: endocrine dysfunction, congenital metabolic disturbances, malnutrition, and disordered protein metabolism; another hypothesis is that the pregnant woman fails to secrete hormones properly or adequately because of poor physical health or age. In keeping with the latter, it is a fact that Down's syndrome babies are commoner among older women. This was crystalized in 1968 by a report from Cornell University Medical College geneticist James German, M. D. that infrequent coitus, especially in long-married couples beyond the age of 35, may be a key factor. Infrequent intercourse, he said, may result in the sperm penetrating the oocyte late in the egg's limited (perhaps 24 hours at most) period of fertility. At this late state, Dr. German suggests, it is probable that the egg is undergoing some deterioration. If this is so, as it seems to be in animal eggs, there could be chromosomal changes leading to a birth defect, such as Down's disease. Increased incidence of this condition among infants of mothers older than 35 might result from decreasing frequency of sexual relations after several years of marriage.

Besides the Oriental faces, these infants have a small skull that is flattened posteriorly, dry and sparse hair, a large, fissured tongue that usually hangs from the open mouth, squat and broad hands with the fifth finger commonly short and curved inward, small genitalia, a large abdomen, and limbs that seem rubbery because of inadequate control of muscles and ligaments. Sometimes there is palatal deformity. Prior to the advent of antibiotics, infants with Down's disease usually died of intercurrent infection before the age of three. Nowadays, thanks to these agents, they are living and growing up so that research is concentrating on their potential so far as training is concerned. These retardates are very affectionate and imitative, with a jolly disposition.

4. Trauma. Traumatic brain damage, prior to, during, or at birth, may result in mental retardation, depending on the site and extent of brain damage. Whether the lesion is transient or permanent determines the extent and duration of retardation. Prominent in this category is *cerebral palsy* (CP)—more accurately "palsies." The cause is unknown. There have been many nosological terms, but the most enduring has been "Little's Disease" (congenital spastic paralysis) named for William John Little, English physician [1810-1894]. The manifestations include spastic paralysis of the extremities, various degrees of lifetime incoordination which may be materially aided by an early start of training and prostheses, but mental retardation may not be present. However Drs. A. R. Shands, R. B. Raney, and H. R. Brasher* state that *"statistics have shown that the mentality of from 30 to 50 per cent of all cerebral palsy patients is either seriously retarded or otherwise defective, and that approximately 75 per cent have a mentality below average."*

5. Infection. Pre- or postnatal infection may cause mental retardation, the severity depending on the area and extent of brain involvement. This category, however, has been decreasing since the introduction of antibiotics.

6. Metabolic Disorders. Within the past few years the discovery that defective metabolism can cause mental retardation has raised hopes that continued research will unearth many other etiological factors; what has been found, unfortunately, is a very minute fraction of the whole.

---

* Handbook of Orthopedic Surgery, C. V. Mosby Co., St. Louis, 1965

Phenylketonuria (*PKU*) is marked by mental retardation and the presence of phenylpyruvic acid in the urine. The latter is due to enzyme failure to metabolize phenylalanine. It is now routine to test for this at birth—the "diaper test"—and the condition is controlled by a diet low in phenylalanine.

Cat Cry Syndrome (*cri du chat*) is seen in infants and young children and is marked by mental retardation, poor physical development, microcephaly, and a laryngeal deformity resulting in the patient's crying like a cat.

Oral-Facial-Digital Syndrome is a familial disorder, and marked by cleft tongue and palate, "pug" nose, narrow upper lip, multiple or short or webbed fingers and toes, and mental retardation.

Maple Syrup Urine Disease, due to faulty fat metabolism, is characterized by albinism, mental retardation, respiratory difficulty, convulsions, diarrhea, and a pungent odor of the urine. In England the syndrome is known as *oast-house disease.*

Idiopathic Hypoglycemia causes mental retardation; however, zinc glucagon, a pancreatic hormone, effectively counteracts the condition of low blood sugar by enabling the liver to convert its stored glycogen into glucose. Research seems to indicate that young adults whose blood contains an abnormally low quantity of adolase may be carriers of Tay-Sachs disease.

Tay-Sachs Disease.   Formerly known as amaurotic family idiocy, this is, as the latter name suggests, a familial, congenital disorder, characterized by blindness, paralysis, severe mental retardation, and a cherry-red spot on the macula lutea which is regarded as pathognomonic of the syndrome.

7. Endocrine Disease.   The outstanding example of this category is *cretinism* whose characteristics include thin, strawlike hair, dry thick skin, puffy face, and severe mental retardation. Institution of thyroid extract therapy as soon as the physician is certain cretinism does, for a fact, exist, goes far in correcting this endocrinal defect.

8. Neoplasm.   Here, new growth implies "multiple" growths which are most often observed as nodules. A prominent example is *tuberous sclerosis* which is characterized by nodules in the brain and other parts of the body, epileptiform seizures, and severe mental retardation. It is rare, and infant mortality is high.

9. Heredofamilial Disease. Like many medical terms, this is a misnomer. Heredo- is self explanatory; familial ("occurring among several members of a family") often causes confusion. Medical dictionaries define heredofamilial as "hereditary in some families," which is highly uninformative because so many disorders are handed from one generation to another and affect one person or, in the next generation, more than one. Hemophilia is an example. Heredity implies a defect or disorder passed on from one generation to the next through the genes and involving, possibly, factors such as RNA and DNA. Sometimes a condition arises which can be traced to a cytoplasmic factor; this is observed, however, mainly in lower animals. Chromosomal and genic deficiencies have been shown to cause some abnormal conditions in man. These defects include partial or total deletion of a chromosome, faulty chromosomal pairing, tripling instead of pairing, and all taking place at an intracellular level.

10. Idiopathic. Here, of course, are the many instances of mental retardation for which there isn't even a hint as to possible etiology; they remain, therefore, as "of unknown etiology."

Intelligence

Intelligence is the general capacity of the individual to adjust his thinking to new and unexpected requirements encountered in the environment. This contrasts with instinct which may be regarded as the innate capacity to cope with environment. Intelligence depends on memory, association of ideas, perception, and execution. Intelligence in the adult person is the result of his mental ability interacting with his environment. If environment is less than optimal, his genetic endowment will not be realized; his ultimate intelligence will be less than its potential.

"Intelligence" and "mental retardation" trigger the popular term "I.Q." Many regard intelligence testing as the unquestionable criterion by which mental capacity is determined. True, intelligence inquiries are indispensable, but none is scientifically exact or specific, and they are used as guides to be incorporated in the total clinical assessment of an individual: the holistic approach to mental retardation. Sometimes the intelligence quotient is disproportionate to the clinical "impression" as, for example, in the *idiot savant* who, despite moderate or mild retardation, manifests an unusual adeptness in one particular field of endeavor such as repairing watches, assembling radios, etc. Therefore, no program for any mentally retarded person can be exclusively promulgated on the I. Q.

Returning to the matter of man and his environment, mentioned above, one asks: Can man manipulate society for the richest genetic return and environmental improvement? This is a challenging question because it implicates the individual's rights and the matter of defining what is meant by a "good" society. It also smacks of sterilization as a means of preventing mentally retarded births. On this question, physicians—among other scientists and clergymen—have been squabbling for years. We must remember that people "unfit" to bear children include many other categories besides mentally retarded potential parents. On sterilization, Dr. Arthur P. Noyes said, "*[It] is not an effective means of halting mental retardation, and its usefulness is more individual than racial. Sterilization as a general policy is a superficial method of approaching the problem of mental retardation since it ignores the need for special investigation and research as to its cause and prevention.*" Time has proven Dr. Noyes correct.

Intelligence tests, at most, indicate whether the subject is subnormal, normal, or above average in intelligence. The most widely used test, and one that has stood the trial of time, is the Terman-Stanford Revision of the Binet-Simon Scale (originated in France) which quite effectively measures the mental capacity of children of school age. In testing adults, the Wechsler-Bellevue Intelligence Scale has considerable merit. It must be borne in mind, however, that all intelligence tests are "relative" measurements, that is, the measure of intelligence of a subject refers to his mental capacity compared to others of a large group. Social adjustment is equally important as a yardstick. As Binet and Simon, the creators of modern intelligence testing declared: "*A peasant, normal in ordinary surroundings, may be considered a moron in the city.*"

In addition to the ordinary intelligence tests there are special ones for blind, deaf, and uncooperative subjects. There are *performance tests* for various age groups; *mechanical tests* for subjects who cannot, for one reason or another, be tested by ordinary inquiries; *aptitude tests* currently popular among military and collegiate leaders, and more specialized tests that measure reading ability, skill in manipulating blocks, mastery of words, etc., in order to determine I. Q.

Signs and Symptoms. Criteria for the identification of mental retardation were established many years ago by Dr. Clarence Potter, as follows:

1. Is the patient socially inefficient? (Is he a child who cannot adapt himself to routine or to the school situation? Is he an adult who exhibits antisocial behavior, etc.?).

2. Does this socially ineffective state depend on maladjusted intelligence?

3. Has this maladjusted intelligence originated during the developmental period of life?

Answers to these three queries enable the psychiatrist to determine not only if the patient is mentally retarded, but also to what extent the retardation may prevent his possible social adjustment. These answers make possible a long-range treatment and training program tailor-made to the individual.

The chief signs and symptoms of mental retardation are tabulated as follows:

Some of the features in the table deserve elaboration. By "faulty integration of activities" is meant a failure to respond to environmental sitmuli. "Play ineffectiveness" refers first to toys, and later with other children. "Inferiority" is actually secondary personality reactions due to the child's feeling that he is different from others. Dr. Potter used to call this "feelings of indifference," but because the word was often interpreted as "apathy" instead of "being different," he dropped the term.

Emotional Equivalents. Certain emotional disturbances that are manifested as intellectual deficiency are sometimes mistaken for mental retardation. An example is *strephosymbolia* which is a reading defect in which a child fails to learn to read in response to

SIGNS AND SYMPTOMS OF MENTAL RETARDATION

MENTAL SYMPTOMS		PHYSICAL SYMPTOMS	ENDOCRINOPATHIES	NEUROLOGICAL
Common to All Mental Retardates	More Individualized			
Faulty comprehension. Poverty of ideas. Weak, illogical reasoning. Immature foresight. Superficiality of observation. Emotional immaturity.	Delay and retardation in motor functioning and growth. Delay in dentition. Faulty integration of activities. Play ineffectiveness. Delay in acquiring excretory control, eating habits, social behavior, and cleanliness Inferiority: shyness and other behavior reactions as compensation for inability to learn.	Flaring, patternless ears. Congenital cataracts. Defective palatal arch. Irregularly erupting teeth. Spina bifida. Ocular imbalances. Congenital heart defects. Horseshoe kidneys.	Depending on which glands are involved: dwarfism, extreme obesity, scaly skin, thin, brittle hair, etc.	Muscular weakness. Palsy and paralysis of extremities. Pathological gait. Reflex changes. Alterations in sensation. Incoordination, etc.

traditional classroom methods, and is due to an emotional conflict. It is not to be confused with neurological organic lesions that produce *alexia* (word blindness). In strephosymbolia, the child's unconscious conflict results in his "seeing letters which mean no more to him than what a Chinese laundry ticket means to us," as one child psychiatrist put it. In *word deafness* there is also an unconscious conflict at play: there is no organic deafness; the patient hears everything said to him but the words are meaningless to him. Thus, he may be told, "Please open the door," and in response straighten his necktie or, more often, simply sit still and stare at the speaker.

Types of Mental Retardation. The three types of mental retardation are: mild, moderate, and severe, once known, respectively, as moron, imbecility, and idiocy.

Severe retardation is defined by the American Psychiatric Association as an individual who *"is unable to guard himself against common physical dangers."* In a crude colloquialism: *"He doesn't know enough to come in out of the rain."* Severe (low-grade) retardates are untrainable; less severe (high-grade) retardates may be taught the simplest routine procedures such as bladder and bowel control, but not to dress and bathe themselves. The severe retardate understands only the simplest commands. Many of these patients have such extreme muscular weakness and/or incoordination or are so congenitally paralyzed that they are bed-confined and must be spoon-fed. Some of these patients are extremely overactive, noisy, and destructive; others lie in their beds or cribs, hour after hour, day after day, staring vacantly at the ceiling. Most severe retardates engage in some kind of repetitious, stereotyped movement, such as swaying from side to side while sitting on their haunches, or rhythmically twisting the head back and forth.

Moderate retardation is found in a person who *"is able to guard himself against common physical dangers, or can be taught to do so, but cannot profit from ordinary teaching."* Occasionally, a high-grade moderate retardate can be taught to read a few words, help in some simple task, and to wash and dress himself. He cannot support himself economically. Most moderate retardates are quite pleasant, affectionate, faithful, and obedient, but they are wanting in inborn curiosity and the spontaneous vivacity of normal children of the same chronological age.

Mild retardation may not hinder a child from progressing very slowly through the first two or three grades of elementary school. Sometimes a high-grade mild retardate manages to reach high school before his deficient intelligence is detected. Mild retardates can be taught to perform simple chores, routine tasks, errands (distribute leaflets from door to door, deliver messages, etc.). Because they are very suggestible, these mild retardates are often exploited by criminals who easily train them to be killers. Mild retardates are, as a rule, sulky, sullen, irritable, but extremely responsive to presents and flattery.

The following table furnishes a *psychometric classification* of mental retardation and other intelligential levels, but it is to be regarded as an arbitrary guide, at best:

TYPE	I. Q. (CHILDREN)	MENTAL AGE
Severe	Less than 20	Less than 3 years (completely dependent)
Moderate	20-49	3 years to 7 years 11 months (trainable)
Mild	50-69	8 years to 10 years 11 months (educable)
Borderline	70-79	
Dull	80-89	
Average	90-109	
Superior	110-119	
Very Superior	120-139	
Genius	over 140	

The vast majority of institutionalized mental retardates is composed of acute and moderately retarded groups. They require inpatient care because of somatic and psychological handicaps. No more than 10 per cent of patients in a civil institution for retardates are there solely for schooling. This is the undeniable statistical rebuttal to well-meaning but uninformed parents who believe the panacea for institutionalized retardates is special education. This and other misconceptions have blocked state mental hygiene departments from having the legislatures approve changing "state school" to "state hospital and school," which acknowledges the need for integrated medical, neurological, endocrinological, and psychiatric care for most patients.

A few physicians are quite uninformed about retarded children. Too often does an obstetrician or a pediatrician exhort mothers, upon delivery of a mentally retarded infant to *"put them away and forget them."* Dr. Clemens E. Benda, authority on mental retardation, comments on the consequences of such advice: *"When one of these mothers is summoned months or years later to the institution because of child's critical condition, or need for surgery, etc., she invariably exclaims: 'Is this what I was told is a monster—this pretty, lovable child who happens to lack normal intelligence?' And, very often such a mother, in reaction to guilt for rejection of her baby, suffers an emotional or psychic disorder."*

This point of view is especially applicable to the infant with Down's disease. If the infant's retardation is the sole psychic and physical handicap, it will fare far better with its mother, for such an infant does not require more or different care than a normal baby. From a cold economic view, if every Down's diseased child were placed in a civil institution, there would have to be a new such establishment constructed every five years to care just for New York City's 400 who are born every year.

Autism. Only in the past few years has recognition been given to the autistic child who is very easily diagnosed as mentally retarded or schizophrenic. Autistic thinking is that which is mainly subjective and detached, and which aims at gratifying desires without regard for the limitations of reality. Objective reality is obscured, distorted, even excluded. The autistic child who is diffident, withdrawn, asocial, regressed, and "mute," is understandably a potential candidate for a diagnosis of mental retardation, although these same symptoms can be caused by psychosis, extreme neurotic preoccupation, severe infection—and mental retardation. Because it is difficult to gain the child's cooperation and hold his attention, an I. Q. test may "reveal" mental retardation while the subject may be a brilliant child! Nowadays, snap diagnosis in mental retardation is shunned, and intense investigation encouraged. It is amazing to find a child with an I. Q. of 30, when the cause of his "retardation" is discovered and corrected or eradicated, to test out at 110. Dr. Lauretta Bender, authority on children's psychological and psychiatric disorders, maintains that more and more of these autistic children are turning out to be victims of schizophrenia or organic brain disease. Most child psychiatrists agree with Dr. Bender that autism in an infant is a herald of schizophrenia. This is the baby who, seemingly aware of persons in his immediate environment, does not react to them. He keeps himself "alone," he does not "stretch his muscles" at four months or begin to babble incoherently as babies at that age usually do, while they grimace and smile. Nor does he tense back and neck muscles when he is picked up. After he learns to walk and is thus physically able to "mingle" with others, he is asocial and remains by himself; he will react with irritability if an attempt is made to interest him in his environment or if his seclusiveness is violated. Eventually he is seen as the star-gazing, daydreaming child who has an almost pathognomonic compulsion for sitting hour after hour, rocking back and forth rhythmically.

Treatment

Not too long ago treatment of mental retardation could be summed up in one word: none. Research has shown that this hopeless attitude is entirely unwarranted. For example, if mentally retarded identical twins are separated after birth and one is exposed to specialized intensive training and education, he will actually develop an I. Q. higher than his untutored twin. We also know that more can be done with and for the mental retardate, and that therapeutic results are more gratifying. It is also true that premature deaths among retardates from intercurrent (even mild) infection have almost been eliminated completely by antibiotics. The object of therapy is not to attempt the impossible, i.e. raise the I. Q., but to attempt to train the patient to be socially adjustable and acceptable. There is a strong psychic factor to be exploited: the innate drive for love. This is met by enabling an individual to gain social recognition, security, and a chance "to do," and to enjoy new experiences. Dr. Walter E. Fernald always maintained that the retarded person has a right to have his needs understood and to be treated accordingly, instead of being classified and isolated on the basis of his I. Q.

The American Association on Mental Deficiency recommends that the first step in planning a treatment program is the collection of as much clinical data as possible: the I. Q., physical and mental examination, the patient's own response to his anatomical, physiological, and neurological situation; an estimate of his behavior, social adjustment, biological background, social heredity; and a careful study of his entire developmental history. In addition, there may be X-ray and laboratory examinations indicated. These add up to an inventory of the patient's total assets and it is these that the treatment program will exploit to the limit.

Therapy for the severe and moderate retardate is mainly custodial and physical. The moderate may benefit by training: dress, bathe, and feed himself, avoid ordinary dangers of the environment, and be taught not to be destructive. Such a program can be successfully accomplished in the home. More and more the idea of day treatment centers is taking hold. Here mothers learn how to care for their mentally retarded children. After all, there is no substitute for a mother's love.

Institutionalization. Placing a mentally retarded child in a civil or private institution does not have as its goal the lifetime segregation of the patient; it is considered a temporary and fortunate chance to expose the child to highly specialized training and education, with the ultimate view of creating an adjustable, acceptable, economically and emotionally independent citizen.

Of course, the institution includes occupation and recreation as complements to academic training, but there is a subtler attitude: filling the child with a sense of self-esteem and pride rather than feelings of inferiority and futility and, above all, of being rejected. It is team work that concentrates on this: the psychiatrist, psychologist, nurse, teacher, ward aide, special therapists, and volunteers who carry out this program with a sensible balance of firmness and sympathy, understanding, compassion, and kindness. The child is rewarded when he deserves it; he is reprimanded and checked as circumstances dictate—but at no time is he struck or deprived of food. He is made to feel that he *is* "somebody," not a "nobody," and within his capacity, he is taught that it is his right and privilege —nay, his obligation, to be a member of society—"out there" where the others are. Group activity is a wonderful implement of treatment. A child may not understand how a seesaw works if it is explained, even demonstrated, to him when he is alone. But let him see two children enjoying it and he promptly "catches on." Likewise, group participation teaches him to adjust to the group, to cooperate and to subjugate his egocentric drives to the will of the majority. It is, in essence, the lesson of interpersonal reaction.

Often, placing a child with older persons answers the need for parent "surrogates," something the actual parents do not understand—and resent—when they visit their child at an institution. He may have failed to "grow up" in a ward with others of his age, but in a ward with older persons he is stimulated to abandon his infantile ways.

Day Centers. The last chapter of the American Medical Association's book *Mental Retardation* states, on page 79: *"No type of retardation in itself is an indication for residential care."* This is irrefutably true, it is underwritten by psychiatrists and by others who are specialists in mental retardation. Unfortunately, this truism fails to register with obstetricians and pediatricians (they who are the first to advise mothers when they give birth to retarded infants). They persist in subscribing to the antiquated idea that such children are "utterly hopeless" and should be "put away."

Dr. Benjamin D. White, a well-known authority in the field of mental retardation, supplies powerful rebuttal of this outmoded sentiment. He declares that the most neglected persons among the mentally retarded population are those judged to be within the custodial or profound category. He says that many physicians and educators, as well as other professional persons, continue to believe that such patients can not benefit from training and that, when retained at home, they are a serious threat to the family unity and integrity. This has resulted in a disproportionate growth of institutions beyond need and out of proportion to the need for expanding community services. It is difficult to convince these obstructionists that in many instances the families prefer to keep the child at home, regardless of the severity of his mental retardation. This is statistically borne out by the fact that only a small number of the estimated total number of the mentally retarded are in institutions, in spite of the widespread tendency of many unqualified "experts" to advise institutionalization.

An outstanding refutation of this attitude is the project of Dr. White and Miss Ella J. Beattie of the Division of Community Services for the Mentally Retarded, Maryland State Department of Mental Hygiene, Baltimore. They initiated a state-wide day-care program for severely—note, *severely*—retarded individuals which was developed as part of the services of local health departments. The first center opened in September of 1961 with 10 children and in four years had grown to include over 400. In the case of children, the program is oriented to care and training; parents are given guidance and counseling. By relieving the parents for 5 to 6 hours a day of the burden of caring for this special type of child, the entire family structure is fortified.

Combining and using various health department services, with services for the child being performed as indicated, the basic structure of the Maryland day-care program is consummated. Before admission to a center, a retarded child is examined physically, psychiatrically, psychologically, and socially; he is then screened and evaluated by a day-care board-appointed committee. A child who is admitted is re-screened each year thereafter to determine if he is benefiting by day-care, if he shows improvement or has regressed, or warrants transfer to another type of installation for the mentally retarded. The exceedingly gratifying results of this day-care program and, in particular, the enthusiastic acceptance by the general public, indicate that this type of community care, supervision, and treatment should be expanded in the field of mental retardation.

Toward the Future. While certain definite and rewarding advances have been made (the discovery of PKU, e. g.), there are pessimists who sneeringly refer to these as mere "drops in the bucket." They are only drops. But, if only *one* drop fell into the bucket, would not that be a positive and real advance over an *empty* bucket? Biochemists continue to work on the challenge of improving learning and memory chemically, as previously mentioned. There is more than a suggestion that malnutrition, particularly proteins, plays an important role in etiology. For example, in a huge investigation of children in Africa recently—thousands, not a handful—it was decided to try a well-balanced diet at birth on these children who are underfed from the day they are born and, with rare exception, show poor learning capacity. Infants who were exposed to such a dietary advantage did, indeed, grow into childhood with perfectly normal intelligence and learning ability. Further, if the balanced diet was witheld until the infant was six months, it did *not* enable the child to achieve normal intelligence and learning capacity. At Johns Hopkins University investigators have demonstrated that a low birth weight, irrespective of socioeconomic status or race, city or rural environment, is often the only observable feature in clinical histories of elementary and high school students who show deficient learning capacity, particularly for arithmetic.

CHAPTER TWELVE

Epilepsy

EPILEPSY IS A DISORDER of consciousness and motor control, with or without convulsions. It is one of the oldest disorders in recorded medicine, and ancient physicians' clinical observations are still valid. Hippocrates, circa 400 B. C., furnished diagnostic criteria that have stood the test of time. It is a disease found in every culture, and has victimized such notables as Julius Caesar, William Pitt, the elder, Feodor Dostoevski, and Vincent Van Gogh, to mention a few.

Etiology. The brain constantly functions whether the organism is conscious or unconscious; this ceaseless activity is manifested by electric currents which are detectable and recorded by electro-encephalography (EEG). It is this mechanical device, in fact, that converted hypothesis into truth, i. e., that epilepsy is basically disruption of the electrophysicochemical activity of the discharging cells of the brain. The question, however, is: what causes this disturbance? There is no argument when the obvious etiology is discernible organic pathology such as general paresis or intracranial neoplasm; the debate centers on epilepsy which to date has no observable cause—better, an undiscovered cause. For some, idiopathic epilepsy is a neurological disease; for psychoanalysts and psychiatrists, it is a somatic expression of an inner emotional conflict.

Epilepsy is both a symptom and a syndrome. The definition provided at the beginning of this chapter is applicable to both phases of epilepsy. When it is a "symptomatic" manifestation of an established disorder, such as cerebral arteriosclerosis, its role is merely one of several indications of a pathologic process. When it shows up as "convulsions" for which etiology is lacking, it becomes "idiopathic" epilepsy. It is this latter variety that this chapter deals with. Idiopathic epilepsy is most frequently observed—in three out of four instances—before the age of twenty. Also in the debate as to epilepsy's "owner" (neurology or psychiatry) is the matter of heredity. For many years the compromise to the argument was: the *tendency* to the disorder is heritable. But EEG disturbed that idea. Normal persons whose parent(s) are known epileptics may produce typical epileptic EEG patterns when so examined, and never suffer any form of the disease throughout life. No one has the explanation for this phenomenon.

Varieties. The main types of idiopathic epilepsy are: grand mal, petit mal, and the associated conditions, psychomotor equivalent, narcolepsy, and cataplexy.

Grand Mal Epilepsy. Grand mal is epilepsy with convulsions. The attacks are unpredictably and irregularly episodic: the patient may suffer a seizure on two successive days, then not again for a month, then a week later, and so on. In at least 60 per cent of grand mal patients there is a definite pattern to the attack. The patient first experiences a prodrome (the "aura") which may be perceived in an endless number of ways: numbness and tingling in some part of the body, a flash of colorful lights, a piercing headache, nausea . . . anything. Almost immediately thereafter he utters a piercing shriek (the "epileptic cry"), and drops to the ground or floor unconscious. For a few seconds to a few minutes his musculature is in steel-like rigidity (the "tonus") and this then is succeeded by the "clonic phase." There is violent jerking which may be of the entire body, or start in one arm and spread to all parts. This may be accompanied by biting of the tongue and by incontinence of bladder and/or bowels. At the height of the convulsion, his lips are flecked with foam which may be blood-tinged from biting the tongue. Clonus quickly subsides, leaving the epileptic utterly limp and he falls into a deep sleep from which he wakens minutes to a few hours later.

Not infrequently the patient hurts or burns himself when he falls, depending on the site where the seizure occurs. When he regains consciousness, he is confused ("clouded sensorium") and has complete amnesia for the attack.

Jacksonian epilepsy (named for John Hughlings Jackson, English neurologist [1834-1911]) is a type of grand mal epilepsy in which the convulsion commences at one focal point (the angle of the mouth, the thumb and index finger, e. g.) and swiftly spreads to encompass the entire body. It is a common component of neurologic symptomatology.

Status epilepticus is a dramatic and serious succession of grand mal seizures which defies the usual anti-epileptic measures. Because its exhaustive potential can easily terminate in death, emergency treatment is directed toward the preservation of life: intravenous administration of a barbiturate, 300 to 500 mg., repeated as necessary, and, according to some authorities, spinal drainage to relieve intracranial pressure.

Petit Mal Epilepsy. Nonconvulsive epilepsy has been subdivided by W. G. Lennox (a pioneer, with E. L. and F. A. Gibbs in electroencephalography) into three subtypes:

Myoclonic Epilepsy is characterized by single jerks of flexor muscles; consciousness is not lost.

Akinetic Epilepsy is sudden loss of postural control or may be nothing more than nodding of the head. The patient may fall to the floor, but he will arise at once.

Pyknolepsy ("true petit mal") is observed as momentary immobility, or as a few rhythmic muscular jerks, with several seconds of unconsciousness. This type of epilepsy is often unnoticed. For example, such a person may be speaking to someone, suddenly stop for a couple of seconds, and then say, "Where was I? Oh, yes. Now, I remember," and continue the conversation.

Associated Conditions. Certain conditions are found in which there is a strong resemblance to epilepsy but the manifestations are mild and not diagnosed as true epilepsy. For example, a patient who has typical manifestations of schizophrenia *and* suffers epileptic seizures from time to time raises the diagnostic chicken-or-the-egg question: Is this schizophrenia with idiopathic convulsions, or psychosis due to epilepsy? Since the causes of both are unknown, the symptomatic treatment of the two conditions is simply combined.

Psychomotor Equivalent is marked by momentary unconsciousness (partial or complete), or by amnesia, with purposeful movements, and sometimes, an emotional outburst of violent rage or utter fright. Automatic behavior may be seen, such as a fugue (see page 52), or anger up to the extreme of homicide. There are many possible variants of psychomotor equivalents, but it is the typical EEG epileptic pattern that pinpoints diagnosis.

Narcolepsy is really a type of sleep disorder, psychogenic in origin. It is a sudden, irresistible desire to sleep no matter where the individual is, no matter what he is doing. It is not syncope, it is natural slumber that lasts from a few seconds to a few minutes. The sleeper can be roused but he promptly falls asleep again. When he does awake he feels completely refreshed. This unusual affliction is found, in the main, among obese young males who are sexually impotent. Amphetamine controls narcolepsy satisfactorily, but the danger of addiction to this drug is always a potential hazard of the beneficial treatment.

Cataplexy is sudden loss of posture, often triggered by excitement, and is related to narcolepsy. Although the patient is completely conscious during the attack, he is unable to speak.

Electroencephalography (EEG). There may be occasions when, in making a differential diagnosis, you refer a patient to an electroencephalographist. EEG waves are seen as four types of rhythm. *Alpha* or *Berger rhythm* or *waves* are found in normal tracings; the interval is 8 to 12 waves per second, with the subject at complete rest. *Beta rhythm* or *waves* constitute a pattern marked by a wave rate of 18 to 35 per second. Beta rhythm is more persistent in the frontal lobes and is a guide to the subject's brain activity so far as reception of sensory impulses and initiation of motor impulses are concerned. *Delta rhythm* or *waves* (bradyrhythmia) occur in an EEG at less than 7.5 per second. It is here that the 3-per-second waves, especially if they are "spiked," are the specific indicators of petit mal epilepsy. *Gamma rhythm* or *waves* is EEG rhythm of 40 to 60 cycles per second, recorded from the anterior regions of the brain; its clinical significance has not yet been determined.

So far as these reports are concerned, there are two rules of thumb: (1) EEG is diagnostically specific *only* in petit mal, and (2) it is highly (85 per cent of cases) suggestive in grand mal. Petit mal epilepsy EEG shows "slow" (3-5 per second) *spiked* waves, that is, delta rhythm (also known as *bradyrhythmia*). Grand mal is marked by rapid, spiked waves. These latter waves are seen in electroencephalograms of other conditions, such as psychomotor equivalent (see above).

The Epileptic Personality. There are no distinctive personality characteristics that set aside the epileptic's personality from other personality patterns. However, it is traditionally marked by overwhelming narcissism and anithetic traits. These were colloquialized years ago by Dr. C. MacPhee Campbell, an authority on epilepsy, who said of the epileptic: *"He works for praise and not for pleasure; he preaches religiosity while he steals your watch."*

Epileptic Deterioration. After many years, a few (5 per cent) epileptics deteriorate to a vegetative existence and personality. This, some authorities believe, is a reflection of ultramicroscopic cellular changes in the cerebrum which may be due to convulsive "attrition," drug therapy, or the psychic trauma of social and occupational ostracism because of the disease.

Neurotic (Hysterical) vs. Feigned Epilepsy. Both types must be separated from true epilepsy, especially in potential draft dodgers, "goldbricks" in the military, and prison malingerers. The hysterical epileptic invariably has a typical neurotic personality; the sociopath (or psychopath) has a long history of antisocial behavior and all the other unsavory traits described previously. Both, however, do not show the typical tonic-clonic succession in their convulsive seizures, both do not bite their tongues or suffer incontinence during an attack, and both do not fall where injury to themselves is a possible complication. Electroencephalography is the outstanding means of separating the malingerer from the true victim of epilepsy.

Treatment. Every physician is acquainted with "first aid" for the epileptic: loosening tie, belt, and tight clothing, placing a padded tongue depressor or wadded handkerchief in the mouth to prevent biting of tongue, putting something protective under the head to prevent skull concussion or fracture, and allowing the patient to remain where he is until he "comes out" of the seizure. It is recommended that persons who are subject to rather frequent grand mal attacks carry an identification card that states his affliction, in addition to his name, address, physician's name and address, etc.

The epileptic needs "psychic" support. He should be encouraged to do what most people do, but in moderation, whether it is working, socializing, or eating. Likewise, when he comes to you for the first time, paint a bright picture of his prognosis, for this is the result in almost every case. A good deal of successful treatment depends on a healthy body, which the physician determines in his initial examination. Most authorities continue to ban alcohol and similar stimulants from the diet. It is reported that children are materially aided by the ketogenic diet (low protein-carbohydrate, high protein regimen).

Without going into details, physicians know the usual pharmaceuticals that are used to control grand and petit mal seizures. In the former, compounds of diphenylhydantoin and mephenytoin are the most successful. Recent reports claim that the tranquilizing agent Librium (trade mark for chlordiazepoxide HCI) is quite useful. There is a therapeutic oddity about medication of grand mal epilepsy: the same dosage may be completely effective at one time of day or night whereas it is ineffective when given at a different time. The optimum times and dosage are worked out by the physician and patient. Psychomotor equivalents and petit mal epilepsy respond very well to phenacemide (trade name Phenurone). Phenurone, however, is—as the manufacturer warns—a dangerous drug because of the possibility of blood dyscrasia. Patients receiving Phenurone should have blood counts at regular intervals.

Currently under trial are electric shock therapy and supersonic surgery and cryosurgery. In the former, the idea is that convulsions induced by EST are replacements, that is, a "planned" seizure is supervised and substituted for the unpredictable one which the patient may suffer where it causes him injury or embarrassment. Neurosurgical procedures extirpate a part of the temporal lobe which, it is believed, bears direct provocative relation to the epileptic seizure.

The psychic profit of completely controlled grand or petit mal is self-evident. It is always worthwhile to talk over the patient's illness and the therapeutic objectives with his family to enlist their cooperation in the overall scheme of encouraging him. Should epilepsy be complicated by an emotional or a mental disorder, treatment for the latter is the same as presented under these psychiatric conditions in previous chapters.

Your opinion may be solicited by employers as to the advisability of hiring or re-engaging an epileptic. Industry and commerce should not bar any epileptic person from work (except, of course, hazardous assignments) on the sole grounds of his affliction after it is under control and you so certify. Even the employee who suffers an occasional attack and has an aura that grants him ample time to retire to a rest room to "see out" his attack (grand or petit mal) should not be deprived of the right to work. Hundreds of years ago, Julius Caesar did just that. When he sensed an aura, he called for a recess of the senate and withdrew to his "special room," had his epileptic attack, and, upon recovery, rejoined his fellow solons.

Your opinion may be solicited in the case of licensing epileptics as automobile drivers; the inquiry is an official questionnaire by a state department of motor vehicles. The time a candidate must be under complete control varies from jurisdiction to jurisdiction. It has been my experience that any epileptic who is *completely* under control (by medication, of course) for two or more years, is eligible, so far as his epilepsy is concerned, to be licensed as a driver. However, if a patient suffers as little as one petit mal attack within that time, I refuse to certify him for licensing.

Treatment of epilepsy is the same as the therapeutic philosophy in controlling a diabetic patient: the individual can enjoy a long and happy life as long as he faithfully follows the prescribed treatment regimen, reporting to you from time to time for any possible changes in the program that may be indicated.

CHAPTER THIRTEEN

Child Psychiatry

BECAUSE A CHILD PSYCHIATRIST treats children he is not, *per se*, a pediatrician. First, the physical, emotional, intellectual, and social problems of normal children differ greatly from those of normal adults. Second, there are even more radical differences between psychiatric problems of children and adults. Of course, a faulty adjustment to environment marks a neurosis in both child and adult, but this has special significance in youngsters because it may shape unfavorable and adverse thinking and behavioral attitudes and patterns in later life. Some children survive the emotional battle with environment; some develop relatively minor emotional reactions; still others suffer gross faulty reactions requiring intensive psychotherapy.

The child with a psychiatric disorder reacts to frustration or anxiety directly or indirectly. The former is manifested as "open" behavior: stealing, lying, running away, or some other type of anti-social activity; these are known as *behavior disorders*. Indirect reaction implies sublimation of rebellion and hostility which is overtly manifested as a psychoneurotic or psychosomatic syndrome: tic, enuresis, stammering, food dislike, somnambulism, and pavor nocturnus (night terrors).

The National Institute of Mental Health (NIMH) reports that about 3,000,000 children suffer with emotional problems; of these, 20 per cent receive some sort of care, approximately 14,000 are in civil institutions, 3,000 in residential centers, and 600,000 are receiving therapy in psychiatric clinics or in psychiatric services maintained by children's (juvenile) courts. The public cry is that there is a dearth of these facilities; the concern should be over the quality of treatment. In 1967, of the thousands of board-certified psychiatrists, only about 400 had sub-boards in child psychiatry!

Etiology

As in all psychopathology, causes may be exogenous, endogenous, or both; the manifestations of these forces may be somatic, psychic, or somatopsychic (psychosomatic). In child psychiatry, we speak of intrinsic and extrinsic factors—more or less, for purposes of "location." Thus, the child's response to intrinsic factors may be a physical disorder or an emotional or mental illness; the latter said to be the youngster who "carries his environmental problems around with him." Extrinsic factors may also be physical (lack of playgrounds, an unsavory home milieu, etc.) or psychic (domestic strife, hostile interaction with a teacher, etc.).

Organic Causes. It is frequently the nonpsychiatric physician who first elicits these. A mother may bring her "misbehaving" child to you and your physical examination may reveal mental retardation, for example, due to (at least a suggestion of) brain trauma, malfunctioning endocrines (especially pituitary and thyroid), juvenile paresis, and the many other etiological factors presented in the chapter on mental retardation. Something as simple as chronic sinusitis may cause a youngster to be irritable and given to temper tantrums. The child with faulty vision or a hearing defect may be referred to you as an unmanageable pupil in school who, when corrective measures are provided, promptly becomes a student no different from the others in the class.

Faulty Discipline. In an early chapter it was shown how mismanagement of an infant in his first two or three years may be reflected later in his personality development. Faulty discipline is a broad term, but it implies deviation from the middle-of-the-road course of moderation: from indifference to oversolicitude. When a child is referred to you because of emotional or behavioral difficulties, your questioning of parents should probe into the method (or lack of method) pursued in disciplining the patient as an infant.

Did he, for example, receive adequate affection? Was he made to feel secure? Was he encouraged when he learned something new? Was he truly accepted at home and abroad (by his "fellow men" when he first goes out, at the age of three, "into the world")? If the answer to the last half of the latter query is "no," you can be sure that he lacks poise and self-confidence because the child first learns how to form and maintain interpersonal relationships at home. It is possible that too much "blame" for a child's behavioral and emotional problems is placed on mothers and fathers, but hundreds of thousands of clinical experiences undeniably reveal that *the most frequently occurring factor behind childhood psychiatric problems is an unsatisfactory parent-child relationship.*

Neglect and Solicitude. This is another way of saying "deviations from the midline of moderation." Disturb or distort a child's normal psychological progress and an "incomplete" segment is left in his personality. It is incomplete because the youngster has failed, or he hasn't had the chance, to resolve his problem, and this incompletion remains in his personality as a springboard for anxiety. Similar or symbolically similar challenges that arise in later life stir the embers in the unconscious of the old fear of failure and the outward manifestation of this inner turmoil is a personality disorder or a neurosis. In many of these adults' clinical histories, a lack of maternal affection and guidance turns up as a background feature. Either the parent didn't "have the time" or, in all truth, just didn't care. What the unconscious expects and doesn't receive is thereafter demanded. The under-loved child spends the rest of his emotional life seeking love. This doesn't mean he is a misfit or a psychiatric wreck. He may be the "big kid" who just lacks the ability to form interpersonal relationships on a mature basis. The reverse also results in adverse personality traits. "Smothering" mothers simply deprive their children of self-confidence, and thereafter he just can't make a decision or plan a course of action without advice—from everybody. One of his or her stormiest eras of life is in the middle years (see Chapter 14).

Environment. Physicians are well acquainted with the adverse factors that can arise and flourish in the home: cruelty, overprotection, alcoholism, parental disharmony, hostility, overambitious parents, oversolicitude, desertion by the father (or no father, or "multiple" fathers), sibling rivalry, stepchild vs. stepchild, etc. With the older child, the most influential adverse factors are those of the neighborhood: the ghetto, poor school facilities, race problems, unemployment of parents, religious prejudice, unsanitary housing. There has been considerable debate over the matter of an infant or child feeling rejected when left to the care of a babysitter, a relative or a hired parent-surrogate. The answer is obvious: moderation. Parents are entitled to "a night out." But if babysitting is a frequent practice, adverse results may ensue. It is unfortunate that many mothers must work and leave their children in day nurseries or in the care of others. There is a potential psychic hazard involved, and all the mother can do is to "convince" her family she loves them dearly when she is with them by concentrating her non-working time on the children and showing genuine interest in what they say and are doing.

Lack of Love. In addition to faulty management of the baby's first years, there are other means by which lack of affection may occur. A mother and/or father who has a paranoid, sadistic, fearful, or punitive attitude toward the world cannot possibly be capable of loving the child since there is no love for anyone. Frustrate and deprive a child's normal desire for love and the chances are excellent that he will be a hostile and obnoxiously aggressive adult. He may, however, sublimate these reactions and regard the whole idea of love disdainfully; as an adolescent he may be the black-jacketed, swaggering, sneering bully who becomes involved in delinquent pursuits.

Psychiatric Disorders. Whereas an adult may manifest his conflict in a neurotic reaction, a child, in a majority of instances, expresses his disequilibrium emotionally: anger, fear, jealousy. Furthermore, they are all-or-none expressions; anger is violent, fear is abject. Very common are fears in reaction to vivid stimuli: thunder and lightning, rigid parents, growling dogs. These are *conditioned* fears; whereas there may be phobias or internal or *neurotic* fears which, by the mental mechanism of projection, may be externalized onto someone or something in the environment. Neurotic fears are commonly seen in utterly frightened, panic-stricken children. Again, a child's protracted state of fear, particularly that of insecurity (arising from overprotection), may be disguised in its outward expression by aggressive behavior—as is the case with the juvenile delinquent.

What we have just described are best considered as "personality disorders," and they are commonly encountered in almost every area of medical practice. Two other childhood psychiatric disorders are: behavior (conduct) disorders and psychosomatic illness.

Behavior (Conduct) Disorder.   Conduct disorders are protests against an unfavorable, antagonistic, or painful life situation—the protest can be the same in neurosis. The disorder, however, is not a mild violation of law and mores; it is violent: cruelty, criminality, running away, truancy, fighting. This is the toughie who, when stopped or apprehended in his misconduct, glowers sullenly and feels not one iota of remorse or guilt. In fact, at that moment he's planning what he'd like to do to the person who has caught him. Whatever the behavior disorder, it is the outward—and ultimate— expression of a will to master a specific situation: to dominate a mother, to "thumb the nose" at teachers, to combat social rejection, etc.

Psychosomatic Disorder.   The mechanism, the results, and the psychopathology of childhood psychosomatic disorder are the same as explained in Chapter 5. The commonest ones are enuresis, grimaces, tics, nictitation, and sniffing.

Enuresis is involuntary urination. Though not unknown in adults, enuresis is of particular significance in child psychiatry and encountered in youngsters with *special symptom reactions.* The latter is a subcategory of *personality disorders,* comprising learning and speech disturbances, sleepwalking, enuresis, and other abnormal conditions. Enuresis is regarded as an indirect manifestation of rebellion, in the same way that the child externalizes his hunger for attention through a tic or stammering (*habit disturbances*). The enuretic youngster is usually unhappy and anxious, and his failure to master bladder control may be traced to fear, hostility, or jealously. Enuresis may have an organic basis, as in the elderly, where it is due to loss of sphincter elasticity. Obviously, the pediatric patient referred to you for enuresis must be physically "checked out" first to eliminate organic pathology.

One out of four enuretic children has been night trained in his past but relapses to bed-wetting. Clinical histories reveal that this most frequently occurs when a sudden traumatic shock is experienced, such as the arrival of a new sibling, death of a parent, divorce, etc. Physical disease accounts for rare instances of enuresis, and in such an instance, there is usually daytime incontinence. Many nighttime wetters are tense and insecure and as the doctor examines them they keep their suspicious eyes on his every move.

Treatment is based on reassurance and encouragement when the first night is slept through "dry." If a plan is adopted whereby there are no fluids given the child, say, after 5 p.m., (a regimen not generally approved by child psychiatrists) he should understand this is meant to help him and is not a punitive measure. Mechanical gadgets, "picking him up" at nights, threats, ridicule—these only tend to more firmly fix the enuresis.

Grimaces, Tics, Nictitation, and Sniffing and other habit disturbances often express the youngster's inner emotional upheaval or hostility. The grimace or tic is gradually separated from its original purpose and becomes an involuntary automatic reaction that is exaggerated under stress. Habit disturbances have been known to result from mimicry, i. e., imitating an older person's tic or grimace.

Stuttering (stammering, logoclonia, logospasm) is uncontrollable repetition of certain consonant sounds in rapid succession. Stuttering is the commonest childhood psychosomatic affliction. All that can be said of it is that it is neurotic in origin and manifestation. Sometimes it is accompanied by simultaneous movements, often bizarre, of the lip, cheeks, neck, etc. Centers, such as New York's Hospital for Speech Disorders, are excellent therapy sources because correctional instruction is simultaneously combined with psychotherapy.

Diagnosis and Interpretation

Nowhere in psychiatry is there greater (really, noisier) divergence of opinion than in the delimited area of child psychiatry. As

promised in this book's FOREWORD, we present the more prominent views without praising or denigrating any of them.

Play technique. This is Melanie Klein's (1882-1960) replacement for the free associations employed in Freudian psychoanalysis.
She applied Freudian concepts about the unconscious to the earliest
period of infancy and decided that Oedipal (see page 7) hostility
and guilt existed before the third year of life; this was the age
Freud believed that the Oedipus situation emerged. Klein was the
first to point out that even a baby can feel hostile and act aggres-
sively toward a parent of the opposite sex. Similarly, she deduced
that since breast feeding sometimes may be inadequate, it can frustrate an infant as well as it can stimulate love (when it cloys the
drinker's appetite). Klein maintained that a child's paranoid reaction (provoked either by a fear of destruction by the father—the
Oedipal competitor—or provoked by the mother who he feels has
frustrated him) begins in infancy. She was convinced that the child
had knowledge of its parents' sexual association. As proof of this,
she referred to a child, for instance, who bumps two play cars
together as the symbolic expression of his unconscious knowledge
of parental coitus, even though he has never seen it. Klein believed
that analysis could assist children in understanding the guilt due
to hostile and aggressive drives. In summary, Melanie Klein felt
that youngsters' neuroses were dependent on inner difficulties in
handling aggression; if instinctual drives are interpreted to them
as early as possible, the result would be ego strength.

Free play technique. This diagnostic-therapeutic methodology
was created by the Anglo-Austrian child psychiatrist, Anna Freud
(1895-   ). She played with her young patients and from their
actions, words, and emotional displays, gained insight into their
conflicts. Free play enhanced rapport between Freud and her patients and went far in gaining the children's trust. She differs from
Klein by the belief that play does not always expose deep unconscious conflicts. Thus, the car-bumping example cited above does
not mean, to Freud, that a child is acting out parental sexuality. It
could be as mundane as the reproduction of a vehicular collision
he has seen that had filled him with consternation. Freud incor-

porated parents into her therapy program to gather data concerning daily events that might be incorporated in the content of the child's play. Klein and her followers (adhering to Sigmund Freud's orthodox views), interpret the deepest strata of the child's unconscious in the belief that this is the dominant therapeutic factor. Freud and her group maintain that the child's ego structure is still developing and that the analyst, therefore, not only should make appropriate interpretations, but should also exert an educational influence on the young patient.

Relationship therapy. It was David Levy, contemporary American child psychiatrist, who pioneered relationship therapy. Like Anna Freud, he allied himself with the youngster and adopted a permissive attitude with the hope that the child would feel less inhibited with the therapist than with his parents in talking of his innermost feelings. Only when other methods fail, Levy says, should treatment be aimed at insight. Levy also originated *controlled play* in which the therapist encourages the patient to re-enact events and circumstances to express the emotion associated with the traumatic events; the method allegedly affords release for tension and anxiety. Instead of free play technique, Levy uses dolls to represent specific persons in defined situations and he takes a more active role in the treatment procedure. His method is based on the idea that the youngster learns by playing how to master certain interpersonal situations.

"Maternal overprotection" is Levy's derogatory designation of "smother" love which he (and other authorities) consider a deterrent to healthy personality development. Overprotective mothers, to Levy, were domineering or indulgent who permit their offspring to "rule the roost" and rarely, if ever, resort to the mildest sort of disciplinary measures. The youngsters, therefore, remain infantile in their demands and anticipations or, as is the case when the mother is domineering, develop shyness, anxiety, extreme submissiveness, and fear, i. e., a neurotic character.

Psychodrama. Psychodrama was presented on page 100; it is the creation of Dr. Joseph L. Moreno. In children this is used in a group therapy setting. Moreno believes that the child who portrays a role derived from either his past experience or his fantasy is able to discharge pent-up emotions through participation in the stage presentation. The patient's intragroup relations are improved because his acting brings him into close association with others (the audience, which is composed of other children).

Permissiveness. Lauretta Bender, contemporary American child psychiatrist, sidesteps intellectual interpretations and emphasizes the importance of a permissive atmosphere in which the child feels free to give expression to his feelings. She uses puppets by which traumatic experiences are reproduced, but this technique allows the patient wider choice than does Levy's which exerts a broader control of the substance of the play. Thus, in this respect, Bender's approach is similar to Anna Freud's. Bender subscribes to the idea of a biological basis for schizophrenia, suggesting that a "maturational lag" in the embryo is the genuine cause of the psychosis and that a later crisis situation merely precipitates an overt schizophrenic process in a genetically predisposed youngster.

Bender divided schizophrenia into: (1) the *autistic child* (see page 173), (2) the *pseudoneurotic child* (who seems to be neurotic but is psychotic), and (3) the *psychotic child* (who appears to be a psychopath because of his delinquency, but actually is deeply psychotic).

Early Feeding. Margaret Fries and Margaret Ribble, contemporary American child psychiatrists, concede that there are differences in the infant's levels of activity at birth, but claim that it is *how* the mother handles the nursing child that determines whether the infant will become overactive or inactive. Fries and Ribble stated that *"painful tension states develop readily in babies who do not have appropriate and consistent psychological mothering."* A disruption in the mother-child relationship often leads to *"exaggerated forms of autoeroticism, such as prolonged thumbsucking, retention of stools, breath holding, and a variety of automatic movements which interfere with the development of the individual."* Ribble stressed that a warm mother-child relationship in the baby's first year protects it from many forms of physiological disturbance and that an unmothered infant will attempt to stimulate itself with rhythmic varieties of body movements, such as excessive rocking and head-banging. Ribble points out that one of the errors in the way newborns are cared for is that after being with a mother briefly, the infant is taken away to the hospital nursery until the following day.

Treatment

It is a very rare occurrence when a child can be separated from his milieu and placed under psychotherapy as an isolated object of treatment. Bender points out that no child is like another, and no child's difficulties and emotional conflicts like another's. She says therapy should emphasize *"the child's needs, strivings, and growth tendencies in a social and cultural background."* Treatment does aim to reorganize the patient's personality on a healthful, firm basis with improved emotional adjustment. The factors which gave rise to hostility, aggression, or insecurity, the factors that retarded his development so that he remained "anchored to his infancy," must be eliminated to permit normal, growth-promoting relationships to flourish.

Freudian psychoanalysis is ineffectual for children—and so Freud pointed out years ago. Question-and-answer protocol may be satisfactory with other children. Regardless of what therapeutic procedure is followed, at least one of the patient's parents should be oriented as treatment advances. One or both parents may require psychotherapy. Often, part of the child's therapy involves changing parental or sibling attitudes, with the elimination of the patient's rigidity of emotions and feeling of rejection to which he has been reacting with behavioral or emotional disturbances.

"Manipulative" (environmental, ecological) treatment enables the child to develop active interests on his own and thereby conquer introversion and shyness. Implements of manipulative treatment include camping, hobby clubs, scouting, dancing, parties, and other group activities. An excellent way to get a child away from over-indulgent parent(s) is sleep-away camp.

In general, child psychotherapy is of three types: (1) psycho-biological, (2) therapist-child relationships, and (3) projective techniques.

Psychobiological Approach. Psychobiology, the brainchild of

Adolf Meyer, the "father of American psychiatry," is known today as *holisticism* (see p. 32).

Therapist-Child Relationships.   Frederick H. Allen was the original exponent of this method of child psychotherapy. It works on the idea that some faulty interpersonal relationship, generally that of parent and child, has blocked the patient's personality development. By means of projective techniques and play the child uses his relationship with the therapist and the therapeutic experience as the means of removing the obstruction to the development and use of his personality assets.

Projective Techniques.   Fundamentally psychoanalytically oriented, projective techniques have the child expressing himself in play as the adult patient expresses himself in words. The child is said to consider his dolls, soldiers, blocks, toy animals, etc., as representatives of his milieu. They become mother, father, sibling, house pet, etc., and the child's emotions are expressed in the "language" of play. He may caress a soldier, hit a doll, etc. This type of expression is simply the mechanism of projection of unconscious emotional and personality features. Very often a child's behavior in the nonpsychiatric physician's examining room is an example of projective technique. A youngster may show no objection to a hypodermic injection or other painful procedure, but, let us say, at the sight of a stethoscope he may shrink from the doctor and howl. It is simply the stethoscope serving as a symbolic reminder of some painful, past emotional trauma. The "little—!" who kicks the physician may well be expressing hostility to his father, although such information doesn't ease the doctor's pain (or anger).

ADOLESCENCE

We have child psychiatrists and gerontologists; but no subspecialty in our field for adolescents. Why not? This segment of our population is attracting more and more publicity and causing more concern than any other age bracket. The adolescent isn't a child, he isn't an adult—he is an adolescent. He is responsible for most of the felonies committed in the United States, for the fantastic rise during the past few years of venereal disease, for the major part of our drug problem, and he constitutes the largest component of the un-employed—and is the drop-out. If these data aren't enough to stimulate thinking about the lack of specially trained psychiatrists for the treatment of adolescents, then consider these: In the 15-19 year age bracket motor vehicle accidents account for 39 per cent of deaths; 18 per cent are due to other accidents; in the 10-14 year age group these statistics are 17 and 25. Put in another way, more than half of the deaths in the 10-19 year-old-age group are due to motor vehicle and other accidents. Equally ominous is the fact that suicide was fifth as a teenager cause of death in 1954; in 1964 it had risen to third. Think what these figures mean for a teenage population of more than 35,000,000.

Because teenagers need the opportunity to talk without check, they want to be heard and, therefore, individual is preferable to group therapy settings. The privacy of the individual session elimi-nates the potential embarrassment the patient might suffer in a group therapeutic milieu; it fortifies the doctor-patient relationship, one in which the parent-surrogate is recognized as an authoritative figure. The psychiatrist's main trouble is avoiding the parents who resort to every subterfuge to get the doctor to reveal what their adolescent is saying (about them, of course). "Does he say I'm mean to him, doctor?" "Does he complain about his father's strict-ness?" How difficult to repress the impulse to answer, "If you weren't 'mean' to him, if his father wasn't excessively 'strict,' you wouldn't ask those questions, would you?" Should the therapist happen to answer parents' queries, you can bet with assurance that when the patient comes home, *they* will hold their own *intime* psy-chiatric session with him—and the transference between patient and psychiatrist vanishes.

If you want to freeze an adolescent the first time he is seen for therapy, just say, "I want to talk to your mother and father first . . . you know, just to get some data about your past history." The patient's understandable reaction is: "Oh, oh. That's all. They'll get you on *their* side." Get the data from the patient and then, if there are things he cannot recall, or if he "doesn't remember" a particular event, inform him that you want to get these facts from his mother or father. Most of the time you can ask these questions of parents in the patient's presence.

Although they are supposed to be hard-boiled, adolescents are very sensitive about handicaps and appearance. In one survey, it was shown that 20 different organic disorders (encountered in 19 adolescent clinics) accounted for 75 per cent of adolescent complaints. The five most frequent diagnoses were *obesity, acne, allergy, convulsive seizures,* and *orthopedic handicaps.* Of course, the dominant emotional manifestation was anxiety. The commonest emotional disorders among adolescents were found to be: difficulty due to adolescence, behavior disorders, personality disturbances, neurosis, and scholastic failure.

Diagnosis. It is not always an easy matter to decide if an adolescent's complaints are indications of psychopathology; the symptoms are so ephemeral that one is torn between the diagnostic labels of mental disorder and behavior disorder. To facilitate diagnosis there have been endless suggestions for nosological terms, to include behavior patterns or conflicts, and to evaluate motivation for change. Another suggestion was to define disturbed behavior as "nonaverage." Now, there's *real* scientific progress! All this does is to bring up the normal-abnormal debate again which we discussed earlier.

It cannot be denied that adolescents react vigorously to their environment; it is their cultural conflict, according to Horney's discipline (see page 95). Therefore therapy should incorporate group forces as well as individual ones. In this category are emphasis on a responsive group environment to facilitate the learning of socially appropriate behavior (which is difficult to obtain in depressed areas), controlled emotional response to promote identification with appropriate adults (which also may be difficult where parents are anything but "appropriate" adults), and encouragement of peer-group forces which stress leadership, responsibility, and foresight (precisely the organizational programs of scouting and the "Y.").

Juvenile Delinquency (J. D.). There is no need to research or hunt for the cause(s) of juvenile delinquency; everyone has the answer—the psychiatrist, the sociologist, the jurist, the policeman, the butcher, the parents, the clergyman—anyone who can talk. Not one proposal has proven to be the unquestionable factor to account for J. D. The dropouts, drug addicts, sex devotees, the immoral, and the criminals do evince a hatred for conformity and authority (psychologically these are the same).

Edgar Z. Friedenberg says that American youth *"is trapped. Youth still depends for protection, as its powers gradually develop, on the insight and responsibility of its elders. They aren't real enough to give it—at least, not in the form in which youth encounters them. In their public life, at least, our 'significant persons' are projected images, though their insubstantial pageant never fades. They are not even meant to deceive or persuade. Their function is rather to provide clues to the underlying power structure, so that bright young men can get with it."*

We hear much about "integrity." It is the lifeblood of community life; it is a highly desirable personality characteristic. Integrity, Friedenberg says, is merely a word in—and a problem to— our society. Above and beyond the illogic of our economic, social, and political systems, those qualities that lead to success (and more of this in a moment) in American life (as well as the inflated value placed on success) make integrity a questionable factor. We talk about it, we say we encourage it, but where is it? If you do not believe this, then examine your immediate world's ethics—your own neighborhood—and see if there isn't any evidence of racism, J. D., unfair labor employment practices, increasing divorce rate, traffic fatalities, and a fear of walking the streets at night—if not, sometimes, during the day. Our national superego is cracking. And this thought leads us to hipsterism.

The Hippies

They are a well-dressed, pleasant, intelligent, middle-class couple. They have come to you because you are a *doctor*. They've known you for years; you can be depended on, not merely for your medical skill but for your counsel. They are in their late forties, perhaps early fifties. The father owns a going textile concern or a dairy or he is an attorney or a physician. They have average interests: community participation, plays, art galleries, reading. They are happy with each other and seldom, if ever, quarrel over anything. You wait. Finally one of them blurts out, "Doctor, you must help us. It's . . . it's George, our son. We just can't . . . can't do anything with him. You see, he's . . . one of those hippies . . . Lives over in East Village."

And you agree to see George. You're going to play psychiatrist, whether you realize it or not. You've straightened out confused young persons before—before hippies, that is. Probably another mixed-up, smart aleck who spouts Nietzsche and Sartre. You smile bemusedly; nothing to it. And so you say, "Sure. Have him come in at three on Friday."

Sit back, doctor, and listen. George is of a different breed; and, no matter your specialty, obstetrics or orthopedics, you're going to see more and more Georges as time goes by. But you'd better do some homework. There are many writers you should get to know. George isn't a befuddled, drug-soaked, "wacky kid." As one whose office is in Greenwich Village where I see many East Villagers, I speak from personal experience; I do not "cite authorities."

Hippies are not a band of juvenile misfits and they are not criminals. They do not constitute a "lunatic fringe." Hipsterism is a movement that is found on every campus and in cities all over the country; not merely in Haight-Ashbury and East Village. Hippies represent an ever-widening schism between their generation and their parents' generation. Hippie garb and drugs may eventually disappear, but the impact they make on our civilization will remain. You must remember the three men of modern times who have done most to change contemporary thinking, all coming from places only miles apart and speaking their pieces within forty years, were Marx, Einstein, and Freud. The buds of their seeds have been growing for some time; the flowers are only beginning to appear, and they are, indeed, incorporated into the "Flower Power." Hippie philosophy incorporates *Das Kapital,* relativity, and psychoanalysis into its tenets and, thus supported, is able to present strong arguments for love-ins, the sex revolution, the "fulfillment of the self," and the fumbling search for relationships. You should know some of the background.

J. H. Plumb refers to hippies as "secular heretics." He also points out that heresy, secular or religious, isn't new. Perhaps it started when the malcontents began to build Babel. Early in the fourteenth century, in Cologne, the Brethren of Free Spirit met secretly, listened to a living Christ, and in the belief that they were one with God, had no faith in Christianity, property, or sin. The logical life, therefore, was love and ecstacy which they pursued enthusiastically and constantly in their church. That was hipsterism.

The peace-loving, charitable Quakers were once hipsters. Three centuries after the Brethren of Free Spirit, they revolted against materialism and "darkness." To indicate their rejection of established church, they wore hats when in houses of worship; they eliminated social stratification by addressing each other as "thou"; they refused to pay taxes, take oaths, or bear arms—and they uncomplainingly went to prison for these violations. As do hipsters.

These are two of many, many examples of "religious heresy." They've cropped up ever since man organized his first social order. Hipsters, as Plumb says, are "secular heretics." They reject society's ethics and turn to their own morality. They reject the values by which their parents live, a frenzied pursuit of material comfort and inane conformity that imbues them with chronic anxiety—and heaven knows, this is the Age of Anxiety. You won't find many hippies in the ghettos or among the wealthy. They are from the middle and upper-middle class—your stratum and mine. Parents in this group have silently rejected this mode of life but continue in it as helpless victims; their children reject it openly and totally and vigorously, sometimes achieving tragic results. Parents will tell you their children do not want to do what they, the parents, want them to do. To the contrary, hippies *are* doing what their parents would have liked to do if they only had the time or initiative. When you judge George, doctor, you judge yourself.

Secular heresy has always erupted when there is affluence. In times of economic depression, all society is too preoccupied with the search for the basic supports of life: food, shelter, and warmth. Invariably, heresy explodes in time of war and social unrest. The hatred of organization, be it discipline, government, or religion, is more than heresy; it is a search for the "unmaterial"—what the hippies refer to as "beauty."

Before you curl your lip and sneeringly refer to hippies as

"pseudo-intellectual bums," please remember that St. Francis of Assisi and Thoreau were hippies. They came from well-to-do, middle-class families, turned against the materialistic, false values of their parents, and decided on their future mode of living, after giving deep thought to it. They meditated—as do hippie disciples of Yoga. There isn't any masochistic self-crucifixion: St. Francis and his followers blithely accepted society's largesse, shelter, and food. So do hippies.

But all prior heretic rebellions were massed power vs. power and, win, lose, or draw, the rebels changed or colored society but never changed a "nation for better or for worse," as Plumb says. Correction or ablation of social and political injustices derives from civil wars, revolution or vigorous and sustained political action. Withdrawing aesthetes in large enough numbers from political activity is one sure way of encouraging totalitarianism.

And therein lies one of three differences between all past heretics and your patients' son, George. Hippies don't "fight." What they dislike, they ignore; that is "flower power." The second difference is drugs. No, drugs aren't new; this was pointed out in Chapter 9. But drugs have never been part of heretical revolts until hipsterism. The third difference is the total lack of a group ideology, of solidarity in principle and action. Their rebellion is not expressed as a coherent philosophy; it lacks concerted action.

Hippies are "getting away with it" because their parents are insecure: their confidence in middle-class institutions and middle-class morality is either waning or practically dead. The solidarity of Western civilization's basic social unity, the family, is splitting. Today's father is not the head of the house his father was, nor is the statutorily emasculated cop the policeman of yesterday, nor are the union-conscious teacher, the fund-raising prelate what they once were.

Finally, although you may be articulate and extremely well-read, you'd better thumb through some of today's recognized philosophers and academicians whose razor-sharp literature speaks convincingly for the hippies. Forget Sartre, Heidegger and Husserl; they're old hat. Get with Marcuse, for example, some of whose views even John Galbraith would not dispute. Read in *Reason and Revolution,* for example, how he combines Marx and love-in. He strikes at smug, middle-class materialism: a comfortable, corporate capitalism imposes *"new, more effective, and more pleasant forms of control"* (Marcuse said this in his *One-Dimensional Man* in 1964). In other words, Western civilization—as the hipster will tell you—has exploited man and shrunken him to one-dimensional *"caricatures of his potential self,"* as Professor Andrew Hacker of Cornell University expresses it. But the Achilles heel in hipsterism even Marcuse cannot conceal: *"In the last analysis, the question of what are true and false needs must be answered by the individuals themselves; but only in the last analysis: that is, if and when they are free to have their answer; as long as they are indoctrinated and manipulated, their answer will not be their own."*

Psychiatrically, this is the peak of egocentricity: "I am dissatisfied and it doesn't matter how many others are, too, or if they see it as I do. I am after my Bluebird of Happiness and don't care if the others find it or not." From any view, by any discipline of psychiatry and psychology, it is anything but "giving"—it isn't love. That's why critics point out that hippies lack "concerted action." They lack concerted action with each other; there are no genuine interpersonal relations. They reject their own social class and their country, yes; but aside from overwhelming narcissism, they suggest or offer nothing philosophical or pragmatic as a replacement. This is the prime reason why hippies *must* have "grass" and "acid." The alibi is "Consciousness-expansion"; the truth is that these drugs crystallize the desire to be alone—out of the world and society they hate. It is, as originally termed by researching scientists, pharmaceutically-triggered schizophrenia.

So, you ask, what will I say to George? What can I do with him? First, you will be surprised; not by his dress: long hair, beads, boots, Indian leather dress, poncho style. It is his attitude. He is polite, attentive, respectful, and never interrupts. He is on the other side of your desk because his parents asked him to come to you. He will answer your questions without hesitation; he will hold nothing back. He won't argue with you—he will "debate" if you wish that. He does not sneer, mock, smirk, or laugh at you. He is extremely intelligent; most have had at least two years of college education. I have several patients who dropped out when they were close to their Ph.D.s. They are not bums. A great majority work because, they frankly concede, they need money for rent and food. Jobs range from salesman in an art gallery, photographer's assistant, all the way to (as in one of my patients) a teacher of music in high school. They are intellectually oriented; not all are genuinely intellectual. Most of them learn to play a guitar. Two of my patients have a musical recording that, at this time, is selling very well. They have one other feature in common: because of the ever-shifting of sexual alliances, gonorrhea is rampant.

When you talk to George your initial reaction is frustration. You feel you're not getting anywhere. You aren't because: (1) his dislike of middle-class society includes you, and (2) you find yourself agreeing with him. Of course you don't underwrite war, crooked politics, the rat race for the unholy dollar, and false fronts. But be patient. Keep probing and, in most cases you'll find that George's outstanding *emotional* problem is that he can't find a real friend, a chick he can really love. He's lonely, he wants someone to lean on and someone to lean on him. He's "hung up" over this and will frankly tell you that when he tries to figure his trouble out he "cops out." So he tranquilizes his troubled mind with "grass." No, he never "trips" alone; but as he begins to soar into the outerspace of fantasy he is alone.

That first conversation will turn out to be pleasant; it is, in most cases. Don't tell George to come back a week from today, *ask* him if *he* wants to come back. If you have lectured, if you have preached, if you have tried to point out it is "everyone's duty to conform," live by the Golden Rule, blah, blah, etc., George isn't going to come back.

If he does return, somewhere around the fourth or fifth visit you ask *the* question that is the genuine trigger to the beginning of therapy. "George, tell me something. What is there in grass or acid that you believe isn't in yourself, or, what do you find in them that you don't find here?" George will stare at you. He may give a feeble answer—and recognize it for its weakness. But what begins to stir within the inner recesses of his psyche are feelings of inferiority. Grass and acid are means of running away—but, you ask, "to what, to where?" George will tell you that he can't orient himself in this world with time or people.

"But, George, you tell me that at the height of a trip you are delightfully unhampered by time or place or person. In other words, you leave nothing in order to go to nothing and return to nothing." You're beginning; George will start to "dig" up material now, and psychotherapy has commenced. But don't expect to proselyte him back to middle-class conformity. In time, if he isn't working, he will. Soon he'll mention that he has a couple of friends with whom he "really can relate." Hippies love that term: relate. If he doesn't tell you, his parents will, that when George comes home every week or couple of weeks, they are "getting on better." It is difficult to put in print what happens and how progress is made, but progress *is* made. If you've played it cool, they develop unqualified confidence in you. They are, amazingly enough, respecters of middle-class authority whom they do not *emotionally* recognize as middle-class. From session to session you see them relax, unbend. One may ask if he can turn on during the interview. Why not? Another will suggest or invite you to tape record the session. They begin to ask your advice: where should this sample of art work be taken? Do you know of anyone who is looking for an assistant in a store? Should I continue with Yoga? Of course you encourage every extraverted activity and proclivity. These are signs of genuine progress: there is giving to and doing for others. Introverted libido is being turned around and directed outwardly.

Hippies have turned out to be the most interesting and gratifying group I have ever encountered in almost 40 years of psychiatric practice. Oh, there are disadvantages. You may receive a telephone call at two in the morning from a scared, "hung up," young man or woman. Interpret this not as a violation of your slumbering comfort; it is a healthy recognition of "authority." You are, indeed the father figure. Such a call means therapy is going well.

And, if parents—even your friends—ask you about hipsterism, you can answer in one of two ways, depending on whose views you endorse. If it is the pessimistic prognosis of Edmund Stillman your reply will be his: ". . . *the wave of the future will not be rationalism and order, but the reverse.*" If you believe in Arnold Toynbee's pessimistic philosophy, you will, as he does, cite Gamaliel's advice to the Sanhedrin: ". . . *let them alone: for if this counsel or this work be of men, it will come to nought: But if it be of God, ye cannot overthrow it.*"

CHAPTER FOURTEEN

The Involution

IN YOUR PRACTICE you must encounter some popular but erroneous beliefs concerning the middle years of life. The well-known phrase, "change of life," for many people implies: (1) a phenomenon of dramatic physiological alteration that applies exclusively to women, (2) the idea that, by some magic of Nature, this period of feminine living occurs with clocklike precision the second a woman turns 45, and (3) the "change of life" is an agonizing time that is the cross every woman must bear. If these myths aren't enough, there is the confusion over terms associated with the middle years which are defined at this point for clarification of what we are about to discuss.

Menopause is the physiological arrest of menses.

Climacteric, according to Webster, is *"a period or point in human life (as among women, the menopause) in which some great change in the constitution, health, or fortune takes place, or is supposed to be especially likely to occur. The critical periods are thought by some to be the years produced by multiplying 7 by the odd numbers 3, 5, 7, and 9; to which others add the 81st year."*

Involution, according to Gould's *Medical Dictionary,* is *"the period of regression or the process of decline or decay which occurs in the human constitution after middle life."*

These definitions (except for the reference to the menopause, of course) do not differentiate between the sexes; no definite year is mentioned (Webster merely cites an old wives'—and unscientific—tale); no suggestion is made that any pathology is associated with the change of life. It is physiologically a fact that *both* males and females experience a change of life somewhere in the fifth and sixth decades. It is likewise fact that this period can be lived through happily and symptom-free.

The involution, of all the ages of man, is the outstanding one of change. Perhaps this is why the French refer to the menopause as *l'âge critique*. It is the narrow channel of human existence between adulthood and senility, the dusk of one period and the dawn of another. Said Victor Hugo, *"Forty is the old age of youth, fifty is the youth of old age."* As in any other period of the average life span, the pre-involutional personality, physical status, and emotional equilibrium determine whether one will glide through the middle years or suffer somatic and/or psychic disturbances.

To choose "settling down" as the criterion of middle age is arbitrary and actually erroneous. Some people "ease off" in early adulthood (Charles Darwin, e. g.); to the contrary, many persons are go-getters to and through the senium. In this latter group are such as Oliver Wendell Holmes, Moses Montefiore, Pablo Picasso, Somerset Maugham, George Bernard Shaw, Pablo Casals, Artur Rubinstein.

Factors of Nature and contemporary civilization produce a "turning in"—an involution—or retardation of function, drive, capacity, and somatic components at different periods in life. Physical stamina is at its peak in youth—soldiers, athletes, ditch diggers, mountain climbers, et al. Mental stamina, on the other hand, seems to reach its peak in later years, examples of which are cited in the next chapter. With this variance in mind, it is now possible to discuss the physiology of the involution.

Physiology

With an understanding of what "involution" implies, we can appreciate that tissue and organ alterations are natural, normal signs that a function or functions have either served their physiologic purpose or have reached a point when they are needed less than in earlier years. In a like vein, normal "wear and tear" of a system or an organ by constant usage demand, like a machine, a let-up, mechanical assistance, or replacement. Thus, as one reaches the forties, he does not dash after a bus as though it were the last one running; thus, the use of hormones; thus bifocals.

Practically every component of the human organism changes in the involution; the menopause happens to be the one most frequently noticed because it is apparently the most "dramatic," and has, through the years, taken on an ominous aura of being a herald of death. Nevertheless, no part of the organism escapes change: eyesight becomes less acute, decay and gum recession affect dentition, hair in women loses its youthful sheen and pliability, and, in men, thins; skin becomes dry and nails brittle. What once was done without effort now requires frequent rest intervals. There are many more changes, all known to physicians.

One of the main reasons for diminished or totally arrested activity is the retarded functioning of the endocrines. For example, the thyroid's contribution in this phase is the dry skin, brittle fingernails, and loss of the hair's lustre. As fibrous tissue and fat replace muscle fiber, physical effort must be decreased and flabby musculature takes the place of youth's steel-like character. The heart lacks the vitality it once had to propel blood through vessels that are becoming sclerotic, whereas they used to be pliable and soft. The only element that is exempt from the involution is the blood; it remains the same from the cradle to the grave.

Seemingly sudden as the involution is, the process of aging *is* a gradual process that commences the second one is born. Autopsies of month-old infants reveal to the microscope's eye arteriosclerosis that is not found in vessels of the newborn, as established by postmortem examinations of stillbirths. Aging implies diminished capacity; it does not mean *finis*. This is something that you may have to point out to patients because of the common belief that involution is equated with the end of sexual drive. All instincts—hunger, race preservation, no matter what, endure as long as life does. Were this not so then the elderly person would not eat or sleep—or indulge in sex. Each of us is born with the same instincts, the same immeasurable amount; the difference between individuals is *how* instinctual impulses are satisfied or deprived of gratification. True, ovarian and testicular hormone production slows with the years, but it never stops. Of course there are exceptions: such function may cease entirely in some. If it does, then sexual activity *does* terminate. The latter is found, for example, in those neoplasms that lead to sex "reversal" of varying degree in either sex, usually the result of abnormally high production of the hormone of the opposite sex which, under normal physiological circumstances, occurs in minute amounts. But, this and similar events are *pathological* occurrences that are not found in normal aging. Sexual activity usually continues despite the march of years. In fact, in some women there is an increase in sex drive immediately before, during, and right after the involution. This will be included in our discussion of divorcées and widows further on.

There are also factors of civilization and longevity and their effects on the climacteric. Women are experiencing the menopause at a later age. Obstetricians are delivering women in their late forties; several births to women in their early fifties are to be found in medical literature. Culture also exerts its influence: In India a girl of thirteen will marry and be an old woman at thirty-five—an age when the average American woman is at the pinnacle of vigor and charm.

The male is often suddenly struck by the psychological impact of the climacterium. One day he requires no eyeglasses; the next he is trying to adjust to bifocals. The well-conditioned golfer suddenly finds that eighteen holes leave him "bushed," even panting and exhausted. The insurance collector who has walked miles every working day for years discovers, one afternoon, that his calves ache and the walk he once took in stride is now too much for him. A great disappointment is his physician's verdict, after examination, that he has "nothing wrong with you—it's just the change of life. Nature is telling you that you must take things at a slower pace. You're not the youth you once were." That's the information that hurts: you are not the youth you once were. It is scientific verification of something he has recently found out for himself: he is not as sexually potent as he once was. And this, too, has been a rather sudden change. Many men are shocked to find that they have trouble achieving and maintaining erection. This is not uncommon, but it does not persist. Within weeks or months, the man who enters middle life and undergoes this ego-deflating disability, recovers his sexual stamina but his indulgence in sexual activity may be less frequent than before. This physiologic evidence of lessened virility explains why emotional and mental reactions in the male in the involutional period are invariably depressive in character.

Psychopathology

Psychiatrically, there are two varieties of involutional reactions: neurotic depression and psychosis, the latter seen either as a paranoid reaction or as a depression (melancholia). At the base of these disorders is an unconscious feeling of inferiority, an inner reflection of the realization that the dawn of old age is the undeniable herald of death. In persons who develop one of the emotional or mental disorders just mentioned, there is a feeling of "it's-too-late" and "unfinished business," a sense of frustration and futility, a fear of dependence, helplessness, and, in some instances, of loneliness. Such emotions may swirl and bubble in every unconscious at the involutional period, but only the immature and incompletely developed emotional machinery will break down because of them. Climacteric psychic states affect only those whose psychosexual development has never attained completion and where adjustment has been faulty.

Involutional Psychosis, Paranoid Type.   This is the projection of unconscious insecurity, inadequacy, frustration, and deprivation as seen by irritability, bitterness, impatience, and delusions of persecution ("the world is against me," "I've been handed a dirty deal," etc.). These ideas are expandable to include organizations ("it's a plot started by the Masons," "the Church has it in for me," etc.). This patient is extremely suspicious, isolates her- or himself from others, and approaches the senium as a sour, contankerous, unloving and unloved person. Very often, the clinical history reveals that the patient's pre-psychotic personality was paranoid; often there is a record of one or more earlier psychiatric disorders. Some authorities claim that the paranoid involutional patient is a schizophrenic paranoid who has managed to maintain quasi-adjustment until the involution, as the "last straw," brings the psychotic reaction into open, discernible evidence.

Involutional Melancholia.   This reaction is characterized by profound sadness, agitation, weeping, death wishes, and often by attempts at suicide. As a reaction to unconscious guilt feelings, the patient frequently insists that he is "worthless," "no good," a "burden on his family and society," that the world's misery and suffering are his fault. This may reach the point where the patient's psychosis permits him to believe and declare that he is dead—or that everybody is dead, leaving only him as the sole survivor to bear the punishment for the sins of this planet. These patients look and act the quintessence of hopelessness and gloom. There is no sun, there is no future. There is nothing they or anyone can do to change the bleak situation; hence, there is no earthly reason to live. And this is the launching pad for the attempt at suicide. He or she who unconsciously—often consciously, too—dreads the approach of the senium and all it implies, who feels that love has been unrequited, or that he or she has not faced life's challenges in youth, is the prime candidate for psychopathology in middle life.

Neurotic depression has been presented on page 55.

Treatment

Many physicians know the experience of having a patient in the involution insist that she must have "hormones." She supports her clinical opinion with a remark such as, "Why, two of my friends take hormones, and they are *marvelous!* No hot flashes, nothing!" Doctors recognize the precise place for hormonal therapy in this period of life, particularly with the woman who suffers, in addition to the "hot flashes," periodic sweats, headache, uneasiness, and tension. Conjugated estrogens are quite useful where there is senile vaginitis. How effective chorionic testosterone is in the male who complains of poor erection, premature ejaculation, and flagging potentia, I leave to endocrinologists to determine.

Involutional melancholia in most instances calls for at least brief hospitalization because of the ever-present hazard of self-destruction. Treatment is the same as previously described for depressive reactions. The melancholic patient, however, is often malnourished (failure to eat properly is, of course, a masochistic mode of self-punishment for one's "sins"), and dietary correction is indicated.

The paranoid patient has a less favorable outlook. Tranquilizers are used simply to make him more amenable and receptive to psychotherapy. Therapy, on the whole, is the same as that for the usual psychotic patient, as presented in Chapter 7. Neurotic depression is treated with antidepressant agents and psychotherapy.

The Widowed and the Divorced

Chapter 9, "Alcoholism," carried the promise of discussing this group at a later time, and this is the time.

Because of a statistical peculiarity, alcoholism is a major problem of widowed and divorced women—*"The Disease of a Million Women,"* wrote Dr. Sidney Greenberg, an authority on alcoholism, some years ago—who are faced with an overwhelming mathematical adversity: of more than ten million divorced and widowed persons, females outnumber males by better than eight to one! There is no doubt that the high rate of coronary disease among men, especially in the fifth and sixth decades, is the responsible factor for the one-sided survival ratio. Certainly, it is immediately obvious that, confronted with this lopsided arithmetical disadvantage, over eight million widows and divorcées face a grim problem of readjustment. It is, indeed, a rat race.

Widows are younger today, but conversely the divorced person (male and female) is "older—more daring—and hardly gay," to quote a newspaper advertisement for a *Newsweek* article on divorce in the United States. Most face the same problem of adjustment: the initial shock, then loneliness, financial insecurity, friends who drift away. Where there are growing children, the problems multiply, especially for the working mother. Statistics reveal that almost one-half of today's divorces break up a home of ten years or more, that more than one-half of these homes have children under eighteen, and that the national average age of the woman at the time of her divorce—often initiated by her—is forty-five.

The divorcée is not the recipient of the same sympathy and solicitous attention that the widow is shown, though both may be subject to the same suspicious glances of wives and "passes" by male friends. A certain aura of the risqué is attached to widows and divorcées by most people. This mental attitude is typified in literature and entertainment: witness *The Merry Widow* and *The Gay Divorcée.*

Coming from the sociological security of married life, both the divorcée and the widow must search for new companions and places for themselves. The divorced man or widower usually has a better time of it socially, though not at the level of firm interpersonal relationships. Most widows and divorcées want to remarry—some to regain the love they once had, others for material support. Of remarriage, Oscar Wilde said in *The Picture of Dorian Gray: "When a woman marries again it is because she detested her first husband. When a man marries again it is because he adored his first wife. Women try their luck; men risk theirs."* Of course this is neither statistically nor, necessarily, psychologically true. And of all persons to pontificate on marriage, Wilde, as a bisexual, cannot be regarded as an authority. Contrary to the quotation, the woman who has been well-adjusted, without feelings of inadequacy, calmly seeks out a man she can love and who can love her—and remarries. Proof of this satisfactory goal is the fact that divorce is extremely rare among persons who marry for the second time. Proof that a widow and a divorcée must find their new mate soon after the loss of the first one is the statistic that eighty per cent of women who remarry do so within three years after their husband's deaths. Thereafter, it is rare for the widow or the divorcée to achieve matrimony.

She quickly appraises the situation; she has no illusions about the difficulties facing her, and grimly sets out to do battle. Men, she discovers, regardless of age, are ever on the lookout for youth in the women they accept for companionship and marriage—and svelteness and pulchritude materially aid a woman's candidacy for matrimony. These men, perhaps because they are accustomed to it, also expect their dates to be "good" drinking partners. The women find out—perhaps, found it out in earlier years—that inhibitions, shyness, reluctance to compete with younger females, magically evanesce under the influence of alcohol. These hesitant and insecure women need Dutch courage, they have to get into a frame of mind where they can kid themselves into believing that they do look extremely attractive in mini skirts, with wild hair-do's and wigs; that they don't look silly twisting and writhing rock 'n roll. Above all, the precepts of childhood, the mores of society—all those lofty principles which have shaped and molded her superego—dissolve in alcohol. Befuddled, uninhibited, and always spurred on by a feeling of desperation—"this is it, or else"—these middle-aged women very often flit from one affair to another whether it is a one-night stand or an "understanding friendship" of months. Very often, when they return to sobriety—usually the next morning, and quite often alone—their superegos berate them as would have their parents. Now, in response to feelings of guilt, there are remorse, self-recrimination, and self-pity. The latter is fully discussed in Chapter 9. What saves the emotional structure of many of these women is a pseudo-philosophy which can be no better expressed than by the following verse by an unknown writer:

> *Said a woman's soul to a woman's heart:*
> *I shall live forever, but dust thou art,*
> *And despite the fires to-day that burn*
> *To-morrow thou'lt die and dust return.*
> *But the heart replied to the soul and said,*
> *Tho' alive to-day—to-morrow dead—*
> *My day of life is worth to me*
> *Thy endless years of eternity.*
> *For I live, and love, and suffer woe,*
> *Yet thou liv'st forever thou can'st never know,*
> *And my day of life, be it bitter or sweet,*
> *No hour of reckoning have I to meet . . .*
> *Flowers shall bloom from my dust and sing,*
> *From the heart that lived but a day we spring.*
> *So, I live and laugh, and sin, and say . . .*
> *It matters not . . . the soul will pay.*

This verse is expressed in less poetic fashion when the widow or divorcée who is emotionally disturbed says to the psychiatrist, quite defiantly, "Well, what's wrong with what I'm doing? I'm free; I don't neglect my children." Dear lady, if your superego believed you were right, you wouldn't ask the question. Your conscience was shaken to its very roots the first time in your widowhood— probably having drunk more than you should—when you bedded down with a man who was, comparatively speaking, just another man. Of this violent emotional experience Freud said, bilingually: *"Ce n'est que le premier pas qui coute. Das weitere findet sich."* (*"It is only the first step that hurts. The rest follows."*)

Alcohol not only enables the woman to indulge in activities she formerly disapproved of, it drowns feelings of inferiority and guilt. Most authorities agree that they know of no group that succumbs to chronic alcoholism more easily than the widows and divorcées who fail to find second husbands. Because they start the journey down a one-way street so late (at least, in their forties), they travel faster and reach the dead-end sign quicker. For a while alcohol enables these women to *think* their consciousness is expanded by alcohol as they behold a whole new vista they have never beheld before, but as with the gray flannel brigade (see page 132) expansion is really contraction. A garish, dazzling, inferiority neutralizing picture that actually shows the same scene time after time is superimposed on its predecessor by liquor. And the hazard of venereal mishaps is exemplified by the patient, Mrs. S. A., cited on page 106.

There is, of course, a more desirable and psychologically healthier solution to the problems of widowhood and divorce. In addition to contacts through church, club, family, and friends, there are many social organizations throughout the country maintained by or for widowers, widows, and the divorced. Other organizations cater to all the "presently single," though usually within the limits of an age group. Computerized dating is not yet popular with the middle-aged; still, the real function of many groups is that of a dating rather than a marriage bureau, and without the selectivity or controls of the latter. Too often, the social functions of such organizations become a free-for-all, sexually and otherwise, and permanent relationships are difficult to attain within the group. Frequently, friendships or affairs between mismatched partners are seen as a result of each one's loneliness. These can lead to social and emotional problems for either partner or both.

Despite the handicaps, the hazards, and the pitfalls, the woman who enters widowhood or divorce with a well-developed, mature psychical and emotional apparatus will see this trying period through to a successful solution, whether it be remarriage or living happily on her own.

CHAPTER FIFTEEN

Senility

ALMOST A HALF CENTURY AGO a renowned American surgeon said that *"medical science is making it possible for man to live longer to suffer more complications."* This statement is well exemplified in the paradox that the more progress is made for the improvement of one end of life's span (reduction in infant mortality), the greater are the problems at the other. In 1900 only 4 per cent of Americans were over the age of sixty-five. By 1975 this figure will be close to 13 per cent of the population, or twenty-five million persons. Two factors are chiefly responsible for the increased percentage: a fall in the number of births and in immigrants, and the prevention and control of infectious diseases.

In the previous chapter it was pointed out that a child cannot be treated as a "younger adult." The same applies to persons over the age of sixty-five; they cannot be regarded simply as "older adults." A man of thirty and one of eighty can manifest identical symptoms, headache and dizziness, for example, but the physician's clinical approach to each cannot possibly be the same. For instance, the younger man may be suffering from labyrinthine pathology; the older man may have severe hypertension.

In 1914 Dr. Ignaz L. Rascher coined the term "geriatrics" to set aside a branch of medical practice devoted to the health problem of oldsters. From this, "gerontology" is derived: the scientific body of knowledge dealing with the process of aging. Dr. Rascher stated that medicine's problem is to restore a diseased organ or tissue to a state that is normal in senility, *not* to a state that is normal in maturity. The motto of the Gerontological Society is: *"To add life to years, rather than years to life."*

Aging is more than "growing old" or "maturing" (as in aging wine). It is a popular belief that progress in medical science has lengthened the life span. However, it is a statistical truism that it hasn't changed much from Psalms, 90:10: *"The days of years are threescore and ten . . ."* In *The Biology of Senescence,* Alex Comfort states: *"It seems quite certain that failing a radical interference with the whole process of aging, the prediction that medicine will give us 150- or 200-year lifespans, which was incautiously made by a number of nineteenth-century optimists, is wrong."* What science has accomplished and what it can be expected to accomplish in the future is that more people will live out their lifespans normally and enjoy better health while doing so. Comfort defines aging as a biological process which causes increased susceptibility to disease; there are many theories why this process occurs, but not one seems to explain it completely.

In a recent survey of aging by the National Institute of Mental Health, a group of healthy older men (ages 65 to 92) was compared with a group of younger men (average age, 21). It was found that the first group was mentally flexible, alert, "vigorous, interesting, and deeply involved in everyday living," and the report added, the old men were "significantly superior" in verbal intelligence. The survey concluded that, as current everyday metabolic diseases of old age are better understood and as progress in geriatric psychiatry continues, there would be "more individuals who are old in years but functionally young by present standards."

The Process of Aging. Physicians must regard the aging process as it applies to tissues and organs so that they can appreciate psychopathology of senescence that results from accumulated somatic handicaps, the general deterioration in bodily functions, and the weight these factors add to whatever emotional traumata have developed within the oldster. The predominant indication of aging is found in tissues where stroma increases while parenchyma decreases. Every organ, every system follows its unique procedure of aging; only blood, as previously stated, remains essentially the same throughout life. Doctors know all the somatic manifestations from arteriosclerosis to cataracts; we need not list them here; not even those endemic to the endocrine glands.

As time goes by, investigators are focusing their attention on the *cell* as the heart of the problem of aging. Old cells have less water and more solids than younger ones. *In vitro,* colloids lose water as they age. These known data imply that the aging of colloidal protoplasm accounts for the toll of advancing years. Likewise, old cells accumulate pigments and lipids which, many researchers maintain, clog cells and impair their efficiency. Other workers point to the reduction of enzymes as the answer. There are many other cellular substances and functions currently under investigation.

Aging alters one's response to stress: the reaction to trauma is slower and less vigorous, and frequently less effective than in earlier life. Therefore, manifestations of pathology are often minimal because the signs and symptoms are generated by the response to trauma and are infrequently due to the trauma, *per se.* For example, an oldster may experience a mild pain in his chest and suffer a hacking cough. These are so benign (to him) that he feels "a couple of aspirin" will correct them, whereas widespread pulmonic inflammation, hyperpyrexia, and associated indications irrevocably indicate pneumonitis which, if untreated or if a physician is not summoned until extremus sets in, may prove fatal. Older persons do not bear extremes well: heat, cold, overeating, malnutrition, and dehydration. "Hale and hearty" are, at best, no more connotative than "comparative well," because the oldster has accumulated many scars from the hazards of life, such as actual traumata—physical and emotional—which are par for the longer courses of life. The longer we live the greater the opportunity to gather (and retain) somatic and psychic souvenirs of the road we have traveled. But life experiences vary in intensity, sequence, severity, and duration; therefore physicians find a limitless variation and divergence in functional capacities among their geriatric patients. The cornerstone of gerontological medicine must be *individualization.* There is no such thing as "routine" treatment.

Psychopathology

While senility and arteriosclerosis are the two outstanding instruments that form the psychiatric disabilities of senescence, more important are the *changes* these conditions evoke. Among these alterations are those of the emotions, intellectual functioning, response to stress, immunity, biochemical equilibrium, metabolism, and structure, to list some. While tranquilizers have proved to be a blessing in treating institutionalized psychiatric patients, this benefit has not accrued to the senile patient. True, they *are* rendered tractable and cooperative by these drugs (at one time many of these patients were "unmanageable, destructive, soiling, and violent"), but despite restoration to comparative emotional equilibrium, the drugs cannot imbue them with the drive to return to a life of competition. There is a strong hint of futility in this: even psychotherapy in institutions speaks of "cure" for younger patients; for the elderly the word is "rehabilitation." As a result, the bulk of long-term patients in our mental hospitals is the senile citizen. In 1930 only 5 per cent of new admissions were over the age of sixty, and these patients lived, following institutionalization, about 2.5 years. Twenty-five years later this admission percentage exceeded 40, and patients were surviving hospitalization for 10 years.

In assaying mental and emotional factors in the elderly we are once more confronted by the normal vs. abnormal problem. Just how much irascibility, suspicion, and "childishness" must there be to warrant a diagnosis of psychosis? Do disorientation, lack of bowel control, intellectual letdown, and carelessness in personal appearance imply mental illness, dotage, or just "simple senility"? Isn't loss of physical vigor enough to provoke a feeling of depression and dejection? When a 65-year-old man, in complete control of his faculties and vigorous for his age, finds that the age of 45 is the limit for employment, is he to be regarded as psychotic and paranoid if, in fact, the "world is against him?" In other words, ecological factors are powerful stimuli for aberrant and deviant ideas. Social maladjustment is rampant among senior citizens; there are insufficient residences, homes, and hospitals devoted to the elderly.

Clinical Syndromes. Senile psychosis and psychosis due to cerebral arteriosclerosis are the two leading psychopathological conditions. Manifestations of these are divisible into physical and psychic symptoms and signs.

Physical Symptoms. Headache, usually throbbing in nature, is a common complaint, with or without tinnitus. There also may be dizziness, a sense of pressure on or in the head, and syncopal attacks. There may be complicating apoplectic strokes with or without paralysis. Examination of retinal vessels reveals arteriosclerotic changes. There may be arcus senilis. Hypertension is present when sclerosis is predominantly arteriolar; it is often lacking when it is chiefly arterial.

Psychic Manifestations. "Mental tension defect" is the commonest indication of cerebral arteriosclerosis. The term implies an impairment of the capacity to think readily and accurately, to concentrate and fix the attention. The patient tires easily—emotionally, somatically, and psychically. There is extreme emotional lability: he may weep over trivial events or show sudden irritability with explosive temper outbursts, even without provocation, but apparently this is a reflection of unconscious realization that he is not as physically and mentally capable as he once was. Arteriosclerosis in and about the thalamus gives rise to emotional disturbances to the point that all control is lost. Memory is poor—it is said to be "patchy"—in that it is clear one day and impaired the next. However, as the patient seemingly returns to his "old self" after an emotional outburst, and his mental faculties seem to be the same, it is a clinical fact that each "return" is to a level somewhat less than the previous one. This gradual deterioration is known as a "step let-down defect." Realization that he is "under par" may lead to deep depression and precautions against suicide are indicated. If he becomes impotent he may project his inadequacy as a paranoid delusion that his wife is unfaithful to him. The patient is subject to delirious attacks, particularly at night, when he is frightened by hallucinations of death, burials, funerals, etc. He may show perseveration, the constant repetition of one thought or word.

The signs of senile psychosis can best be understood when we consider a patient who is, say, eighty years of age. Certainly his years are compatible with senility coexisting with cerebral arteriosclerosis. Therefore, rather than list the indications of senile psychosis, the following table provides the features of each, when one or the other is the predominating difficulty in an older patient:

CEREBRAL ARTERIOSCLEROSIS	FEATURE	SENILE PSYCHOSIS
Occurs earlier	*Occurrence*	Occurs in later years
Brief	*Duration*	Somewhat longer
Apt to be abrupt, stormy	*Onset*	Gradual
Confused	*Intellect*	Clear
Depression and hypochondriasis common	*Emotions*	Depression and hypochondriasis rare
Present but not prominent	*Paranoid State*	Common; may be very marked
Headache, dizziness, apoplexy, syncope, convulsions	*Physical Signs*	Rare
Capricious defects; "patchy"	*Memory*	Orderly retrograde defect
May be elevated	*Blood Pressure*	Not elevated *per se*
Fairly well preserved	*Personality*	Not well preserved

Treatment. This is a misnomer, since it cannot be the goal of helping the elderly psychiatric casualty. The correct term—and the objective—is "control." It is in geriatric practice that holisticism comes into its own. Usually there are one or more organic processes in evidence, chiefly of the "degenerative" type: arthritis, gout, hypertension, diabetes, and a host of others well known to physicians. These, of course, demand medical attention. Meanwhile, the oldster has not only lost most of his immunity to disease, he may even be vulnerable to childhood diseases. In psychotherapy, occupational and recreational therapies are added to encouragement, reassurance, and re-education—but what promise of a "better tomorrow" can the psychiatrist really offer? The aim, then, of geriatrics is to widen the split between handicap and disability or death.

Longevity. Longevity is commanding more and more interest; dissemination of news and information about it also brings, unfortunately, many myths, legends, and distortions of statistics. For example, population experts gravely project the latest rise in census to a prediction that by the year 2000 there will be so many Americans that space will be lacking—or such is the idea one infers. Meanwhile, there is the shadow of the "pill"—the Age of Contraception. For the past six years this country's birth rate has been steadily dropping. What promises to be the case in 2000 is that a larger percentage of our population will be in the senior citizen category.

There has been considerable research on longevity. Raymond Pearl, a well-known geneticist, demonstrated that in fruit flies long-livedness is a dominant factor while short-livedness is recessive. But how this genetic process works remains unknown. Better public hygiene, medical advances, antibiotics, immunization, and other progressive features of recent times serve to extend life expectancy. At the time of Julius Caesar, the average length of life was 23 years. In 1900 this had risen to 46, and in 1950 to 69. To put it another way: it took 2,000 years to double life expectancy but only 50 more years to triple it! Science has shown that natural selection and favorable chromosomal and genic combinations account for longevity, but physicochemical explanation holds that it is not heredity that governs the duration of life but longevity in the sense of a definite amount of life energy. Speeding up or retardation of metabolism, temperature and light may affect longevity because these factors control the rate of consumption of the fixed available supply of energy. We know that thin persons generally outlive fat persons; women outlive men; and, in younger people, a higher mortality rate prevails among those under average height.

Intermingled with and serving to confuse statistics are legends and myths about long life, and these, in turn, confuse socioeconomic consideration of geriatrics. The Bible provides Methuselah and Isaac, and the obstetrical phenomenon of Sarah giving birth at a time when most women are dead. Intellectual interests seem to foster longevity. In literature and science we think of Newton, de Fontenelle, Goethe, de Buffon, and Kant; in art, Titian and Michelangelo; in medicine W. W. Keen, Duverney, Sloane, and Harvey. Hannemann married when he was eighty and was still working eight years later. Walton was writing when he was ninety. *Molecular and Microscopic Science* was written by Mary Somerville when she was eighty-six, and Landor penned his *Imaginary Conversations* when he was eighty-five. Contemporary times include Stravinsky, Churchill, Adenauer, Truman, Picasso, Stokowski. History is replete with notables who were mentally alert and hard working in their old age: Baruch, Victoria, Edison, Ford, Rockefeller, Pius XII, Gustavus V,

Gladstone, etc., etc. giving special due to Sir Moses Montefiore who, on his hundredth birthday, spent his usual day working in his office. It's never what one says, but how. For example, there is probably little if any surprise at the statistic that five ten-thousandths of Americans are aged 100 or over. But some amazement might be provoked by expressing this as: 100,000 Americans are 100 years of age or more. There are about 70 persons past the hundred-year mark receiving Social Security benefits.

Economics and Ecology. Our attitude toward old age is a paradox, difficult to comprehend. Our senior citizens are profoundly concerned with their social adjustments, finances, and health. Legislators, sociologists, economists, and industrial leaders seem to be doing all they can to make social adjustments, financial security, and health adjustments attainable for oldsters. We live longer, we go on pension or retire earlier. A man at the age of fifty is "unemployable." In the previous century a man worked until he died. Today, the aim is (at least in civil service and many unions) retirement at 50 (police and similar persons can retire after 20 years or by the age of 45). Perhaps our grandfathers' lifetime of working smacked of "survival of the fittest"; maybe it wasn't "wholesome," but despite the so-called advantages of modern social progress, social security, old age pensions, and unemployment insurance do not provide psychological benefit—"peace of mind," as Joshua Liebman expressed it. All these do-good programs succeed in breeding are feelings of futility, dependence, and worthlessness. Fifty years ago children were solicitous and patient with their elderly parents, and cared for them at home. Today, children are almost eager to "dump" grandpa and grandma in an institution—any institution. And, should a sensible rehabilitation program restore the oldsters to a point where they can live at home, the children offer an endless array of excuses to duck their responsibility: no room, expenses, the effect on their children, etc. Today, all grandfather has to do is spill a bit of soup from a spoon held by a tremulous hand. The instantaneous—if not jubilant—cry is: INSTITUTION!

This country is casting aside many excellent, skilled workers and alert, capable scientists because of compulsory retirement. According to one insurance report, an investigation of the records of four hundred renowned men, each an outstanding artist, author, poet, soldier, or statesman of his time, revealed that 35 per cent of them recorded notable achievement when they were in the seventh decade, 23 per cent in the eighth, and 8 per cent in the ninth decade!

And why don't men over sixty-five work when they are able and, more importantly, *want* to work? You know the answers: labor's members are increasing faster than jobs do, automation, and all the rest. Most oldsters seek part-time work to supplement social security or pension benefits which, in an era of soaring inflation, are insufficient to support life at a decent level. There is a sore need for research to produce criteria for measuring work capacity, to furnish yardsticks to determine which somatic alterations "must" be accepted as part of normal aging. Habilitation programs meet with a minimum of success because there is nothing for the oldster to "shoot for." Where is he going to find a job, how will he be able to maintain a dignified standard of living, from whom is he to expect love, respect, and sympathy? No wonder so many senior citizens are "depressed" and "futile."

Psychiatrists are discovering that these emotional manifestations are not signs of psychiatric disorder but reflections of social and familial brush-off. A great deal of so-called "social decline" comes from lack of opportunity rather than the ravages of senility. Add to these taxes on his social and psychic adaptability the death of friends, environmental changes, enforced retirement, being compelled to move to less expensive quarters or to live out his years in a "home." That many oldsters' talents are being wasted is borne out by psychological tests that reveal that knowledge, vocabulary, general information, and reasoning are well preserved longer than most persons suspect. When we speak of treatment it is important to include community services, vocational guidance and placement, suitable housing, and recreational facilities.

Physicians must participate in the program, too. There is more than scientific engagement in research, diagnosis, and treatment; the holistic approach embraces ecological and economic features as well. As Dr. R. H. Young aptly said: ". . . *it is imperative to appreciate . . . the geriatric patient as an individual with as many, or more, social and economic problems than medical.*" Put it another way: the senior citizen deserves respect and dignity.

It takes an oldster to appreciate the challenge of geriatrics. The late Bernard Baruch, when he was approaching his ninetieth birthday remarked: *"We must get away from employment policies based on cold arithmetical averages and take advantage of the skills and judgments of older people. How hideous a mockery it would be if, as a result of advances in medicine, surgery, hygiene, and higher living standards, older people were kept willing and able to work— but society deprived them of something useful to do."*

Ecological Strain. The psychological challenge of the senium is, without doubt, greater than the physiological, somatic, and metabolic decline of old age. We exclude, of course, that small minority of elderly creative and performing artists, jurists, professors, and government officials. It is the average senior citizen whose main preoccupation has, for so many years, been his occupation. It gave him great satisfaction which he won't find in a hobby or playing shuffleboard. Besides, in our modern world of materialism, relaxation and personal pleasure cannot be equated with the status of a regular salary—nor does a relief or welfare or old age check carry the psychological impact of a pay envelope.

It isn't too banal a statement that the time to prepare for retirement is in childhood. The development of personality—insatiable curiosity, the spirit of adventure—dictates one's attitude to voluntary or involuntary retirement. Even many of life's basic pleasures are unattainable for oldsters, and that includes sex. Recent surveys conducted among men and women over seventy demonstrated that most of them wanted sex but only a small number were able to find gratification. These few were married or managed to maintain a mutually agreeable "affair." The popular attitude is one of horror, scorn, and derision toward the elderly who have no mate and attempt to find sexual gratification. Any adult whose widowed parent has the intestinal fortitude to hunt for unmarried companionship is either angry or profoundly embarrassed when "the neighbors find out about it." And the senior citizen who is frustrated in this search can only be imbued with feelings of inferiority. He just isn't good enough to enjoy what he's enjoyed for decades. Lack of sexual outlet is the unconscious equivalent of loss of virility. It is as though the unconscious says, "You've had it, brother. You're dead."

Dr. Alvan L. Barach said that senior citizens could really "take it easy" if they could "send appropriate letters of resignation to their instincts as well as their jobs." Dr. Barach adds that oldsters need and enjoy excitement—to a lesser degree, of course—as much as younger persons. Strolling through an art gallery, listening to a concert, working a jigsaw puzzle, embroidering, placing stamps in albums, are undeniable intellectual and occupational sublimations, but they don't provide excitement and vigor . . . and noise.

Prevention of disease, at any age, is always desirable. An important preventive measure was prescribed by Claude Bernard: *"Health comes from harmony between the external environment and the internal milieu."* This sentiment was expressed by Longfellow in his *Morituri Salutamus* (1875):

> *For age is opportunity no less*
> *Than youth itself, though in another dress,*
> *And as the evening twilight fades away*
> *The sky is filled with stars, invisible by day.*

INDEX

(Page numbers in italics indicate where a subject is defined
and/or discussed at length)

A

AA. *See* Alcoholics Anonymous.
abnormal, concept of, 19; *see* normal vs. abnormal.
Abnormal Psychology, 83.
accident, cerebrovascular, *see* cerebrovascular accident.
accident proneness and death instinct, 54.
acid. *See* LSD.
Activity, disorders of, *71*.
addict, personality, 122-123; "typical," 124-125.
addict, addiction; compromise between unconscious and conscious, 118.
addiction, *118-150*; definition, 120; opioid, *138*; drug, *see also* narcotism; *see also* under amphetamine(s), psychic energizers(s), *and* tranquilizer(s).
addictive(s), *see also* drug(s), addictive.
Adenauer, K., 222.
Adler, A., 34, *94-95*.
admission, community, county, or municipal agency certificate, *102*; court certification (commitment), *102*; nonstatutory, *102*; one-physician certificate, *103*; two-physicians, *103*; voluntary, *103*.
adolescence, *196-205*; diagnosis, 198.
adrenalin, and hallucinogens, 31.

affect, appropriate, 70; disorder(s) of, *70-71*; inadequate, 71; *see also* emotion(s).
Age of Anxiety, 49, 205; Horney on, 95.
aggression, and behavior, 9; aggressive type, *112*.
aging, process of, 217-218.
agoraphobia, 51.
akinesis, 181.
alcohol, as an addictive, 120; ambiguities of, 120; personality, 127; among widowed and divorced, 214-215.
alcoholic deterioration, *see* chronic intoxication *under* alcoholism; paranoid states, *see under* alcoholism.
Alcoholics Anonymous, 133, 134.
alcoholism, *124-134*; acute (alcoholic) hallucinosis, *131*; and addiction, 121; alcoholic paranoid states, *130*; chronic intoxication, *130*; and death instinct, 54; defined, 128; delirium tremens, *130-131*; delirium tremens, grim humor, 131; and homosexuality, 115-116; Korsakoff's psychosis (reaction), *131-132*; as a metabolic illness, 29; and narcotism, 146; and narcotism combined, 147; pathological intoxication, *129-130*; psychology of, 127-128; quiet drunk, *132-133*; treatment, *133-135*; chronic, types, 129.
Alexander, F., 96.

ecology, see also environment; see also under senility.
ectomorph, and vagatonia, 32.
Edison, T. A., 222.
education, as a therapeutic adjunct, 98.
EEG, see electroencephalography.
ego, 8; and personality, 9; e. ideal, 10.
Einstein, A., 200.
élan vital, 93.
Electra complex, 2.
elation, 70.
electric convulsive therapy, see electric shock therapy.
electric shock machine, 74.
electric shock therapy, 29-30; 75, 76, 78-79; and depression, 34; see also under epilepsy.
electroencephalography, rhythm, alpha, 182, beta, 182, 183; delta, 183; gamma, 183; wave(s), spiked, 183; see also under epilepsy.
embryotrophy, faulty, 165.
emotion(s), and etiology, 31; and defense mechanisms, 9; see also emotional instability.
emotional instability, and sociopathy, 111-112.
emotional response(s), self-protective, 36.
encephalitis, 24; e. "measles," and mental retardation, 163.
encephalomalacia, 164.
endocrine(s), see under involution.
endocrine disease(s), and mental retardation, 166.
endocrine system, and emotions and psyche, 31.
endogenous factors, and nervousness, 45.
endomorph, in sympathetonia, 32.
energizer(s), see psychic energizer(s).
energy, psychosexual, see libido.
English, O. E., 56.
enuresis, see under child psychiatry.
environment, and personality, 15-16; in schizophrenia, 30; see also ecology; see also under senility.
environmental influences, in schizophrenia, 29.

enzyme(s), and hallucinogens, 29.
epileptic cry, 180.
epilepsy, 19, 179-185; akinetic, 181; amnesia, 182; cataplexy, 182; clonic phase, 180; cryosurgery, 185; deterioration, 183; and driving automobiles, 185; electric shock therapy, 184-185; electroencephalography, 179, 180, 182, 183, 184; etiology, 179-180; chlordiazepoxide, 184; feigned, 183-184; fugue, 182; Librium, 184; diphenylhydantoin, 184; grand mal, 180-181; grand mal, Jacksonian, 181; idiopathic, 180; Jacksonian, 181; ketogenic diet, 184; mephenytoin, 184; myoclonic, 181; narcolepsy, 182; narcolepsy, amphetamine(s) in the treatment of, 182; neurotic, 183-184; normal persons with EEG epileptic patterns, 180; personality, 183; petit mal, 181; phenacemide, 184; psychomotor equivalent, 182; pyknolepsy, 181; and schizophrenia, 182; sociopathy and 183-184; status epilepticus, 181; supersonic surgery, 184-185; tonic seizure, 180; treatment, 184-185; varieties, 180-182.
error(s), see behavior, slips in, and speech, slips in.
EST, see electric shock therapy.
estrogen(s), in treatment, 79.
ether sniffing, 159.
etiology, 24-34; biological, 29; see also cause(s).
ethyl chloride sniffing, 159.
Ewing, J. A., 81.
euphoria, 70.
exaltation, 70.
exanthemata, and mental retardation, 163.
excitement, catatonic, 63.
exhibitionism, -ist, 117-118.
existentialism, -ist(s), 96-97; and ontology, 96-97.
exogenous factor(s), and nervousness, 45.
extravert, 94.

emotional equivalents, 169; and encephalomalacia, 164; and encephalitis, 163; and endocrine disease, 166; etiology, 162-167; and exanthemata, 163; and genes, 167; and heredofamilial disease, 167; and hydrocephalus, 163; and idiopathic hypoglycemia, 166; idiopathic, 167; and infection, 165; institutionalization, 175-176; and maple sugar urine disease, 166; in metabolic disorders, 29, 165-166; mild, 172; moderate, 171-172; and neoplasm, 166-167; and oral-facial-digital syndrome, 166; and phenylketonuria, 166; psychometric classification, 172; and RNA, 167; severe, 171; signs and symptoms, 169-170; statistics, 162; sterilization, 168; and Tay-Sachs disease, 166; and trauma, 165; treatment, 174-178; and tuberous sclerosis, 166-167, types, 171-173.
mental tension defect, 220.
mescaline, 159.
methadone, 150.
mephenytoin, 184.
meprobamate(s), 79; side effects, 80.
Merry Widow, The, 212.
Mesmer, F., 98, 99, 100.
mesmerism, 99.
metabolic disorder(s), and mental retardation, 165-166.
metabolism, and etiology, 28.
Methuselah, 222.
metrazol, 75.
Meyer, A., 195.
Michelangelo, 222.
mind expansion, 159; *see also under* addiction.
mind expander(s), *see under* addiction.
mixoscopia, 116.
Molecular and Microscopic Science, 222.
mongolism, 164.
Montefiore, M., 207, 225.
mores, *see under* personality.
Moreno, J. L., 100, 193.
morning glory seed addiction, 158.
moron, 171.

morphine, as an addictive and a narcotic, 120.
morphinism, *see* opiumism.
Morituri Salutamus, 226.
mutism, 64; in catatonic schizophrenia, 10.
myoclonus, 181.

N

Nalline, 150.
nalorphine, *see* Nalline.
Napoleon I, 110.
narcissistic (narcistic) stage, 6.
narcissistic neurosis, *see* neurosis, narcissistic.
narcolepsy, 182.
narcosis, 120.
narcotic(s), defined, 120, 135.
narcotism, *135-150*; and alcoholism, 145-146, 147; as a metabolic illness, 29; treatment, *147-150*; treatment, attitude toward, 146; treatment, economic factors, 146.
Nation, C., 114.
National Council on Alcoholism, 135.
National Institute of Mental Health, 135; child psychiatry statistics, 186-187; on senility, 217.
Nazism, and Jung, 94.
need for punishment, and conversion hysteria, 12.
negativism, 64; active, 64; passive; *see also* mutism.
neo-culturalism, 95.
neoplasm(s), and mental retardation, 166-167; *see also under* involution.
"nervous breakdown," 46.
nervousness, 35-46.
neuroleptic(s), 79.
neurosis, as a compromise, 49; defined by Horney, 47; features of, *47-48*; evolution of, according to Freud, 47; and psychosis, differentiated, 48; narcissistic and psychoanalysis, 89; cardiac, *see* cardiac neurosis; *see also* psychoneurosis *and also under* child psychiatry; transference, *see* transference neurosis.

pederasty, 117.
peeping Tom, 116.
pellagra, 28; treatment, 78.
penis envy, 7.
pep pill(s), *see under* amphetamines.
pepper kava, 123.
perception, disorders of, 68-69.
perfectionism, -ist, and nervousness, 42.
permissiveness, *see under* child psychiatry.
perseveration, *64*; *see also* stereotypy.
personal unconscious, *8*; 93.
personality, 9, *15-16*; addictive, 121-122; alcoholic, 127; and environment, 15-16; epileptic, 183; and mores, 23; and national cultures, 23; in neurosis and psychosis, 48; "normal," 23; pre-situational, and nervousness, 35; and racial cultures, 23; and sociological factors, 23; sociopathic features of, 110; transient situational, *see* nervousness; *see also* compulsive and passive-aggressive personality.
personality, paranoid, and nervousness, 39.
personality disorders, 109; and alcoholism, 129; *see also under* child psychiatry.
persuasion, as a therapeutic adjunct, 98.
petit mal, in electric shock therapy, 79; *see also under* epilepsy.
pharmaceutical(s), psychiatric, as addictives, 137.
pharmacological combination(s), 84-85.
pharmacotherapy, *see* chemotherapy.
phenacemide, 184.
Phenurone, *see* phenacemide.
phenylketonuria, 166.
phobia(s), 51; as transference neurosis, 89.
phobic reaction, 51-52.
phylogenetic unconscious, *see* collective unconscious.
Physician's Desk Reference, 80, 84, 145.
physiology, and etiology, 31.

Picasso, P., 207, 222.
Picture of Dorian Gray, The, 213.
Pinel, P., 75.
Pitt, W., 179.
pituri plant, 122.
Pius XII, 222.
PKU, *see* phenylketonuria.
Poe, E. A., 123.
porencephaly, 164.
play, play techniques, *see under* child psychiatry.
Plumb, J. H., 200-201.
Practical Clinical Psychiatry.
preconscious, 8.
precipitating factor(s), 26; and nervousness, 44.
projection, *11;* in neurosis and psychosis, 48.
projective technique(s), *see under* child psychiatry.
protein, *see under* antibodies.
pseudocyesis, 54.
Psalms, 217.
pseudoneurotic child, *see under* child psychiatry.
pseudoneurotic schizophrenia, 62.
psyche, and etiology, 31; activity of, according to Jung, 93-94.
psychiatry, child, *see* child psychiatry.
psychic development, 3.
psychic energizer(s), 79-80; addiction, 85.
psychedelic, 151, 154.
psychoanaleptic(s), 79.
psychoanalysis, *88-97;* Freudian, 88-93; in homosexuality as treatment, 116; Freudian objectives of, 92; techniques, 91-92; *see also under* child psychiatry.
psychobiology, *see under* child psychiatry.
psychodrama, *100;* *see also under* child psychiatry.
psycholeptic(s), 79.
psychological therapy, *see* psychotherapy.
psychology, analytic, *see* analytic psychology.
psychology, genetic and Horney, 95.
psychomotor equivalent, 182.